Pinkas Tishevits
(Tyszowce, Poland)

Translation of
Pinkas Tishevits

Original Book Edited by: Y. Zipper

Originally published in Tel Aviv 1970

JewishGen
מרכז עולמי לגנאלוגיה יהודית
The Global Home for Jewish Genealogy

A Publication of JewishGen, INC
Edmond J. Safra Plaza, 36 Battery Place, New York, NY 10280
646.494.5972 | info@JewishGen.org | www.jewishgen.org

MUSEUM OF
JEWISH HERITAGE
A LIVING MEMORIAL
TO THE HOLOCAUST

Pinkas Tishevits (Tyszowce, Poland)

Translation of *Pinkas Tishevits*

Copyright © 2023 by JewishGen, INC All rights reserved.
First Printing: November 2023, Kislev 5784
Editor of Original Yizkor Book: Y. Zipper
Project Coordinator: Moses Milstein
Yiddish Translations: Moses Milstein
Cover Design: Rachel Kolokoff Hopper
Layout: Jonathan Wind
Name Indexing: Stefanie Holzman

Library of Congress Control Number (LCCN): 2023947255

ISBN: 978-1-954176-88-1 (hard cover: 246 pages, alk. paper)

About JewishGen.org

JewishGen, an affiliate of the Museum of Jewish Heritage - A Living Memorial to the Holocaust, serves as the global home for Jewish genealogy.

Featuring unparalleled access to 30+ million records, it offers unique search tools, along with opportunities for researchers to connect with others who share similar interests. Award winning resources such as the Family Finder, Discussion Groups, and ViewMate, are relied upon by thousands each day.

In addition, JewishGen's extensive informational, educational and historical offerings, such as the Jewish Communities Database, Yizkor Book translations, InfoFiles, Family Tree of the Jewish People, and KehilaLinks, provide critical insights, first-hand accounts, and context about Jewish communal and familial life throughout the world.

Offered as a free resource, JewishGen.org has facilitated thousands of family connections and success stories, and is currently engaged in an intensive expansion effort that will bring many more records, tools, and resources to its collections.

Please visit https://www.jewishgen.org/ to learn more.

Executive Director: Avraham Groll

About the JewishGen Yizkor Book Project

Yizkor Books (Memorial Books) were traditionally written to memorialize the names of departed family and martyrs during holiday services in the synagogue (a practice that still exists in many synagogues today).

Over the centuries, as a result of countless persecutions and horrific atrocities committed against the Jews, Yizkor Books (Sefer Zikaron in Hebrew) were expanded to include more historical information, such as biographical sketches of famous personalities and descriptions of daily town life.

Following the Holocaust, the idea of remembrance and learning took on an urgent and crucial importance. Survivors of the Holocaust sought out other surviving residents of their former towns to memorialize and document the names and way of life of those who were ruthlessly murdered by the Nazis. These remembrances were documented in Yizkor Books, hundreds of which were published in the first decades after the Holocaust.

Most of these books were published privately, or through Landsmanshaftn (social organizations comprised of members originating from the same European town or region) that still existed, and were often distributed free of charge. Sadly, the languages used to document these crucial histories and links to our past, Yiddish and Hebrew, are no longer commonly understood by a significant percentage of Jews today. As a result, JewishGen has undertaken the sacred responsibility of translating these books into English so that the culture and way of life of these communities will be preserved and transmitted to future generations.

In 1986, a group of farsighted JewishGenners started a project to pool their efforts together in groups based upon their ancestors from each town and donate money to get the Yizkor books of their ancestral towns translated into English. As the translated material became available, it was made accessible for free at www.JewishGen.org/Yizkor. Hardcover copies can be purchased by visiting https://www.jewishgen.org/Yizkor/ybip.html (see below).

It is our hope that the translation of these books into English (and other languages) will assist the countless Jewish family researchers who are so desperately seeking to forge a connection with their heritage.

Director of JewishGen Yizkor Book Project: Lance Ackerfeld

About JewishGen Press

JewishGen Press (formerly the Yizkor Books-in-Print Project) is the publishing division of JewishGen.org, and provides a venue for the publication of non-fiction books pertaining to Jewish genealogy, history, culture, and heritage.

In addition to the Yizkor Book category, publications in the Other Non-Fiction category include Shoah memoirs and research, genealogical research, collections of genealogical and historical materials, biographies, diaries and letters, studies of Jewish experience and cultural life in the past, academic theses, and other books of interest to the Jewish community.

Please visit https://www.jewishgen.org/Yizkor/ybip.html to learn more.

Director of JewishGen Press: Joel Alpert
Managing Editor - Jessica Feinstein
Publications Manager - Susan Rosin

Notes to the Reader

The images in the original book were reproduced from photographs from the time of the first edition. These reproductions were already of poor quality, being pre-war and at least 30 or more years old. As a result, the images in the book are the best achievable.

A reader can view the original scans of the book on the websites listed below.

The original book can be seen online at the Yiddish Book Center website:

https://www.yiddishbookcenter.org/collections/yizkor-books/yzk-nybc314068/ziper-ya-akov-pinkes-tishivits

OR

at the New York Public Library Digital Collections website:

https://digitalcollections.nypl.org/items/eed852c0-3574-0133-d433-00505686a51c

To obtain a list of Shoah victims from **Tishevits (Tyszowce, Poland),** the reader should access the Yad Vashem web site listed below; one can also search for specific family names using family name option. These lists are continually updated by Yad Vashem, so it is worthwhile to periodically search these lists.

There is more valuable information (including the Pages of Testimony, etc.) available on this website: https://yvng.yadvashem.org/

A list of all books available from JewishGen Press along with prices is available at: https://www.jewishgen.org/Yizkor/ybip.html

Acknowledgement

It is with eagerness, yet some trepidation, that I undertook the translation of the Tishevits yizkor book. The original editor, Yakov (Stern) Zipper, was a highly respected advocate of Yiddish in Canada, and principal of the Jewish Peretz School in Montreal where I was a student in the 1950s. Of all the students who passed through the Peretz *shule*, I'm not sure *lerer* Zipper would have chosen me as his translator. Yet it is thanks to his dedication to Yiddishkeit, and the Yiddish education he strove to impart to his students, that gave me the motivation and ability to undertake the task.

I apologize for any inadequacies and errors that this translation may contain. It was particularly difficult to translate the poetry, and one may ask if it is even possible to do justice to a poem in any translation given the protean, often cryptic and ambiguous nature of verse.

Thanks go to fellow translators Jerrold Landau and Sara Mages. Lance Akerfeld, Director of the JewishGen Yizkor Book Project oversaw the project. We are fortunate to have him leading the yizkor book project at JewishGen with his usual efficiency and care. Also, thanks go to the JewishGen Press team: Susan Rosin, publications manager; Jonathan Wind, formatting; Stefanie Holzman, indexing, and Rachel Kolokoff Hoper, cover design.

Moses Milstein
Pemberton, British Columbia, Canada

Photo Credits

Front Cover:

The family of Rabbi Avraham and Gittel Stern of blessed memory. From right to left, sitting: Daughter-in-law, Sara Stern of blessed memory (Yechiel's wife), Gittel Stern holding granddaughter Esther, Rabbi Avraham Stern, Yechiel Stern, his daughter Hene Marder-Stern, son – Dr. Yisrael Stern, daughter Shifra Krishtalka-Stern, Elka Danziker-Neiman. Absent – Yaakov Zipper-Stern and Shalom Stern, who were already in Canada at that time. Page 33 [Page 57].

Background Photos Front & Back Covers: *Wildflowers* by Rachel Kolokoff Hopper

Poem on Back Cover: *Reciter of Psalms* by Sholem Stern. Page 46 *[Page 80].*

Back Cover:

Upper Right: *Rabbi Avraham Stern of blessed memory, a shochet and teacher of righteousness.* Page 29 *[Page 51].*
Lower Left: *Tarbut school in Tyszowce, Lag B'Omer class 1935-1936.* Page 75 *[Page 120].*
Lower Right: *Gitl Stern a"h.* Page 106 *[Page 162].*

Geopolitical Information

Tyszowce, Poland is located at 50°37' N 23°42' E and 162 miles SE of Warszawa

	Town	District	Province	Country
Before WWI (c. 1900):	Tyszowce	Tomaszów	Lublin	Russian Empire
Between the wars (c. 1930):	Tyszowce	Tomaszów	Lublin	Poland
After WWII (c. 1950):	Tyszowce			Poland
Today (c. 2000):	Tyszowce			Poland

Alternate Names for the Town:

Tyszowce [Pol], Tishevitz [Yid], Tishovtse [Rus], Tishevits, Tishovits, Tishvits, Tishivits, Tishvitz, Toshvitse, Tyszviec

Nearby Jewish Communities:

Łaszczów 6 miles SSE
Komarów 10 miles W
Jarczów 15 miles SSW
Hrubieszów 16 miles NE
Grabowiec 16 miles NNW
Kryłów 17 miles ENE
Tomaszów Lubelski 17 miles SW
Uhniv, Ukraine 17 miles S
Varyazh, Ukraine 19 miles ESE
Uchanie 20 miles N
Bełżec 20 miles SW
Zamość 21 miles WNW
Lubycza Królewska 21 miles SSW
Belz, Ukraine 21 miles SE
Skierbieszów 22 miles NW
Wojsławice 22 miles NNW

Mosty Małe 22 miles SSW
Krasnobród 22 miles WSW
Horodło 23 miles NE
Khlivchany, Ukraine 24 miles SSE
Lipsko 24 miles SW
Narol 25 miles SW
Rava-Ruska, Ukraine 26 miles S
Ustyluh, Ukraine 26 miles NE
Kraśniczyn 26 miles NW
Vul'ka-Mazovetskaya, Ukraine 26 miles SSE
Potelych, Ukraine 27 miles SSW
Sokal, Ukraine 27 miles ESE
Skryhiczyn 28 miles NNE
Chervonohrad, Ukraine 28 miles SE
Izbica 30 miles NW
Sielec 30 miles NNW
Silets, Ukraine 30 miles SE

Jewish Population: 1,898 (in 1895), 2,451 (in 1921)

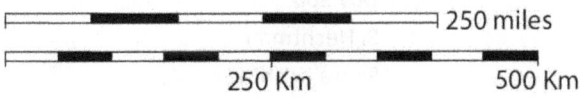

Map of Poland showing the location of **Tyszowce**

Table of Contents

Pinkas Tishevits

(Tyszowce, Poland)

50°37' / 23°42'

Translation of *Pinkas Tishevits*

Editor: Y. Zipper

Published in Tel Aviv 1970

**Our sincere appreciation to Yad Vashem
for the submission of the necrology for placement on the JewishGen web site.**

This is a translation of: *Pinkas Tishevits* (Tiszowic book),
Editor: Y. Zipper, Association of Former Residents of Tishevits in Israel, Published: Tel Aviv 1970 (H,Y 324 pages)

Note: The original book can be seen online at the NY Public Library site: Tyszowce

פנקס טישיוויץ

צונויפגעשטעלט און רעדאגירט

פון

יעקב זיפער

אַרויסגעגעבן פון „אָרגון יוצאי טישיוויץ
בישראל"

תל-אביב תשל"א, 1970

[Page 5]

In Memory of the Shtetl, Tishevits,
One of the Nine Communities of the Polish Commonwealth

Translated by Moses Milstein

For close to 500 years, Tishevits was located in "Lesser Poland," close to the crossroads of Volhynia and Ukraine, surrounded by rushing rivers, dark forests, swampy peat bogs, and sun-dazzled sands.

Tishevits was connected to the world around it, in both territory and time, by bridges on every side, and underground caverns. With extraordinary effort, people lived and looked for answers to the world's problems from their own intellect, and dreamed the dream of the days of the Messiah.

The wonderful deeds, and the joy, and the sad events of the generations that had lived, suffered, and hoped there, were imprinted in her alleys and her narrow interlocking little streets. The realities of today were always connected to and seen through the spiritual mysteries of yesterday.

And then the disruption of the old ways of life, and the beginning of the preparations for a new approach to the world came to the shtetl, but was severed by the storm of horror and catastrophe issuing from the land of the Huns. The horror rampaged through all the streets and bridges, annihilating everyone and everything, destroying the bridges, and sealing the caverns and their waters.

Only in our memories does it shine as it once did.

[Page 7]

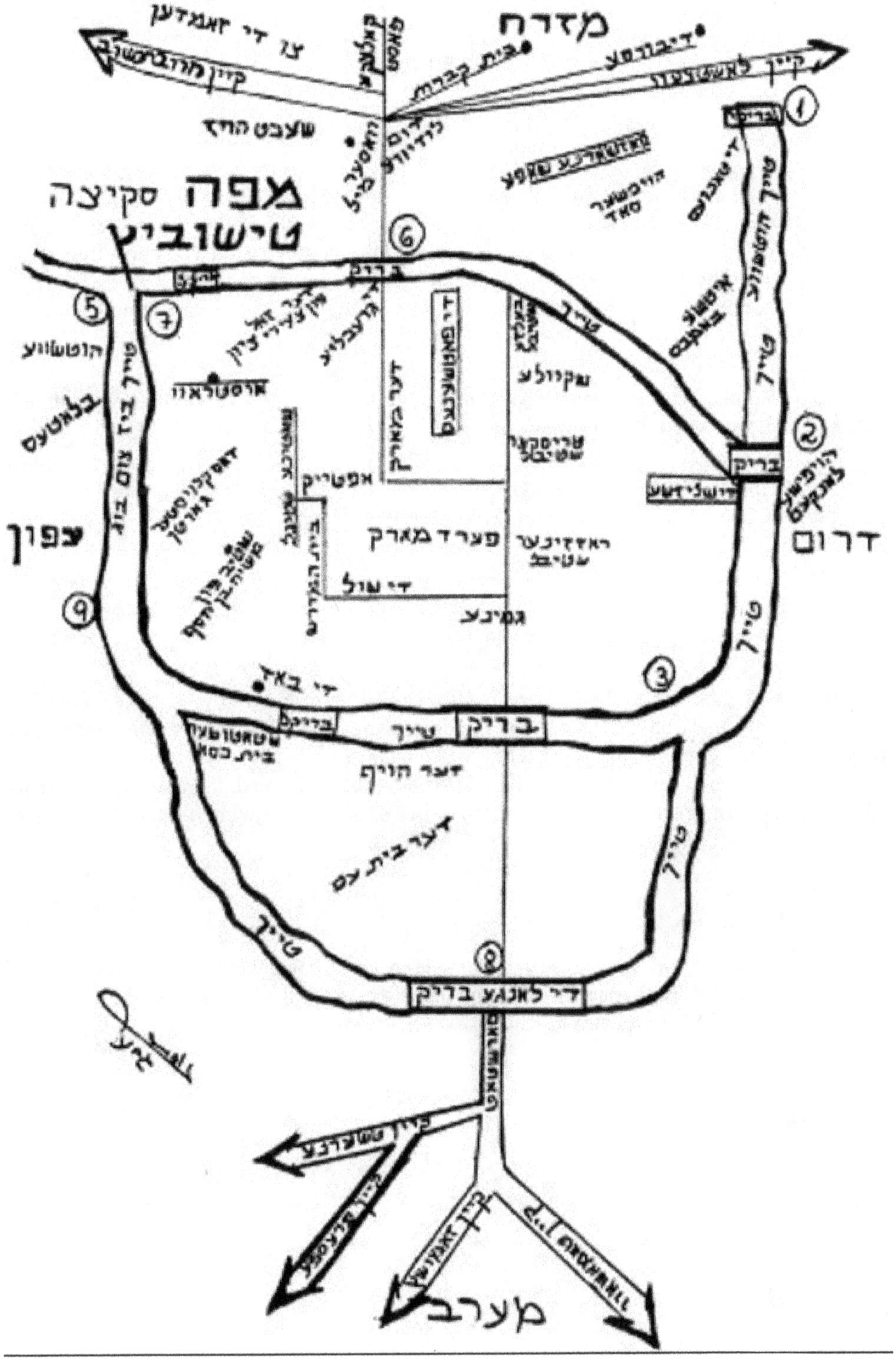

מזרח

מפה סקיצה טישוביץ

צפון

דרום

מערב

צו די זאמדען
קיין הרוביעשוב
בית קברות
דיבורסע
קיין לאשטשעוו

שעבט הויז

בלאטעס
הוטושווע

די באר

שטאטושע בית כסא

דער הויף

דער בית עם

די לאנגע בריק

בריק טריך

[Page 8] [Blank] [Page 9]

Description of the Map Drawing of Tishevits

Pinchas Landau

Translated by Moses Milstein

This is the map of Tishevits as I remember it in the year 1933, when I left Tishevits to immigrate to Israel. As the drawing shows, Tishevits was an island surrounded by the Huczwa river, which flowed in an irregular manner from number 1 through numbers 2, 3, 4, 5 to Hrubieszow, and emptied into the river Bug. The part of the river from 2-7 was dug when the first watermill was constructed. Near the bridge, on the way to the "Klentves," a ramp had been constructed. For that reason, the bridge was called the "Shlizhe[1]." The water to the mill came from number 2 and returned to the river at number 7.

The part of the river, from number 3 to number 9, was dug by farmers from the suburbs. As a result, a bridge had to be built (number 8) which was called the "long bridge."

In the last world war, the Nazis filled the river using Jewish labor so that part of the river, from number 3 to number 9, as well as the long bridge, doesn't exist anymore.

I once heard the Tishevits old-timers say that the name Tishevits comes from the Polish words "Tu szewcow" which means, "Here are shoemakers." The Polish spelling is Tyszowce or Tyszowiec. Jews pronounced it Tishevits or Tishivets.

It is no exaggeration to say that 40% of the farmers in Tishevits made, or knew how to make, boots. This was the kind of special boot made only In Tishevits. That's why the boots were called Tishavanes. They were sewn together by hand using only soft leather, even for the soles. They were made from leather on one side, and after they were finished, they were turned over on the other side. The face of the boot was deformed; there was no difference between the left or right boot. Every farmer knew how to make such boots, and in the winter when there was no outdoor fieldwork,

[Page 10]

they used to make the boots for their own use, as well as for sale. A lot of boots were sold, mostly in the wintertime, in the Lublin area of which Tishevits was a part. And also on the other side of the Bug, in the Volhynia region. Before the first world war, the boots were also exported to Russia.

———

Footnote:

1.   Sluice

[Page 10 - Yiddish] [Page 21 - Hebrew]

Tishevits–Rise and Fall
of a Jewish Settlement in Poland

Dovid Stockfish

Translated by Moses Milstein

1.

In the historical work by Eliezer Feldman: "*The Oldest Information on Jews in Polish Cities in the 14th - 15th Century*," 1538 is the year given as the official and earliest date for the founding of Tishevits. In its more than 400 years of existence, the community underwent many transformations and developments from occasional progress to recurring declines due to war, plague and administrative decrees from central and local authorities. There are only two important historical events of a Jewish and general nature that distinguished this little locality: The Tishevits statute adopted by the *Va'ad Chamaysh Artzot*, Chol Hamoed, Pesach, 1583, and the Polish Confederation against Sweden in 1655.

It is hypothesized that these two historical events, associated with such a small settlement, were responsible for Tishevits being mentioned in various historical sources, lexicons, and encyclopedias, and other books containing a lot of materials, facts and figures in some areas, while in other sources, the story of the shtetl is told in 2-3 lines. After finding and getting to know all these sources, it was possible to construct a picture of the history, development, and fall of Tishevits.

2.

The shtetl is mentioned in the "*Yevraiskaya Encyclopedia*" under the editorship of Dr. L. Katzenelson, volume 15, published in St. Petersburg, in 1908-13; in the "*Algemeiner Encylopedia*,"

[Page 11]

S. Arglebrand, Warsaw, 1859-68, volume 25; in the "*Geographishen Verter-Buch of the Polish Kingdom and other Slavic Lands*," Warsaw 1880-1902, volume 12; in the two-volume publication, "*Polish Cities in One Thousand Years*," published in 1965 by the National Institute; in the *Encyclopedichesky Slovar*," volume 34, St. Petersburg, 1902, issued by F.A. Brokhouse, Leipzig, Y.A Ephron, Peterburg, "*Historical Facts, Questions and Answers* (Historical Works, Vol. 1); *Pinkas Va'ad Arba Artzot*; in "*Sh'eilot Habach v'Maharam M'Lublin*"; in "*Bletter far Geschichte*," issue 1-2, volume 3, January –June 1950, issued by the Jewish Historical Institute, Warsaw; in "*Verterbuch fun Turistisher Geographia fun Poiln*," Warsaw, 1956, and other sources.

There is no doubt that Tishevits occupies a respected place in many other books, but unfortunately it was not possible to access them all. Therefore, we have to use what's available and achievable. Let us hope then that this will be enough to become acquainted with the historical record of a Jewish community in Poland–from its emergence to its tragic demise–during the Second World War.

3.

And now–the sources.[1]

Tishevits, an urban shtetl, previously a shtetl on the right bank of the river Huczwa, Tomaszow county, township and parish. Tishevits lies 28 verst[2] northeast of Tomaszow, 115 verst from Lublin, 21 verst from the highway from

Lublin to Zamosc and Tomaszow, united through the highway with Hrubieszow. The village of Podbor lies on the other side of the Huczwa. The suburbs are Debina and Zamlynie. A forested region.

The settlement contains 3 Russian-Orthodox churches, a Catholic parish church, a synagogue, a shul, a besmedresh, a 2-class elementary school, a township authority with a savings-and-loan bank, a post office, a pharmacy, 43 shops, 465 houses (mostly wood), 4325 residents (1930 Jews, the others–Russian Orthodox and Catholics in equal numbers).

The residents own 2,617 acres land. The population is employed

[Page 12]

in agriculture, shoemaking, and fur working for sale in the local markets. Tishevits real-estate (owner: Yozef Glogowski) in `1836 consisted of the Tishevits settlement, Klatwy ranch, Mikulin, and Przewale.

There is a mill on the Huczwa with a "zamczisko" embankment. The main church in the parish was a wooden one, whose date of construction is unknown, confirmed in 1760 by August the Third. Two wooden churches in the suburbs of Debina and Zamlynie belong to it. The Catholic parish church, named after the holy Leogard, is walled, erected in 1870, and funded by the believers. The parish and the church have been in existence since the 16th century. The exact date is unknown, as well as the date for the town's establishment.

The Mazowiecki prince, Wladislaw, in the hopes of elevating the depressed town, allowed them to cut trees for free in his woods in 1453, fish in the Huczwa, the meadows called Szedlec, and created the "adomarszczizne." When the city was razed by the Tatars in 1502, Alexander Jagiellon exempted them from taxes for 10 years. The leagues who administered along with the *starostve*, wanted to remove the right to be a city from the citizens, and transform them into peasants. It was not until 1555 that Zygmunt August put an end to it, and granted the city the same rights as other cities, allowing Jews to settle there in 1566, and establishing markets and fairs in 1569.

The census of 1571 showed 218 city houses, several houses belonging to the nobility and princes, 27 bakers, and many artisans.

4.

The unassuming shtetl became famous thanks to an important historical incident. On December 29, 1655, the confederation against the Swedes arose, who, under the leadership of the adventurer Karl Gustave, took, almost without resistance, the entire country in the span of barely 3 months, with an army of 17,000 soldiers. Defending Czestochowa had repercussions. The great hetman, Potocki, and the field-hetman, Stanislaw Lanckoronski, left the camp of Swedish General Douglas, led the troops to Tishevits, and proclaimed the Confederation whose goal was to oust the Swedes from Poland. Aside from the two hetmans, they chose as commissars in the army:

[Page 13]

Kszisztow Tiszkewicz–Czernogwer Wojewode, Jendzai Potowski–royal clerk, Jacek Szemberg–Boguslaw starasto, Stanislaw Domaszewski, Waclaw Lanckoronski–colonel. The provincial governors, as part of their association with the confederation, had to choose the commissar. The idea in whose name the confederation arose, brought out unusual heights of emotion in almost all sectors of society. The oath, delivered in Lemberg (Lvov, Lviv) by Jan Kazimierz (April 1, 1656) was the most obvious expression of this feeling. The Swedes would have to leave this land that they captured so quickly and so easily.

The military defeats led to the downfall of the community. The audit of 1665 found a ruined shtetl. In 1765, after several fires, the shtetl was in ruins. In 1827, Tishevits counted 391 houses, and 1977 residents.

The starostve outside of Tishevits found itself in the Belzec voivodeship, Grabowiec powiat. According to the audit of 1628, the starostve consisted of the city of Tishevits and the villages of Mikulin, Przewale, Perespa, and nearby places, which, in the Sejm of 1768, changed into the Hermonow starostve. From then on, the Tishevits starostve no longer existed.

5.

In "Shayles v" Tshuves" we find some responses in which the Tishevits rulings are mentioned. (We bring them here in the original spellings).

שנת שמ״ג

ב. „מן זאל קיין רב או ראשים או טובים או קהל יצ״ו או שאר מנויים שבעולם קלויבן נייארט ברחוב היהודים, דהיינו, אז דיא ממונים כנ״ל זאלין ממונה זיין במוסכם ראשים וטובים וקהל יצ״ו וכפי דת תורתינו, אז מיר אויך קיימים האבן פון מלכים אונ׳ פון אלין שרים ומושליב אונ׳ אויך אז מיר מושבע זיין ועומר זיין מהר סיני. אונ׳ דיא זעלבע שבועה האבן מיר איינצוורדט ווידר מחדש גיוועזין.

אוב איין יחיד או רבים ח״ו וואלסטין אייס פלין אונ׳ וואלסטין דיא שררה יר״ה אונטר ריכטן, דאז דא וער וידר דת תורתינו ושבועתינו וקיומים שלנו, הן בעצמם או על ידי שלוחם, הן על ידי יהודים הן על ידי ערלים, דא זאל דער זעלביג עוברין או עבריינים זיין, אונ׳ האבן אלי עונשים וחרמות וחומרות, אז גימכט אין בתקנות חמש ארצות בק״ק טישוויץ בחוה״מ פסח שנת גשם לפ״ק, כמבואר בתקנה דיא דא לינט במפנקס — — בק״ק לובלין השייך לחמש ארצות, וזא אלי תקנות איין געשריבן. ושם נאמר: דאם יעשה אדם איזה פעילה חדשה אצל השררה, הן יחיד או רבים, הן איש

[Page 14]

או אשה, שיעשו השרים או המלך יר"ה בעניני מינויים של הקהלה אשר יהיה שלא כדת, וגם ירצו
להשתדל אצל המלך הן בעניני רבנות או כל שאר מינויים[2] הנזכרים בתקנה זו, או שירצו לעשות
להם איזה הכנסה בתוך הקהלה, או שירצו להשתדל לפטור א"ע ממסים שלא ליתן חלקם בתוך
הקהלה, או שירצו לעשות דבר מה שיהיה נגד קיומים שלנו ונגד הקהל יצ"ו מכל מה שהספה יוכל
לדבר והלב לחשוב, — אז יהי' האיש ההוא או האשה, יחיד או רבים, בכל מיני עונשין וחרמות
וחומרות המוזכרים בתקנות טישעוויץ הנ"ל. ואפילו. מי שיהיה ממונה באופן הנ"ל ויתנצל לאמר:
הדבר נעשה בעל כרחי או שלא בידיעתי או באונם גם הוא מחוייב להחזיק כפי התקנה של טישעוויץ
הנ"ל.

ג. "ואם רב מעיר אחרת או הרבה רבנים ביחד או רבים יכתבו לכאן איזה חרם הן על עסק
יחיד הן על עסק רבים מבני קהלתנו יצ"ו, מחוייבים הרבנים מפה (קראקא) ורו"ט וקהל יצ"ו לומר:
"אדרבה", ויטילו הם חרם על אותו יחיד או רבים כפי התקנה הנעשית בטישעוויץ בענין זה".

ד. "חען איינער ח"ו נפטר וערט אונ' לאזט יורשי' קטנים אונ' ער העט בחייו קיין אפוטרופסים
ממנה געווען, דא זאלין רבנים ורו"ט ממנה זיין אפוטרופסים; דארף קה"ק יצ"ו דז געלט, דא זאלין
זיא ריבית געבן כנ"ל אונ' דיא אפוטרופסים זאלין אלי ב' שנים חשבון געבן (מקבל זיין). וונש
הוט נימען נישט צו דען אפוטרופסים בעולם, כתקנת שלש ארצות בקק"ק טישעוויץ".

ה. "אוב זיך איינער וואלט אויש ריכטן אפוטרופסות ע"י גוים[5], דא זול מן זיך קיגן איהם הלטן
כפי התקנה בכל אופן ועונשים, דיא דא שטיין אין דער תקנה של טישעוויץ, הן ער וויל מבטל זיין
אפוטרופסים דיא אביהם של יתומים האבן ממנה געווען, הן דאש ב"ד הנ"ל האבן זיא ממנה
געוועזין, דער זאל זיין בכל עונש התקנה הנ"ל רו"ט אונ' כל הקהל יצ"ו זיין מחויב אים
אנקיגן צו גין, אז דאז ניט צו גישטטן איז בכל אופן כללי".

ו. "שדכנות דרפן דיא משודכי' ניט מין צו געבן אז איין שדכנות כנ"ל, וען שון מין אז
איין שדכן אין, אונ' וער דיא רעכטן דין ובורר כפי התקנה הנעשית בטישעוויץ, ומהעשיריות לפי ערך
המאות כנ"ל".

ז. "שכירות שדכנות כנזכר לקמן אצל חתונות וכפי התקנות הארצות יצ"ו. שכירות סרסרות
מכל מאה חצי זהב מכל צד וצד. וען איין סרסרות אין אונטר חמשים זהו' זול מן געבן מן שגי זהו'
איין חצי גדול. מצוביל וריס וביבר טובים ואבנים טובים ומרגליות מכל מאה איין טאליר
מכל צד וצד. וכן סרסרית מבתים. ומכל עשיריות לפי ערך המאה. וכל דין סרסרות במתחיל ונומר
זול זיין כדי שדכנות כנזכר בתקנות טישעוויץ".

6.

The emptying out of Tishevits forced the king to issue the following privilege:

Whereas it is desired that the city should consistently achieve better conditions through an increase in population, we allow the Jews, those living in the city, and those outside, to occupy houses, gardens and bathhouses, to buy and sell various goods by weight and measure: produce and sell beer, mead, and alcohol, engage in ritual slaughter and sell the meat, and benefit from the freedoms and the responsibilities together with the city's residents.

[Page 15]

We forbid them, however, from ever occupying any municipal office. In order for the Jews not to experience any interference with their commercial activities, markets will be held on Tuesdays, as is customary, and if ever the day needs to be changed, it will not be a Saturday.

On the basis of a privilege from Zygmunt August, no more than 16 Jews were allowed to live in Tishevits. In the 1571 census there were "31 Jews in Tishevits, because in 1570 many of them had died of a plague."

According to the surviving tax records paid by the city residents in the Belz voivodeship in 1630, Tishevits had: 1,140 Christians, 190 houses, 280 Jews, 10 small houses, 2 large houses.

7.

Before–a city, now a village, the home of the village national council in the Tomaszow powiat[3], located by the Huczwa River, a tributary of the Bug River, 26 km northeast of Tomaszow-Lubelski, near the "little train" line Laszczow-Hrubieszow, and the intersections of secondary roads to Zamosc and Tomaszow.

In 1453, Tishevits received city rights from the Mazovian princes who, until 1462, farmed the Belzer lands as vassal payments for the Polish kings. The origin and development of Tishevits probably had a connection to the revival of the trade routes from Lemberg through Tishevits in the direction of Poznan and Wroclaw. Consequently, Tishevits had an importance as a trade center in the 15th and 16th century. In 1578, the city counted 84 houses and 420 inhabitants.

The armed confederation against the Swedes was proclaimed in Tishevits. The city became a total ruin as a result of the wars in the 17th century, and didn't recover until the end of the 18th century. In 1810, the city only counted 1,704 residents, but by 1886, it had reached 4,910 residents.

The residents were employed in agriculture and handwork in which shoemaking and making products of hide were the most significant. In the second half of the 19th century,

[Page 16]

Tishevits lost its city rights, and as a settlement, had an agricultural character until modern times.

During the period of the German occupation (1939-1945) Tishevits was simply destroyed. Most of the people were killed, the buildings burned (about 60%), so that by 1959 there were 950 residents, mostly farmers. Of the trades, shoemaking continues the tradition.

8.

During the Republic era, a shtetl in the Belz voivodeship. In order to increase the population, in 1565, king Zygmunt August proclaimed a number of privileges, allowing Jews to buy and sell houses in the city, profit from free trade, engage in brewing (cooking wine), and possess all the same rights as city residents.

Markets were to take place every Tuesday, and could be held on any other day except Saturday, because it might interfere with Jewish observance.

In 1570, many Jews fell victim to a plague. According to the census of 1570, 31 people survived.

In 1583, the Va'ad[4] of Five Lands took place in Tishevits (Lithuania did not yet have a va'ad), and affirmed local autonomy and freedom of voting for rabbis.

In the 17th century, Tishevits had to endure many problems that led to the decline of the city.

According to legend, in 1765, the city counted 925 Jews. For the right to have a rabbinate, Jews had to pay an annual sum of 666 Zlotys and 20 groshen.

In 1856, there were 1669 Christians, and 940 Jews. In the census of 1895–2201 residents, of whom, 1898 Jews.

9.

Tishevits–a settlement in the Lublin gubernia, Tomaszow district on the Huczwa River, tributary of the Bug to the west. 5002 residents, significant trade, 2 steam-mills, a post office and telegraph office.

[Page 17]

10.

Tishevits–a village, earlier, a city, Tomaszow powiat[5], Lublin voivodeship, lies on the Huczwa River, left bank of the Bug, nearest train station–Tuczapy, on the narrow gauge line Werbkowice-Laszczow, 4.5 km from the city. Other than that, bus connections to Zamosc. The name of the community, according to local tradition, comes from Tuszewce (here shoemakers). The people of Tishevits had long been employed in tanning leather, and shoe manufacture. Tishevits is also known from the confederation against the Swedes during the Swedish invasion of Poland in 1665.

11.

End of Jewish Tishevits

Before the war–3,800 Jews. In March 1941, 1780 Jews (1690 local, 90 new arrivals). In September 1941–2,090 Jews. In April 1942–2,050. In June 1942–1,090.

In 1941 there was an expulsion of Jews from Lublin. May 25 1942, 580 or 800 Jews were sent to Belzec from Tishevits.

Footnotes:

1. Part gathered by V. Bernstein, z"l, in New York, and G. Zipper in Montreal ed. note
2. A verst is an old Russian unit of length equal to 1.07 km
3. County or district
4. Council. Autonomous body regulating Jewish life in Poland/Lithuania 16th to 18th century.
5. County

Supplementary Material Regarding Tyszowce

(Collected from Y. Z.)

Translated by Jerrold Landau

·Extracted from the research work "Collecting Testimony in Questions and Answers" by Zalman Rubashov (Shazar, president of Israel), published in historical works, volume I, YIVO, Vilna; Questions and Responsa of the Mahara'm of Lublin – in the book "Lightening the Eyes of the Sages" (published in Venice 5478 – 1618) Number 115 (our count) in which he testified as Mr. Moshe the son of Reb Yaakov of blessed memory: Thus did several Cossacks say several times that the *ritzer*[1] the Jew Bercha (Berko) came in so defensively. They beat him and stabbed him with the *kordem*[1].

116 – this is the words of the witness: "A Jew named Bercha the son of the k'r[1] Reb Aharon of Tyszowce leaped up against our soldier… His father had served

[Page 18]

among them in the army unit on three horses. There, he jumped on to his horse two or three times, as is done during war." (Also brought down in Yevr. Starina b. 1, and by B. Tz. Katz in his History of the Jews in Russia, page 45, where the year was accurately identified as 5371, 1611).

Number 126 – Old Responsa of the Ba'ch 57 (Rabbi Yoel Sirkis, Lublin 5321, 1951 – 5400, 1650)

– We householders were in the army, and a Jew Bercha the son of the holy Aharon of Tyszowce leaped up. He served on three horses, and he leaped against the Muscovite unit two or three times in warlike fashion… In any case, I shortened the content of the testimony from the full body of testimony that is brought down at length in the book of chronicles of the aforementioned committee in front of the rabbinical court of the community of Florianów on Monday, 25 Kislev 5374.

Editor's Remarks:

In the old cemetery in Tyszowce, near the two large monuments of the two merchants, there is also a monument upon which we can barely read "The martyr Reb Aharon Koza." It was said that he lived during the times of Chmielnicki uprising… According to the Responsa, it can be derived that he and his son served in the Polish army years earlier.

Names of Authors and Rabbis

The author of a commentary on the book *Bechinat Olam* – – – see title page.

In the list of authors and rabbis in Zamość by Yaakov Dov Mandelbaum, published in Pinkas Zamość, the following is mentioned:

Number 14 – Reb Binyamin the son of Zeev Bechar David, the author of the book *Ben Oni*. Torah thoughts from his grandfather (the renowned, wholesome sage Aharon of Tyszowce who died in the holy community of Turbin on the Sabbath of Rosh Chodesh Kislev 5471) -- are included in the introduction.

31 – Among the givers of approbations on the book Yad Tzvi-Shalom is the approbation of Rabbi Moshe Yaakov Chopa'k of Tyszowce, 7 Av, 5639 [1879].

55 – The author of the book *Pnei Ari Zuta* concludes his introduction as follows: These are the words of apology and pleading of the insignificant Aryeh Leib the son of the great Rabbi Avraham Cordovera, may the memory of he holy be blessed, a native of the community of Tyszowce, called Reb Leib Tartshiner, on account of my previous place of residence, the community of Tartshin in the region of Volhyn, may he be remembered forever, in the community of Zamość.

75 – In the book *Tiferet Tzvi*, section *Even Haezer* [one of the four volumes of the Code of Jewish Law] by Rabbi Tzvi Hirsch (Bishko), may the memory of the holy be blessed, from Zamość, there is an approbation from Rabbi David Wohl, the head of the rabbinical court of the community of Tyszowce, the son-in-law of the grandson of the author. In these notes it is mentioned that the author had also been a rabbi in Tyszowce during his younger years. The book was published in 5626 [1866].

[Page 19]

Rabbi Leibush Adamczyk of blessed memory (Kozhane Rabbi), the author of the book *Gan Raveh*, a commentary on *Pri Megadim*. He left Tyszowce after the First World War. He was considered to be a *Maskil*. The rabbi and rabbinical judge Rabbi Yaakov Ginzburg of blessed memory. Died on 7 Iyar 5667 [1907]. The author of the book *Zichron Yaakov*, a commentary on the *Pri Megadim* and *Yoreh Deah*, laws of salting [of meat], meat and milk, and mixtures.

The preacher Pinchas Nota Ginzberg of blessed memory, son of the rabbi and Gaon Rabbi Yaakov Ginzberg of blessed memory. He was the author on the book of sermons Der Veinshtok "The Vine Shall Give its Fruit," Warsaw 5690 [1930]. He was a well-known preacher and popular speaker. His influence on the youth of the city during a certain period was poetically described by Yaakov Zipper in his book "Between Rivers and Seas."

Rabbi Shimshon of blessed memory, died in the epidemic during the Second World War.

Rabbi Aryeh (Rabbi Artshele), may G-d avenge his blood, son of Rabbi Shimshon of blessed memory, the last rabbi of Tyszowce.

Rabbi Avraham Stern of blessed memory, shochet and rabbi, author of the books *Edut BeYisrael*, novellae on the Babylonian and Jerusalem Talmuds; *Kvutzat Kitvei Aggada*, an anthology of letters to the children in Yiddish and Hebrew, with Torah novellae and reactions to daily progress; as well as a treasury of folklore material *Chutim Meshulashim*, Hassidic stories and novel ideas in learning. All were published in Montreal, Canada, where he died on 8 Adar 5715 [1955].

Yaakov Zipper-Stern, son of Reb Avraham and Gittel Stern, peace be upon them, born in Szczebrzeszyn (Shebreshin) and educated in Tyszowce. He was in Canada since 1925. He was a prose writer, teacher, and an administrator of the Peretz School in Montreal. To this point, he has published the following works of his own in Yiddish and Hebrew: "There Was a Man," five stories about the Baal Shem Tov; "Across the Bug River"; "Between Rivers and Waters"; and a poem "I Have Come Again to my Destroyed Home." He also publishes stories and articles about literature, themes on pedagogy and society in the important Yiddish and Hebrew journals. He has won two literary prizes for stories published in *Zukunft* of New York, and *Di Goldene Keit* of Tel Aviv.

Yechiel Stern, son of Reb Avraham and Gittel Stern, peace be upon them. He was a teacher and administrator of Yiddish schools in Calgary and Edmonton. He is the main teacher of the Peretz School and administrator of the Yiddish teachers' seminary in Montreal, Canada. He wrote important works on Yiddish education and published the fundamental research work "Cheder and Beis Midrash," for which he won the Lamed prize for literature.

Shalom Stern, son of Reb Avraham and Gittel Stern, peace be upon them. He is a poet, essayist, and teacher. He has lived in Canada since 1926. To this point, he has published seven books on anthologies

[Page 20]

of poems. Among them are two epic poems "Canada" in two parts, and "The White House" that has now been translated into Hebrew. He is considered as one of the talented Yiddish poets. His poems have been translated into Hebrew, English, and French. There are also recitals songs from a number of artists.

Dr. Yisrael Stern, son of Reb Avraham and Gittel Stern, of blessed memory. He is a poet and prose writer, a Yiddish teacher and professor of mathematics. He writes in English and Yiddish under the pseudonym Ish Ya'ir. To this point, he has published two collections of poems in English, which have received very good reports from the critics. He has received the poetry medal from the international union of poet laureates from the president of the Philippines.

He edited and composed the "Poet" feature dedicated to Yiddish poetry. That journal [in which it was published] is international. It is published monthly in India, and is dedicated to poetry in various languages. His daughter Eidel Stern writes poems in English.

Shifra Stern-Krishtalka, daughter of Reb Avraham and Gittel Stern, peace be upon them. She is a teacher in the Peretz School in Montreal. She primarily specializes in preparing learning material and educational questions. Her sons Aharon and Leibel write poems and stories in Yiddish and English. Aharon's first book of poems, "Good Morning to the World" was published at the time of his Bar Mitzvah in 1955.

Hene Stern-Marder, daughter of Reb Avraham and Gittel Stern, peace be upon them. She writes poems in Yiddish and English under the pseudonym Avi-Goel.

Tyszowce is perpetuated in a number of works of the Stern family. All members of the Stern family live in Montreal, Canada.

A. Slutzki, son of Shlomo and Rivka Kreiner, may G-d avenge their blood. He is a poet. He writes in Polish. He published a number of poetry collections in Polish. A number of his poems have been translated into Hebrew.

Sinai Licht, born in 1884, immigrated to North America in 1905. From there, he went to South America. He published a number of works of humor. He also wrote poems and articles under various pen names, among them Yossele Tyszowcer.

Hershel Tzvilich, the son of Meir, lives in Lima, Peru. He writes articles and stories in a humorous fashion in Yiddish and Spanish. He has published two anthologies of prose in Spanish. He plays an important role in the societal life there.

Tyszowce and Tysowiczer types have also been perpetuated by Peretz in his writings of his journeys, in the volume "Images and Sketches" in the section "Bitachon," and in Isaac Bashevis [Singer's] work "Tysowczer Story." Sh. Ansky also wrote abut his visit to Tyszowce during the time of the First World War.

Translator's Footnote:

1.   I am unsure of the meaning of this word.

[Page 26]

The Year 1920 in Tishevits

by M. Dornfeld, z"l

Translated by Moses Milstein

Report by M. Dornfeld, secretary of the Jewish community in Tishevits, delivered to Dr. Itzchak Shiffer, Sejm deputy (translated from Polish):

On August 23, the Bolsheviks retreated towards the river Bug. On the same day, 10 *Balachowtses*[1] entered the city and aimed a *Kolemjat* at the Jewish houses, demanded 30,000 Marks, and ran riot through the city.

Moishe Itzchak Dornfeld, z"l

[Page 27]

In the span of half an hour, they stole money, jewelry, and other goods worth half a million Marks. It wasn't until their senior officer received 5,000 Marks from the community that they left the city, and warned that they would be back at midnight for 20 wagonloads of clothing, 16 pairs of boots, and two wagonloads of hay. The Jewish community prepared everything. The Jewish community was awake all night waiting in fear for the "guests." They never arrived. At the same time, the local priest, Adolf Naczinski, and Dr. Waclaw Miller displayed some compassion for the Jews, and together with other Christians, they guarded the Jewish houses every night.

On August 27 the second regiment of Don Cossaks, the Cossacks of General Balachowicz, and 3 artillery pieces arrived in town. They brought with them two barrels of whiskey. The commanding officers got together at Reuven Bicher's residence, and invited the Jewish musicians to attend. They drank, played and danced. The officers forgot about what was going on, and in the meantime, Budyonny[2]'s cavalry was sitting on the outskirts. When a patrol informed the drunken general staff that the Bolsheviks were already on the outskirts at Dabrowa, the Cossacks hurried to hitch the horses to the artillery, and went off after the cavalry. The commander, completely drunk, fell off his horse. In such a disordered fashion the two regiments set out against the Bolsheviks. It was, however, too late. The Bolsheviks attacked the Cossacks from several sides with koljemats and hand grenades to such an extent that the Cossacks had nowhere to flee to. The battles took place in the city. The Cossacks left behind some tens of dead, and 50 wounded at the "Rinek,[3]" and fled in great disorder as far as Komorow, some 14 versts from Tishevits. They left their artillery behind at the "Rinek" as well. Arriving in Komarow, they took out all their anger on the local Jews, and perpetrated a terrible slaughter. Sixteen Jews were murdered, and over 100 wounded. They robbed and raped. The Balachowtses, not being able to explain their defeat to the army heads, and wanting to wipe way their shame, leveled the well-known libel against the Tishevits Jews, accusing them of shooting at them from windows and balconies, and throwing grenades.

They told these kinds of lies in every city in which they did their devil's work, saying, "This is for Tishevits. When we return to Tishevits, we will slaughter every Jew." This was related to us by the returning hostages.

On the 29th, the Bolsheviks left the city again, and wanted

[Page 28]

to take with them the local priest, Adolf Naczinski and the writer of this letter, along with another Jew, Noah Taub. When I found out about this, we immediately warned the Christians—Catholics, and Jews. The latter immediately went off with me, and the Christians supported us. With great effort, tears, and a lot of pleading, we succeeded in keeping the priest from leaving. We, the Jews, later the Christians, signed a protocol which contained a warning that if they wanted the priest, and he was not in Tishevits, the "*Wojenkom*"[4] would shoot 100 Jews and 50 Christians. We were not frightened by this, and signed the report, and saved the priest in this manner. With great joy, he pressed my hands and kissed them.

On August 31, our shtetl was captured by the Bolsheviks for the third time. The Polish army neared the city on September 1st. During the shooting, which lasted 2 days, almost all the houses were damaged. Miraculously, only 10 people died and a similar number wounded. The following Jews were killed: both Richter sisters, the 65 year-old Dovid Kiperstock, and the 16 year-old Akiva Oifer. Two women lost their legs. The Bolsheviks quickly retreated, and the city was occupied by the "*Hallerczikes*."[5] Two hours later about 100 Balachowicz "heroes" showed up, and began to remove the men from their homes threatening to shoot them. When the number of Jews reached 50, I, along with Noah Taub, went to see the priest where the chief of the 10th Polish Division—a colonel—happened to be staying. With tears in our eyes, and kissing the hands of the priest, we finally convinced them to go to the Cossack "*sotnyk*[6]," and they convinced him that the libel against the Jews in Tishevits was an empty one. The following Christians corroborated it under oath: Antony Dudzinski, Gustav Maslowski, Antony Szikarski, Jan Meliszewski, Winarski, Ksaveri Zukawski, Franczisek Miller. Thanks to their attestation, the colonel categorically ordered the sotnyk to immediately send the Cossacks out of the city. That's how the Tishevits Jews were saved from slaughter at the hands of the Balachowtses. After leaving our city, the Balachowtses went to Laszczow, 8 verst from Tishevits, and carried out there what they were not able to do in Tishevits. The entire shtetl of Laszczow was plundered in the span of 3 days, from September 3rd to the 6th. All the women, from 12 to 50 years of age, were raped. One who resisted was shot.

[Page 29]

Nevertheless, in all the nearby villages (possibly also in the Polish press), the rumor went around that Tishevits Jews, using hand grenades, fought on the side of the Bolsheviks against the Polish soldiers.

I will not, Herr deputy, point out what has to be done in order to remove this suspicion from Tishevits Jews.

The Jewish community expresses its heartfelt thanks to the priest, Adolf Naczinski, and the head of the 10th Polish Division, as well as the other Christians for their testimony on our behalf in avoiding a slaughter of the Jews.

A special thanks goes to the commander of the 2nd Lublin detachment for maintaining order in our city from the 14th to the 18th of August.

Respectfully, secretary of the Jewish community—M. Dornfeld

2.

Sholem Bicher, 27, a merchant from Tishevits, reports:

Monday, probably August 23, a patrol of 10 people entered Tishevits. They entered my father Ozer's dwelling, and asked where they could get leather. They took the opportunity to steal several hundred Marks from my father. After leaving our house, they accosted Pinchas Ginsburg in the street, and took 3,000 Marks in cash off him. It's quite likely that they also robbed the passerby, Motl Zuker from Laszczow, from whom they took, as he reported, 15,000 Marks. Not far from us, they grabbed Perl Kraut, and stole the rings off her fingers. They continued to rob a bunch of people like that. Finally, they asked for the Jewish *soltis*[7], Shieh Katz, and ordered him to prepare, before evening, 20 shirts, 12 pairs of shoes, 3 bushels of oats, a wagonload of hay, and 100,000 Marks. Aside from the hay, the Jews got together all the items demanded as well as 5000 Marks. The Balachowtses got the money in the evening. As for all the other items, they did not get any of them, having been forced to leave that very night.

Thursday, August 26, a new patrol of about 8-10 Balachowtses appeared. They went around stealing all day.

The following day, Friday August 27, two regiments of Cossacks from Balachowicz's army entered, with officers at the head. The general staff took over the home of Reb Bicher (my father), and they drank alcohol all day that they had brought with them from pillaged "Gozelnie"

[Page 30]

in Labunie (Zamosc powiat). At the same time, the Cossacks were robbing the town. The officers demanded that Jewish musicians be brought, and when they arrived, the officers went out onto the balcony and watched as groups of Cossacks danced on the "Rinek." Around three o'clock, the colonel demanded 4 cows from the Jews. The Balachowtses did not manage to take them with them or to slaughter them, because around six o'clock in the evening, the Bolsheviks entered the town, and the Cossacks, most of them drunk, fled in great confusion toward Komarow. The Bolsheviks stayed in the shtetl until Thursday, September 2nd. Thursday, Tishevits was shot up by the Polish army. The sisters, Nechama, and Feige N., and a boy, N. Oifer were hit. Many people, Jews and Christians were wounded. That same day, at noon, the Polish army entered the shtetl, followed by the Balachowicz Cossacks. They captured 40-50 Jews, brought them to the Rinek, threatening to shoot them, because the Jews of Tishevits had thrown bombs at them, and poured boiling water on them. At the request of the Jews, the priest intervened on their behalf with the colonel of the 44th Regiment of the Polish army, and the Jews were freed.

For fear of the Cossacks, the Jews hid with Christians, and the abandoned Jewish houses were plundered by the Cossacks, and people in Polish uniforms. The plundering took all of Thursday. In the evening, Polish patrols were set up, and the plundering ceased. For a period of several days, until Tuesday September 7, bands of Cossacks entered and carried out robberies. That week, Polish police arrived, and then things calmed down.

About 800 Jewish families lived in Tishevits, and there were barely any that were not robbed. The damages were huge, reaching several million Marks. Most afflicted were Leib-Ber Rotenberg (textile store), Miriam Crystal (restaurant), Ozer Bicher (iron work and household utensils), Tsalke Zweig, and others. It is said in the shtetl that there were many cases of sexual assault against Jewish women, but their names were kept secret for obvious reasons.

Sh. Bicher

3.

Moishe Blonder, municipal council representative in Tomaszow, 28, reports:

Sunday August 29, I went on private business to

[Page 31]

Tuczapy. That same day I left Tuczapy for Tishevits, 6 verst from there, and stayed for several days.

During the robbing in Tishevits, the Balachowtses argued that they were exacting revenge for the losses they suffered from the Jews who had thrown bombs at them. I was present when the priest intervened with the Balachowtses not to carry out any pogroms against the Jews.

I myself was robbed by the Balachowtses. They stole a silver cigarette case, a leather briefcase with documents, 125 Russian rubles, and 220 Polish Marks. I received, as well, a sword cut on my arm, and a torn coat, smock, vest, and clothing. I was not wounded. [Sic]

M. Blonder

The picture shows how we hosted the Catholic bishop. He greeted us warmly for our reception.

Footnotes:

1. Soldiers under the command of Stanislaw Bulak-Balachowicz known for perpetrating vicious pogroms
2. Semyon Mikhailovich Bedyonny. 1883-1973, Russian. Founder of the Red Cavalry
3. Market
4. Military commissariat (original translator)
5. Polish soldiers under General Haller. Many recruited from USA and Europe. Associated with antisemitic actions
6. Cossack military officer subordinate to a colonel
7. Village magistrate

[Page 32]

Tishevits, as it was

Yehoshua Shtengel (Israel)

Translated by Moses Milstein

Our little shteteleh, Tishevits, lying between the regional-cities of Zamosc, Tomszow-Lubelski and Hrubieszow, was not even marked on the map. Connection to the bigger cities was primitive, largely via horse and carriage. The carriage drivers would bring merchandise to the city, and at the same time carry passengers back and forth. The roads were unpaved. Only in later years was the road to Zamosc paved. The "little train" station was also not in town but several kilometers away in the village of Tuczop.

Naturally, the difficult communication conditions had some influence on the evolution of the Jewish population, and particularly on the youth. That is not to imply that they were less advanced than in the bigger cities. On the contrary, as far as social and cultural areas are concerned, it is possible that the youth of Tishevits were even more developed and diversified.

Our shtetl was an old one, with a history going back hundreds of years that young and old took pride in. The old legends, like the story about Moshiach ben Yosef, brought a lot of prestige to the rich past. The Polish population took pride in their " Konfederacja Tyszowiecka," and in the various big battles in the time of Poland's grandeur. In particular, they were proud of the things they produced in the shtetl: boots of hide, hand sewn, which extended above the knee. In winter, the farmers would wrap straw and rags around their feet, and draw their boots over them which warmed the whole body in the cold and snow. From this the name Tishevits derives–that is, "Tu szewcow," "Here are showmakers." One can infer from that that the population

[Page 33]

expressed a certain independence, not looking for some prestigious name from the aristocracy, or the gentry.

The city was built in the form of a square. The streets were diverse, the one-story houses built mostly of wood. The roofs were shingled, later also of tin. In the middle of the shtetl there was a large building built of bricks, called the "*Rinek*." It was in the center, and divided the square into two separate halves.

On the north-east side of the square, a street, which we called the "Greblie," stretched all the way to the river, and went on further to the suburb called Majdanek, and from there to the nearby villages. On the southwest side, there was a similar street called "Zamlinie" that led to the Zamosc road.

Aside from that, there were streets and alleys on all sides. On the west side, there was a little street that led to the besmedresh and the shul, as well as to various Chasidic shtiblach. Below them there was the bathhouse and the mikvah. The streets were given special names like "bath street," and so on.

Seen from above, the city looked like a beautiful garden with many green "lawns." Due to the crowded conditions, and the lack of a sewer system, spring and fall were very muddy. "*Kladkes*," narrow boards, led from one street to another. For toilets, people mostly went to the "*Pasheh*"[1] on the other side of the river, behind the bath, and also in the darkened alleys.

The Huczwa River flowed by the city and stretched far beyond Hrubieszow, all the way to the Bug River. The population consisted of three nationalities: Poles, Ukrainians, and Jews. The Christians mostly lived in the suburbs. The churches for Catholics and Orthodox were located there. That is where they had their fields and businesses. The previously mentioned "Rinek," was the site for stores and shops of all manner of goods. The pharmacy and several taverns were also located there.

The Jewish population provided all the necessary goods for the surrounding villages. The market was held once a week on Wednesday. Preparations for the market went on all week. The farmers and the Jews awaited the Wednesday. The farmers used to bring their wheat, horses, cows, and other animals, as well as fruits, vegetables, butter, cheese, eggs and flax.

[Page 34]

The whole shtetl would be full of wagons coming to the market. Here, the Jews displayed their goods. Stalls and tables displayed merchandise in a certain arrangement: clothing, manufactured goods, haberdashery, shoes, etc. Jewish merchants with their goods also came from the nearby towns of Laszczow, and Komarow. The market was an important contributor to the economic life of the shtetl.

With time, some big and small merchants made names for themselves. There were thoughts of expanding sales to other cities; they began to look for external markets. Artisan work also developed, especially tannery, and rope making. It really took off after WWI. Ways of thinking also changed. Different ideas and interests developed.

Social and cultural life in the shtetl was varied. It can be viewed from two aspects. On one side–the foundation of the past with its deeply rooted traditions. On the other side–a more progressive development among the young who were beginning to look for other ways of living. The past had its spiritual center in the shul, the besmedreshes and the shtiblach. These places served not only to study Torah and to pray, but also as houses of meeting and celebration. A center of Torah, and wisdom, and a full life, in one. The big shul was renowned throughout the whole region for its beauty. The shul was used for davening on Shabbes and holidays only. The congregation of the shul was mostly the businessmen, as in the besmedresh, and also, so to say, the more common "worldly," dressed in modern clothes with hats and short jackets. They davened in the Ashkenazi style.

The shul was artfully painted with various artistic-historical works: the twelve tribes of Israel; the Leviathan with the Shorabor[2], objects from the Beis Hamikdash, and other historical paintings, always bright and neat, instilling respect and honor.

The besmedresh near the shul was built simply, in the folk tradition, always open to all and anyone. Large windows, and long tables with sturdy long benches. Near the doors, was a large, wide oven that, in winter, used to warm the whole building, and everyone would warm themselves near it. The poor would be positively revived by it. Jews who arrived from other cities, would make the besmedresh their first stop.

[Page 35]

Cantors, prayer leaders, preachers, and others, would also visit the besmedresh first. The besmedresh was the backbone of the poor. Here they could find their place and some peace. Men would also come here to "get in" a chapter of psalms, or a section of mishnayes, or a kiddush or yorzeit. The city rabbi prayed here as well as other notables. It was also the site for various gatherings like Moes Khitin[3], Hachnoses Kallah[4], fixing the fence at the cemetery, mikvah, etc. Gatherings of a more general nature took place there–voting for the Sejm, or local congregation affairs.

Child rearing was the same as in other shtetls. It was understood that a three-year-old child would start cheder. Twenty to thirty children would sit in a room all day, the rebbe at the head with a pointer. There were teachers for the littlest, Chumash teachers, and Gemara teachers. And that's how they were taught until the age of thirteen, and then they went on to study either alone at the besmedresh, or at a shtibl, or travelled to a yeshiva. Others had to interrupt their studies and learn a trade, or help their father in the store. The very poorest, not being able to pay for tuition, left school before reaching 13 years of age.

Thus the population's way of life was somewhat insular. No sign of anything new. Everything according to the old standards, according to the traditions and ideas of the past. Everything in a Jewish way, even the clothing. It was not until WWI that change began to arrive in educational methods. The "Powszechne szkole"[5] –elementary government school–was compulsory for all children, and the cheder had to adapt to becoming an afternoon school. New schools of our own also were established, like "cheder metukan" (the pious spelled it with a *samach*, "*msukan*"), "Tarbut." The old educational ways struggled and managed to keep the upper hand for years, but in the end had to accommodate themselves.

The years following WWI brought major changes to Jewish society in the shtetl. The October Revolution in Russia, and many other events and changes in the world brought new ideas and problems to shtetl society. Our own economic situation changed as well, and we had to take a stand on all these changes.

Understandably, the youth were very aware of these issues. Their lives were at stake. Studying and learning about the historical changes became the main focus. Many of the adults and especially the youth undertook to deepen

[Page 36]

their understanding, and study on their own. They read everything: books, brochures. Clubs and groups were formed, and in time, parties were established with all kinds of ideas and world-views, and thus, more opportunities to express the differences in opinions, and at the same time, to improve their understanding of world problems. There were many parties that were established later, but among the first were Poalei Zion, the Bund, and the Communists.

The young, and the adults as well, yearned for a new society, and many abandoned the above-mentioned education and behavior. They clung to the party believing the party would provide them with wider opportunities in the future. The honor of being the first in this must be given to the Poalei Zion party that brought new energy to the young in the task of rebuilding life. The library, organized by the party, became an important center for the thirsting youth. Frequent meetings, literary, political-historical, and other issues were held there. Poalei Zion was the first to elucidate and establish the Zionist idea. The party later organized the youth in pioneer spirit, and prepared the Hachshara in order to be the avant-garde in immigration to Israel. The youth organizations, Freiheit, Scout, were renowned in the shtetl. The leaders of the party: Moishe Motl Shaler, Itzchak and Pinchas Landau, Shloime Shtengel, Itzchak Kalinberg, Moishe Barg and others, worked hard for the movement. The Bund was not especially popular as a political party with us, but was more a part of social life thanks to the Peretz library whose founders were Bundists.

The Peretz library was one of the most important cultural institutions providing the opportunity to read books, and was a source of knowledge for all those who were interested in Haskala[6], and wanted to gain more knowledge. There were many classic Jewish books as well as translations from Polish literature, and scientific books about philosophy foundational concepts, etc., as well as journals and newspapers.

The library also was the site of the drama club under the leadership of Mendl Singer, z"l, who achieved a lot putting on plays with great success from time to time. Discussions of a political nature often took place there because it was free for all politically inclined to be members.

In time, the Peretz library became the cultural center of the shtetl.

[Page 37]

It was the place from which the ramifications of political maturity originated, later diversifying into all the parties and groupings that developed in the shtetl.

The Communist party and the needle union also attracted a lot of the young who were in trade. More and more trades organized: tailors, shoemakers, carpenters, millers, boot makers, and others. The most popular trade in shtetl was the needle trade. The workers in all these trades were not organized. They worked for very low wages with no defined work hours. There were of course some adults and youth who were well off, and did not work. Although there was no particular antagonism between the two naturally opposite groups, the clear differences between them, social and spiritual, were noticeable. In time, the workers began to look for ways so as not to be so exploited by the bosses. Then the professional union was formed. The needle union became the guide and defender for all workers in the shtetl. An 8-hour workday was instituted, and better wages; they fought against laying off workers, and against strike-breakers. In addition, the union carried out political-cultural education.

This kind of work was naturally not favored by the Polish authorities, knowing who the leaders were. In fact, the needle union was under the influence of the Communists. Under those conditions it was no small thing to organize and influence politics, spiritual matters, and economic matters: teaching the workers and the youth to celebrate workers' holidays, stopping work and parading on May 1st. Under the conditions of harassment and violence, it was heroic!

There were times when the police terrorized the leaders, imprisoning them even without any valid evidence against them.

The Communist Party was not satisfied with its links only to the Jewish community. It had contacts with Polish and Ukrainian workers, and farmers. Clubs and cells were organized. Illegal assemblies often took place in the forests. They demonstrated at all the political events, and took a stand on all the actual problems. The wave of arrests did not deter the leading cadres. In 1926,

[Page 38]

arrests of communists occurred, and again in 1932, and in 1935. The fearless leaders of the movement spent their best years in jail, among them: Itzchak Zwillich, Israel Eitel, Abraham Eisen, Moishe Krempil, Yehoshua Shtengel, and others.

In particular, we should mention here the first party leaders and activists: Favish Alboim, Yosl Shtengel, Wolf Messer, Ephraim Itzchak Shoichet's son, and many others who were not even well known in the shtetl.

There were other parties and organizations that played a big role such as: the Left Poale Zion, the General Zionists, Mizrachi, Agudat Israel, Folks-Partei, handworkers union, savings and loan bank, and almost all of them had a youth wing. Most of the youth, however, grouped themselves around the three aforementioned parties with which I was more familiar.

The lively youth, unfortunately, is no more. The shtetl is in ruins.

Footnotes:

1. Pasture
2. Legendary giant ox whose flesh will be eaten by the righteous in paradise
3. Contributions to the poor for Passover
4. Communal help for young girls without resources to marry
5. Primary school
6. Jewish Enlightenment

[Page 39]

Tishevits—My Shteteleh

by Hersh Ben Mair and Breine Zwillich

Translated by Moses Milstein

Not on paper, but on parchment, with a goose quill, like the old scribes, is how I would have to write about you, my dear little shteteleh. Every letter must be holy and pure. Your shul and besmedresh, your Chasidic shtiblach, your youth unions, were all so full of charm. You, my shteteleh, forged our souls for generations in poverty, and raised whole generations on Torah and hard work.

You were a small shtetl, surrounded by a small river that quietly flowed on to somewhere in the wider world, half-fallen houses reflected in your waters, and in your summer evenings, the willows by the river whispered a prayer.

It is necessary to write about your death with tears and blood. There was once a shtetl, we would have to tell our grandchildren, a shtetl that lived without commotion, without clamor. Everyone worked hard to earn enough for bread and challah for Shabbes. With their last pennies, they sent their children to cheder, yeshivah, and did hard physical labor to be able to marry their children off with proper respect. There were Jews like oaks in the Lipowic Forest, with wool tallises and silver crowns. There were Jewish business owners who worked very hard to make a living; there were Jewish merchants and store-keepers who waited for customers in order to be able to earn enough for a pair of shoes, and clothes for their children. There were the Jewish youth who left the besmedreshes and filled the culture unions, and swallowed whole chapters of Tolstoy, Mendeleh, Sholem Aleichem, and Peretz with the same enthusiasm with which they consumed the yellowed pages of the Gemara. There were quiet love affairs, and Saturday dusky evenings somewhere among the mountains. There were children, with torn shoes and patched trousers singing the *"V'Ani"* by the light of tallow candles, exactly as if they were living in Bethlehem by mother Rachel's tomb. There were *dorfgeyers*[1] who dragged themselves around for weeks in the

[Page 40]

villages, and came home for Shabbes with a sack of potatoes on their shoulders, a little barley kasheh, and beans.

But everything was annihilated all at once, killed off violently, and from the whole shtetl, nothing was left but a mass grave somewhere in the forests around the shtetl.

I stand orphaned on the ruins of my shtetl, and say Kaddish for you, my shtetl!

All along my wandering ways, you stand before me. I see the besmedresh with its long tables covered with religious books. I even see the barrel of water by the door where the men would wash their hands before saying, *"Asher Yatzar."* I see Yasheh Shammes warming his back at the stove; I see the proud shul with its symbolic paintings, and my grandfather, Chaimtche, shoichet and chazzen, standing at the lectern in his white smock on Yom Kippur evening during Kol Nidrei. I see the Husiatyn shtibl from which you could always hear the monotonous melody of *oi, oi, amar Raba*. I see the Belzer shtibl where Hershl Velliyes sang the *"Yaalot"* with such sweetness. I see the Trisker chasidim, going around the shtetl on Simchat Torah singing *Shishu v'Simchu*, and the tall Leibish shouting out, *"Tzon Kidoshim,"* and the children running after screaming, "Meh, meh." I see Nathan-Dovid Zuker standing in his little store, his wife the breadwinner, and he only paying attention during the Wednesday market, his shortsighted eyes always buried in a religious book. I see Yechiel Asher with his wide tallit-katan wandering around the market looking for bargains. I see Leibish Shtuden, always worried, standing by the door of his store, dragging on a cigarette butt in his stained yellow fingers. I see Hersh Braun with his groomed beard hurrying Friday night to daven, and telling the tardy Jews to close their stores in order to prevent a desecration of the Sabbath. I see Moishe Motl Shaler chewing his nails, always lost in thought, Shloime Kreiner, the *maskil*, with a buttoned up collar, always smiling. More than once, I see in my dreams my rabbi, R' Abraham Shochet, who lived on a narrow street, a Jew a great scholar, always with his snuff, peering into a religious book, and when he finds the proper interpretation, his face breaks out in a smile, and he asks his wife to bring him a bowl of hot potatoes with the peels that he peels with his long nails which he also uses to slaughter fowl. We, his students, also enjoyed the hot potatoes, as well as the verse "*kol habassar*" in *Holin*[2]. I can see before me Leibish Wassertreiger, a Jew with a broad beard, bent over, carrying two large pails of water from the river dangling from his shoulder yokes. Somewhere on a *prisbe*, Feige-Leah the Meshugene used to break out in a song

[Page 41]

with a sad melody, "Gold and silver are left alone, and if you are called, you must come." I can see standing before my eyes the nobleman, Krant, the Tishevits aristocrat with the groomed beard, a *vinkl advocat*[3], as he looks down from the balcony of his aristocratic dwelling on the dyke. I see the Tishevits bathhouse, a half-ruin, and I hear the men shouting from the highest bench, "Hot, another scoopful," and the steam creeps up to the highest bank where they whip themselves with little brooms. I see my grandfather, Moishe-Nachman Yosef's, with his long white beard, reciting every Shabbes at the *Melave Malkah, Tikon Eliyahu*, in order to be certain of a place in the world to come. I see the old cemetery with the legendary tombstones from Meshiach Ben Yosef, and the two merchants from Lublin, and Jewish women praying fervently at the graves pleading for health and prosperity. I see Leah Henye's, the stout woman, who leads women services in shul. I see Shmuel Sofer, with his wide, blonde beard, scratching a goose quill across a sheet of parchment, and I hear the baritone voice of White Aharon reciting the parsha of the week in the Torah in the big besmedresh. I see Cheneh Melamed, a *Bontche Schweig*,[4] who is delighted with the little bit of grits his wife gives him for dinner. I see Leib Ber Kolenberg, the Chasidic aristocrat, who, alas, has trouble from his children, who are beginning to hang around the unions. I see Nechemiah Hitlmacher, the little well-dressed man who was very musical. I see Nachman Yidl, dressed-up, carrying the newspaper *Heint* on the sidewalk of the dyke. His son, Shmuel Saver, is yelling at him for getting his trousers muddy. I see Nachman Spodik wearing his tefillin, rocking back and forth with an old torn siddur. I see Simcha Shtuden with his white bushy beard, his hands in his belt, his head turning from side to side. I see so many children carrying flags with red apples on Simchat Torah at night in the besmedresh. I see Black Riva going home from the library with a book, sneaking a peek at the first page while walking.

I see before me how we performed theater at Dotche Zhibivitser's attic. We are performing, I think, *Motke Ganif*, by Sholem Asch, or *The Ganovim* by Bimko, or *Die Shchite* by Gordon, and Sureleh Nachman Yidl's is our primadonna.

It's Saturday morning in the shtetl. Everyone's asleep after the cholent. Groups of young people are promenading on the *krinitza*. Moishe Zalman is standing with his yarmulke and big tallit katan near his door, yawning in the direction of the market towards the pump. Near the pump, a pair of Jews stand refreshing themselves with a drink of cold water. Kopl Kellenberg is walking slowly, in his Shabbes clothes, listening to Abraham Shoichet. From Moishe Liebe's house a voice is heard studying a chapter of Mishnah by Itzye Rov. Malkah Dvore and Gitl are sitting on the sidewalk.

[Page 42]

Avrumtche Eitl, dressed-up, goes by, and winks at Malkah, and continues on to the water mill. A little while later, Malkah Rov gets up and goes into the house to change. Raizel Nachman Yidl's goes arm-in-arm with Yenkeleh Nuster on a short walk by the *klentwes*. Shabbes is spread over the shtetl in all its beauty. Near the administrative office a couple of Jews are groaning while reading a Polish notice about a new tax.

I see the shtetl where Leib Steinshreiber sits in his cramped store on the dyke, and sews visors onto caps, and gets in a chat with Leib Eitel about Bucharin's ABC of Communism. And Moishe Motl Shaler explains the paradoxes of Max Nordau to me. I see Chantsieh-Dotche Ozer's read, with tears in his eyes, *Der Schwartzer Yungerman* by Dinezon, and I can still hear Shloime Goldman giving a talk in the Tzeirei Zion group about workers and labor. So long and so far away from my shtetl, yet while writing, everything comes to life in my memory, as if I were right there. I even see the pigs that wallowed in the mud near the bathhouse, and the children throwing stones at them. I see Abish Czuma harnessing his horse and wagon to drive to the kolejka,[5] and Basheh chatting with Velye Tsap's wife about how the challah came out for Shabbes. I see the market women sitting and selling frozen apples, warming themselves by the firepot, and waving sticks at the city Billy goat with his two dried-out horns and goatee, trying to eat the apples in the stall.

It is Yom Kippur eve. The cries and voices of women reciting blessings over the candles issue from the houses. The sun goes down somewhere in the Tishevits Forest. Men are rushing from the mikvah with wet beards. The shtetl is quiet and in holiday mood. The tall wax candles cast their light through the windows. Children snuggle up to parents. The melody of Kol Nidrei is heard from the shuls. At every turn the spirit of the Days of Awe is felt.

I also see Chaveh Chaim-Yosl's standing at the post office waiting for a letter from her husband, Chaim-Yosl from Cuba. Maybe there will also be a small check with a few dollars for winter clothes for the kids. I see my brother, Yehoshua, gluing paper purses for sale, in order to save my mother who lies paralyzed in bed begging for death. It's Wednesday—market day. Hundreds of Christian wagons with pigs, sacks of potatoes, corn. The city is noisy. Bnimeleh is bargaining with a goy over a horse sale. He opens its mouth and looks at its teeth, while nearby a young colt is prancing, kids plucking hairs from its tail. Stalls with "*Tishavyanes*," boots with wide bootlegs, hanging.

[Page 43]

Jewish men are slapping hands with the goyim negotiating prices like that. A resounding slap is the sign the sale is done. A goyeh takes out the money from a filthy knotted kerchief, and the goy walks away with new boots on his shoulder. Leizer Gantcher is examining a hen, blowing into the feathers to see how fat she is, a rooster crows, and somewhere a goyeh drops a basket of eggs, and the yolks get mixed into the mud.

In Dotche Zhibivitzer's teahouse, farmers sit at long wooden tables sipping boiling hot tea, eating black bread with lard.

The holidays are over. The autumn rains fill the gutters. People gather round the wagons of wood, every log stored for the winter like a piece of gold. Wood chips are collected and kindling is chopped for heating the ovens. Children start to go to cheder at night, and study chumash and Rashi by the light of smoky lamps. They go home in lantern light. Later, the cold, frozen winter comes with snow knee-high. The windowpanes become steamed up and covered with frosted flowers. The river freezes over. Youngsters with warm scarves slide on the ice. The besmedresh is warm. Men sit by the stoves and tell stories about the Baal Shem. My grandfather, Chaimtche, tells, for the hundredth time, how the Radziner found the snail.[6] Sometimes a magid[7] comes and delivers a sermon in the traditional magid melody, and the people groan when he describes hell so that you can almost see the flickers of flames, and the audience gives him some groschen by the light of a tallow candle. Moishe Dutche, the town's rich man, drives out to the forests in a new hooded fur cape. Black crows fight over fat pieces of intestine a Jewish woman threw out onto the snow, making a chicken kosher for Shabbes. Aharon-Berish Laks comes riding back from the forest in a thick scarf, his beard and moustache sprouting pieces of ice, his breath misting in the air. Fishl-Leibish Shtuden's opens his shop and sweeps the piles of snow away from his door, and Getzl Kuperstein comes from davening in his skunk fur, his tallis and tefillin under his arm.

Winter passes. The snow melts and fills the ditches with water. At Shimon Nadel's they are beginning to make matzes for Pesach. Lilacs are beginning to bloom in the gentile gardens. Soon the Rosh Chodesh radishes will appear. The Jews start to whitewash their houses. Sheets with matzes are carried through the shtetl in honor of Pesach, and children are wearing their new shoes for the holiday. Spring rushes in from the *klentwes*.

[Page 44]

Eggs are available from Abraham Glatter. Schmaltz for Pesach is taken out of the cellars. People are running around with wrapped-up spoons, burning the chometz. Passover wine is pressed from raisins for the four cups. The shtetl acquires a new soul. Wagonloads of lime to cover the floors are brought in from Koczer Mountain. Birds begin to build nests under the roofs, and the first stork stands on one leg on Peretz Krant's roof. After Pesach, Getzl Kuperstein and Moishe Shtuden travel to Warsaw to buy flowers for summer. Gentile women start to be seen in the streets with their kerchiefs, selling *tsiprinkes*, and radishes, and trees begin to bloom in the orchards. People are beginning to eat tsiprinkes and sour cream for breakfast, the poor, radishes with soured milk, and frugal wives use even the buttermilk.

The beloved summer comes, women begin to bake knishes with blueberries. Canaries sing in the summer dawn. The Jews begin to move out to the orchards with wagons full of bedding, benches, tables, plates and kettles. Meshugener Yani runs around the streets singing, "The holiday times are beginning to appear," accompanying himself on the mandolin, and groups of youngsters follow him to the "long bridge." Yakov-David Shoichet, and Yitzchak Shoichet meet at the *kontzeleria*,[8] share a pinch of snuff from one snuffbox, and quickly run back home, because the women are already waiting there with chickens to slaughter for Shabbes.

I see you, Tishevits, with all your streets and alleys, from the watermill to Pinye Landau's house where pots and pans were manufactured. I can still smell the smell of the orchard in the court, and the mud. I still see the ruin where according to legend, Meshiach Ben Yosef lived. I see the cellar room where old Zelikl lay paralyzed for years, and hear his constant groaning, and where Peretz Parach gave him a little grits to eat that some housewife donated to sustain the soul of the sick man.

I still see Gershon Melamed's cheder opposite the besmedresh, where he taught children. He also chiseled the letters on tombstones. I remember when Yosef Meirtsie went around buying dollars and loaning to Gemiles-Chasidim. He used to hide the dollars in his tefillin sac when he saw a policeman in the distance.

I remember when Hershl Moishe-Liebe's son in law, Moishe Itzchak Zuker's son, a young man, a Torah scholar who used to daven Shabbes in his shtreiml, was murdered in a village, and was brought to town Friday during the day in a wagon. The shtetl mourned, and Herzke Garber from the Chevra Kadisha carried the burial board,

[Page 45]

and wept bitter tears, and when they were carrying the stretcher, the whole city followed in the funeral procession. At the cemetery, Krimmer Dovid was standing with his gnarled stick keeping people from stepping on the graves. Youngsters took advantage of the moment when Krimmer Dovid was preoccupied protecting the graves to fill their pockets with apples from the cemetery. I see Deaf Shieh who was "soltis" for years running around the city with his long goatee carrying notifications concerning taxes, and in the days of Russian conscription, Deaf Shieh was the carrier of the sad news that so and so had to report.

I left my shtetl in 1927, said good-bye to my friends and family. I said goodbye to my grandfather, Chaimtche, already an old man in his nineties, in the Radziner shtibl. Half blind, he was still telling his tales of the Radziner court. The only thing my grandfather told me, with tears in his eyes, was to make sure to enter the new land on the right foot. I parted from my sick mother who covered me in tears, from my brother, Yehoshua, who was choked-up with tears, and one Sunday at dawn I was already seated on Abish Czuta's wagon travelling to the kolejka[1], and from there on trains and ships to Cuba, to start a new life on this exotic island.

When I returned in 1930, I saw for the first time how poor and lonely our shtetl was, the houses more sunken in age. Even Yankl Paniche's brick building in the middle of the market, that workers especially brought in from Russia had built, had lost its charm. Peeling paint, the roof covered with patches, the doors screeching. Peretz Krank's house on the dyke had lost the color on its walls, doors and windows. The shtetl looked old. Chaim Rubele's hobbled along bent over, Artsheleh, the city rabbi, still a young man in his forties, already had grey hair under his worn-out shtreiml. The stores were half empty. In the new cemetery, new rows of tombstones. A lot of my friends had left the shtetl, some to the kibbutzim of Palestine as it was known then, some to Argentina, others to America and Canada.

From then to now, after years of wandering, I still have not left my shtetl. I see it in dreams, I see it when I close my eyes. Not New York, not London, not Paris, not Buenos Aires, and not years

[Page 46]

in beautiful Lima, Peru have been able to erase my shtetl from memory.

May these words be a Kaddish, and may the winds carry them to my shtetl Tishevits, and to the ruins of my shtetl, to the mass graves of our martyrs. May my Kaddish be heard and may the trees answer, amen!

Lima, October 10, 1965

———

Footnotes:

1. Literally, "village-goers,"¹ people who made their living going to and trading in villages
2. Talmudic tractate
3. An unlicensed lawyer
4. Bontche Schweig is a character of great meekness in a story by I. L. Peretz.
5. Narrow gauge railway
6. Snail believed to be the source of purple dye
7. Itinerant preacher
8. Administrative office

———

My Shteteleh Tishevits

by Ruth Sherer (Rita Felz), Israel

Translated by Moses Milstein

I will shut my eyes, and go back in my mind to my little shtetl, Tishevits.

How alive it all seems before me. Little wonder, because the most beautiful, carefree years of our lives, years that will never return, were left there, along with our nearest and dearest.

A shtetl like all the other shtetls, with a shul, a besmedresh, and many chasidim, shtibls as well as synagogues. There was a Jewish community, and a Polish community, a *gemiles chesed* bank in the handworkers union, a bath and poorhouse, a cinema, a Catholic and Russian Orthodox church, and a courthouse.

There were four Polish schools, and many cheders. There were many organizations, both of the left and right, and a Y. L. Peretz library which served all classes of society. Physically, our shtetl distinguished itself from others. Nature had imbued it with a special charm. The center of the city was the market, and around it all the side streets.

The river Huczwa encircled the town and separated us from the suburbs. The center of the shtetl was where the Jews lived with some Christian families here and there. They mostly lived in the suburbs where there were a few Jewish families too who drew their livelihood there. Bridges connected us to the suburbs. North of the market stretched the so-called Ostrowa. To the south, a bridge separated us from the so-called *klentves*. To the west, we were separated by a small bridge and a long bridge.

[Page 47]

Beyond the small bridge was the so-called "court" where only Jews lived. After that came the long bridge, and the outskirts of Zamlynie. To the east, there was a bridge near the water mill, and then came the suburb that was divided in three. One way, stretched through a bridge and a meadow where the slaughterhouse lay. The second way led to the "*bursn*" where the old cemetery was, and opposite it was the "court" orchard. After that came the school and the Russian church. The third way led to the so-called Debina. There was another school here, a Polish church, and the pretty, so-called *krynica*—where, climbing up to the highest hill, you could see a mixture of green colors which really caught the eye—beginning with dark green grasses to light yellow flowers. From a distance, it looked like a beautiful carpet laid out as if a painter had arranged the appropriate pretty colors.

Hard by the bottom of the hill there was a well with spring water that had a special fresh taste.

Those beautiful childhood years that everyone longs for, we spent there. Those were memorable, but in other cases Tishevits can be mentioned in less positive terms, because, in every corner, you could find backwardness, and frequent antisemitism that humiliated us. The houses were built of wood. There were very few brick buildings. The houses were pressed so close to each other that you might think they were unable to support themselves, and that may indeed have been the case. The market and several streets were paved, and that gave it a little bit of a big-city feel. There were two pumps in the middle of the market, and they provided water for the city. The city was lit with a few gas lamps that did not always function.

The houses used naphtha lamps and some gas lamps, and near the mill there was electricity.

They heated with wood, coal or peat. You were lucky if there was enough fuel, because in some houses there was not enough. There were different classes of people. A few rich families; a small number of middle class; the greatest part, poor, and very poor. People lived together peacefully, in spite of the fact that most were large families with sharply delimited comforts. There were about 300-400 families. There were merchants of forest products and wheat, and smaller stores, and businessmen who were good tradesmen: cobblers, tailors, tanners, carpenters, and masons.

[Page 48]

The only good day to make money was market day, Wednesday, and on all other days of the week, the shtetl was quiet. Storekeepers yawned, and tradesmen left their apprentices to do the work, and wandered out to the street where you could run into someone, or a child even. Market day was especially happy. Early in the morning, wagonloads of farmers would come in from around the city, as well as merchants from nearby. The hog butchers occupied quite a respected place, and stunk up the shtetl with their cooking and roasting pig meat. It was really suffocating when you got near the place. Near them, the shoemakers set up their shops with their regular boots, as well as the special boots with the long white bootlegs called *Tishevianess.* On the other side were the old-clothes dealers, and other stands with various merchandise like, glassware, knitwear, toys, locks and keys, and so on. In the midst of all this, farmer women pushed through the crowds selling chickens, beans, onions, garlic, and other greens. Jewish women were out looking for bargains. Everyone in their own way lauded their goods. There was such a crowd that you could barely hear yourself talking, and in among the horses neighing, the pigs squealing, the ducks quacking, the hens crowing, and just the general racket, a pair of male and female singers with a harmonica set themselves up in the crowd. They both thought they would be heard over the noise, but their echoing songs did not succeed in overcoming the din.

For us, still young at the time, it was a special satisfaction to push yourself into the whole crush, and inspect the new merchandise brought in from abroad, and to listen as one tried to shout over another touting his wares in a not-very-good Polish. Women with nice smiles put on their faces, invited you into their stores. Everyone tried to earn a few zlotys.

Toward evening, everyone dispersed, and it was quiet again, and very dirty, as they barely cleaned up.

We didn't have much to brag about regarding transportation. Mostly people travelled by horse and buggy. For longer distances, the train was used, but you had to get there by horse. The train station was far from the city. The last year, there was also a bus from Tishevits to Zamosc, leaving at 8:00 AM with few passengers, and returning in the evening. The bus was greeted by a gang of kids with shouting and noise that echoed through the shtetl.

[Page 49]

The roads, it can be said, were quite quiet. Nevertheless, we heard of bad accidents from time to time. Mostly it happened in broad daylight, when a goy wanted to have some fun, and raced through the market with his horse and wagon, and hit a child or an adult. People would come running from all over the city, quickly grab the victim, pour water on him, gave him some to drink too, and everything would return to normal.

We also experienced plenty of fear every summer while bathing. Every year something had to happen. The Jews would interpret it as the water required a person. I never understood this, and I was too shy to ask. I knew that a person could not live without water, but water not being able to exist without a person, I still don't understand.

We also suffered from frequent fires that occurred in the summer nights in the suburbs. The whole shtetl would be illuminated by the fires.

The holidays and Sabbaths had their own special charm. Friday evening, as soon as Mecheleh the shammes banged on the doors of the stores with his hammer telling everyone that Shabbes was arriving, all the storekeepers shut their stores, and the street was empty of stalls, and everyone started to get ready for Shabbes. There was a special homey atmosphere. After the candle lighting, the shtetl looked like a Sabbath queen. There was a ring of lights shining from windows around the whole market. The streets were neatly swept. The children, hair washed and dressed in Shabbes clothes, hurried with their fathers either to the beautiful big shul, or to the besmedresh, or to the Chasidic shtibls. There was such a sort of holiday atmosphere that it seemed in those moments that all the problems of the Jews had ended. The goyim looked on at this holy atmosphere with respect. And also we, the so-called free thinkers, regarded the religious part of the city with tolerance.

I remember that we, the youth, had little patience for the drawn-out ritual of the Shabbes table with the kiddush and the zmires, and the serving of food. We wanted to get the meal over with quickly so we could go out and join our friends, some to an organization, others just to have a good time, others to go listen to a political discussion. We had a beautiful youth that was cultural as well. We didn't have a high school, nor did we have any

[Page 50]

opportunities to study. Nevertheless, we had young people stuffed with knowledge like a pomegranate, and achieving it by themselves. The library was always full of searchers. Everyone came to hear something, to absorb something, a little news, a little knowledge. We were many, but few survived.

Oh, how alive you all appear to me, you beautiful, sweet young girls, and goodhearted boys. You are as dear to me as my own life. As long as we are alive we will remember you. All of you live on in us!

You are with us everywhere, in every joyful moment, and in sorrow. But why do I always see your eyes filled with tears and longing, your arms outstretched? Why do I see the small children, weary, languishing, with tears running down their emaciated faces? Why do I see you, fathers and mothers, grandfathers, and grandmothers, and aunts, with defeated faces, with eyes full of despair. You give me no rest. I always see you as if you are begging for help, for mercy from us. It was a time when we too were sentenced to death, escaping by the skin of our teeth. We could not have helped you. Our conscience is clear. We, the survivors, will never forget you. The spilled blood of innocents will not rest until the murderers are annihilated.

The Tyszowcer Messiah the son of Joseph[1]

Reb Avraham Stern of blessed memory

Translated by Jerrold Landau

(Excerpted from the book "Anthology of Aggadaic writings"[2])

Blessed be G-d, 18 Av, 5684 [1924], Tyszowce.

To my honorable son Mr. Yaakov Zipper, may his light shine, Shalom.

You know of course that it is a tradition in our city that the Messiah the son of Joseph is resting in our cemetery. You have been there many times and seen with your own eyes the wonder of the bent monument over his grave. There is a tree growing beneath it that is just as bent as the monument,

[Page 51]

which is holding it up. You also know that with us in the city, as well as in the entire region, this grave was regarded with great holiness. Every Jew goes there to pray. One does not approach within four ells, and there are no other graves in a large surrounding area. You will be wondering what type of news I am telling you? I will answer you, for your younger brother, Mr. Shalom Stern, may his light shine, showed me in the Der Lodzer Tagesblatt newspaper where a writer gathered together some sort of legend regarding the Tyszowcer Messiah, full of lies, with a bit of truth that also got

Rabbi Avraham Stern of blessed memory,
a shochet and teacher of righteousness

[Page 52]

twisted around, with its head down and its feet up. Therefore, I found it necessary to give over to you, also for the future generations, that which I have heard here, from older people who received it from their parents and grandparents, going back to the generation of our Messiah about whom we are discussing here. My childhood *melamed* Reb Chaim Hirsch Harpen, the father-in-law of your childhood *melamed* Reb Gershon Lerech, peace be upon him, also told me such. (He died at over the age of 80 when I was 15-16 years old.) When he was young, his father-in-law, also a *melamed* of young children, described what he had seen with his own eyes in the city *pinkas*. The *pinkas* was burnt in the house of the rabbi of that time, Rabbi Avraham Yaakov, peace be upon him, the father of Rabbi David, peace be upon him, the father-in-law of Rabbi Shimshon Mordechai Yaakov, peace be upon him, the father of the current [i.e. most recent] rabbi, Rabbi Aryeh Glancz, may G-d avenge his blood.

As a preface to the story, I wish to mention to you the Gemara of Sukka, 52, who are the four craftsmen[3]? Who are the four craftsmen who will, G-d willing, speedily in our days Amen, cast off the horns of the evil nations who specifically oppress the Jews? The Gemara answers there, the Messiah the son of Joseph, the Messiah the son of David, Elijah, and the righteous priest – Shem the son of Noah. In *Sanhedrin* 98b, one finds that every student believes that his rabbi is fitting to be the Messiah, and hopes, and also searches for, hints in the Bible that this is the case. It states there that Rabbi Shilo's students said, "His name is Shilo, and found a hint, 'until Shilo comes' [Genesis 49:10]. Rabbi Yannai's students stated that his name is Yannai, and found a hint, 'Before the sun his name is Yinon'" [Psalms 72:17]. Similar to Yannai was Chanina Chizkia, as it states there, Rav, from Rebbe's numbered students who gave their opinions, as is said in *Gittin* 59a – if he is from Chiya, he is from our holy rabbi [Rabbi Yehuda Hanasi], and if from Matia, such as Daniel the man of pleasantness[4]. This means, it was clear to him that the Messiah could be one of the living *Tzadikim* in the generation, who is fit to host the soul of the Messiah (The Admor of Husyatin, may he live long, once said in the middle of a discussion, "The Messiah will not necessarily come down from heaven. It is possible that a *Tzadik* may be sitting at the table, take a nap, place his head in his hands, and began to say that he is the Messiah, saying the last words as he is resting his head in his hands.") He could also be from the deceased *Tzadikim*, who will be the first to rise at the Resurrection of the Dead, and will become the Messiah to lead the Jews to the redemption. Therefore, Rav chose his rabbi from amongst the living – for he was also the rabbi of all the Jews as he was the compiler of the six orders of the Mishnah, and was called "Our Holy Rabbi" [*Rabbeinu Hakadosh*] due to his great holiness. And from amongst the dead? He chose Daniel the man of pleasantness, for the last verse in the Book of Daniel, chapter 12, is "And now Daniel… And you will arise[5] – i.e., he will rise during the Resurrection of the Dead, to his destiny at the end of days

[Page 53]

(see Rashi *Pesachim* 56a, starting 'End of Days'). It can be derived from all this that in every generation, there are two living *Tzadikim*, one of whom is fitting to become the Messiah son of Joseph, and the other the Messiah son of David.

Now, to the story. On the gravestone, it is etched, "Here is buried a righteous, faithful man, Reb Elyakim the son of Reb Shmuel, in the year 5319 [1559] or 5332 [1572] – i.e. from the generation of the *Ariza'l* [Rabbi Yitzchak Luria], who was already living in Safed in the Land of Israel. It was told that on a specific Friday, a rumor spread forth in Tyszowce that a poor *Latnik* – that is a tailor who fixes and patches all garments – died, and so that he will not remain [unburied] over the Sabbath, the *Chevra Kadisha* quickly gathered together with *Chevra Nosim* to perform his rites. To their surprise, they found two unknown guests in his poor house. They were honorable people, suffering from severe tribulations, who did not want to leave the deceased, as he was a holy Jew. They summoned the rabbi of Tyszowce of that time, who made a compromise that they were to prepare the shrouds with the casket, bring them to the cemetery, and then the usual people who conduct the funeral arrangements would do what they do, under the condition that each of those involved would first purify himself and immerse himself in a kosher *mikveh*. However, the *tahara* [preparation of the body for burial] and dressing of the body would be done by the guests who had stated that the deceased was a holy person.

At the request of the rabbi of Tyszowce, they explained what was happening, that from Heaven they had been informed by their rabbi, the *Ariza'l*, that the Lubliner rabbi from that time, the Gaon the *Maharsha'l* of blessed memory, along with the rabbi of Krakow, the *Rem'a* of blessed memory, were conversing between themselves, that on a certain Sunday they would blow the shofar in Lublin and also in Krakow, and – Heaven forbid – place he *Ariza'l* under a ban of excommunication, for he established a new method of study of the wisdom of Kabbalah. In order to prevent this plan from taking place, the *Ariza'l* sent them to the elderly Gaon, the *Maharsha'l* of blessed memory, as well as to the younger Gaon, the *Rem'a* of blessed memory.

When the rabbi of Tyszowce had invited the guests to his place for the Sabbath, they answered that they must get to the *Maharsha'l* in Lublin for the Sabbath. The rabbi asked whether this was possible? The distance between Tyszowce and Lublin was almost 200 kilometers. The elder of the two guests, Rabbi Chaim Vital of blessed memory, responded that their rabbi , the *Ariza'l* had designated a cloud to bring them here. We left Safed first thing this morning, and, G-d willing, with the same cloud, we will soon be in Lublin. Now, we are travelling,

[Page 54]

G-d willing. We will write to you from Lublin about all the details from there and here.

That is what took place. They wrote to the rabbi of Tyszowce of that time from Lublin. He wrote in the city ledger: Rabbi Chaim Vital had once asked the rabbi, the *Ariza'l*, to state where is the *Tzadik* from amongst the living who is worthy to be the Messiah the son of Joseph (he did not ask about the Messiah the son of David, for he believed that his rabbi, the *Ariza'l* was himself suitable for this). He responded, "I have received an announcement from Heaven to fulfil all your requests. I ask you to revoke your request, for the *Tzadik* is a hidden one, and it is a great danger to reveal him." (Regarding this, there is a note in *Sefer Shivchei Ha'Ari*, also in *Sefer Shivchei Rabbi Chaim Vital*). When Rabbi Chaim agreed that the rabbi should reveal it to him, the *Ariza'l* promised him to inform him at the appropriate time, when the opportunity arose to send the emissaries to the *Maharsha'l* – and Rabbi Chaim Vital was to be one of them – the *Ariza'l* fulfilled his promise. He informed them that the Messiah the son of Joseph of that generation lives in Tyszowce, a town in the Lublin Gubernia. He gave them a sign that if they wish to find him in the house, nobody would be harmed, stating: (with that sign, one can well understand the Gemara in Yoma 71a: When he finds the High Priest in the marketplace, they say to him, my master the High Priest, we have fulfilled your mission. If he finds him in the house, they say to him, the One Who Grants Life to the Living, we have fulfilled His mission[6]. Various books quote the *Chizkuni*[7], that the Torah refers to the messenger from Azazel as *Ish Iti* [the appointed man] because, although the High Priest was an expert in astrology, he required the Holy Spirit to choose a person who would certainly die that year[8], i.e., the *Ish Iti*, for his time had come to leave the world. During the time of the Second Temple, it was also uncertain whether the High Priest himself would survive the year, for it says earlier on page 8 in Rashi, that the sign is that if the emissary found the High Priest in his house, he and the emissary would survive, and he would be able to state that the mission was faithful in the name of G-d, and for the good, as it says "The Giver of Life, we have fulfilled Your mission." That means that we have fulfilled the mission of the Blessed G-d in accordance with the request of the Torah – that influences the living that they may remain alive. However, if they find him on the street, it is not a good sign for himself, and perhaps not for the High Priest. Given that it is bad, one must not mention the name of the Blessed G-d. Therefore, he refers to the mission in the name of the High Priest, granting the honor to him. He says, "My master the High Priest, we have fulfilled your mission. However, unfortunately when they arrived at the house, he was in the *mikveh* in honor of the Sabbath. When he came home

[Page 55]

he did not say one word. He just washed his hands, greeted the guests, took a bit of straw from the bed, spread it on the ground, lay down upon it with his feet toward the door, and immediately died. Thus it was, and it remains the custom in Poland to place a bit of straw on the ground beneath a deceased person, and to position him with his feet toward the door.)

When they arrived at the synagogue of the *Maharsha'l* in Lublin, they entered as the people were standing for the silent *Shmone Esrei* of *Mincha*, prior to *Kabbalat Shabbat* [the service that welcomes the Sabbath]. They entered the synagogue and remained standing at the door. One of them said to the other, "The local rabbi is riding on a wheel in the middle of *Shmone Esrei*." People from that time heard this, and interpreted these words as a violation of the honor of the rabbi. However, they saw that the guests were of fine form, with a splendid countenance, so those who heard did not dare to hurt them. They passed the words of the guests on from bench to bench, until they reached the monthly administrator [*Parnas*] who stood near the *Maharsha'l*. The *Parnas* alerted the prayer leader that he should wait to begin the repetition of the *Shmone Esrei* even after the *Maharsha'l* had concluded the silent *Shmone Esrei*, until he could tell him the words of the guests who had impinged upon the honor of the rabbi.

When the *Maharsha'l* finished, the *Parnas* told him everything. The *Maharsha'l* immediately ordered that the *Shmone Esrei* be started, and that *Kabbalat Shabbat* be recited immediately thereafter. After the services, the *Parnas* presented his complaints to the rabbi, asking why he did not react to the insult to the honor of the Torah? The *Maharsha'l* responded, "It is my custom every Friday to take account as to how the week went. I did so today, but in the middle of the silent *Shmone Esrei*, I recalled that a Torah judgment between two wagon drivers regarding a wheel came my way this past week. I thought about whether I had given a correct verdict in accordance with the claims of both sides. Since the guests sensed this, they must have the holy spirit, so how can one punish them?"

The *Maharsha'l* invited them to his house for the Sabbath. He made kiddush himself, and fulfilled the obligation of the guests regarding kiddush. After washing the hands in preparation for eating, the *Maharsha'l* passed the knife over the *challos* and wanted to recite the *Hamotzie* blessing. Rabbi Chaim Vital took out a cloth and swished it over the eyes of the *Maharsha'l*. Then the thought in his mind increased a thousandfold that from the mite that he had cut when he passed the knife over 'the bread', it seemed that he had killed the largest living creature, and he remained in a fright. Rabbi Chaim took out his 12 *challos* that he had brought with him from Safed and placed them before the *Maharsha'l*. The *Maharsha'l*

[Page 56]

recited the *Hamotzie* blessing upon them. Seeing that the *challos* were fresh and still warm, he felt hurt. Rabbi Chaim summoned up the rabbi's *challos*, giving them the special charm of the shewbread [*Lechem Hapanim*], that remain fresh to be used on the day they are divided up. In I Samuel 21, and in the Gemara *Chagiga* 26b, it is taught that they were baked on Friday, and removed from the table of purity on the second Sabbath thereafter. They remained as fresh and warm as when they had first been removed from the oven.

After *Havdalah*, the *Maharsha'l* asked what they wanted from him. They answered, "We were sent to you from the *Ariza'l*. Together with the *Rem'a*, you will prevent the excommunication from taking place, so that nobody will be harmed, Heaven forbid. The *Maharsha'l* then proposed to debate with them on Kabbalistic wisdom. They agreed on the condition that the debate be held in the cellar. During the debate, the *Maharsha'l* recited a statement of the Kabbalah to them. They responded with the verse, In the beginning, the L-rd created the heavens and the earth [Genesis 1:1] The cellar became like the heavens and new earth. They stated, "This is how our rabbi learns Kabbalah." The *Maharsha'l* promised that he and the *Rem'a* will hold back from controversy.

After that, in Tyszowce, they asked regarding the wife of the Messiah, whether she had seen wonders from her holy husband. She responded that every day, when her husband went to the synagogue for the *Mincha* and *Maariv* services, it was not light for her in the house, for they did not have the possibility to purchase candles or oil due to their great poverty. However, when her husband returned home, he always brought with him many very fine guests, and it again became light in the house. Thus did they study an entire night. They asked her, why did she not tell this earlier? She responded innocently that, because she believed that this is what happens in the home of every Jew.

There is an interpretation in Rashi on *Shabbat* 118a that the birth pangs of the Messiah is an accusation against the scholars. That means that the *Tzadikim* and wise men of the generation fight amongst themselves, thereby delaying the arrival of the Messiah. That is what the birth pangs of the Messiah mean. The pain of the Messiah! The Rizhiner, may his memory be a blessing for life in the World To Come, once said that the Rambam of blessed memory was fitting to be the Messiah of that generation. However, on account of the great disputes surrounding him, even in his time, such as one sees in the strength of the glosses of the Raava'd of blessed memory against him[9], the redemption was deferred until later. In later times, there was a dispute between Rabbi Moshe Chaim Luzzatto, may his memory be a blessing for life in the World To Come, and Rabbi Yehonatan Eybeschutz of blessed memory. After that, [there was a dispute] between the Baal Shem Tov, and of Rabbi Ber with their students. In recent times, there was the great dispute between Sanz and the Rizhiner descendants, may their memory be a blessing for life in the World To Come.

[Page 57]

Let us hope that our prayer of "He Who makes peace in His heights, may He grant peace to us and to all of Israel" be fulfilled in the near future. The prophesy of "And they shall seek God... and David their king" [Hosea 3:5], and "A redeemer shall come to Zion" [Isaiah 59:20] shall be fulfilled speedily in our days. Amen, as the prayer of your father, Av Br'y[10].

The family of Rabbi Avraham and Gittel Stern of blessed memory

From right to left, sitting: Daughter-in-law, Sara Stern of blessed memory (Yechiel's wife), Gittel Stern holding granddaughter Esther, Rabbi Avraham Stern, Yechiel Stern, his daughter Hene Marder-Stern, son – Dr. Yisrael Stern, daughter Shifra Krishtalka-Stern, Elka Danziker-Neiman. Absent – Yaakov Zipper-Stern and Shalom Stern, who were already in Canada at that time

Translator's Footnotes:

1. A Jewish Messianic figure, who is expected to die in the pre-Messianic wars, making way for the Messiah the son of David. See https://en.wikipedia.org/wiki/Messiah_ben_Joseph .
2. There is a footnote in the text here: A collection of letters in Yiddish and Hebrew. Written to the children during the years 5683-5687 [1923-1927]. Published in Montreal in 5707 – 1947
3. Figures related to the Jewish Messianic vision. See https://en.wikipedia.org/wiki/Four_Horns_and_Four_Craftsmen
4. I cannot find this quote.
5. The final verse of the Book of Daniel, 12:13, from Sefaria: But you, go on to the end; you shall rest, and arise to your destiny at the end of the days.
6. This refers to a conversation between the man appointed to bring the scapegoat (The goat for Azazel) to the desert on Yom Kippur, and the High Priest. For the full Talmudic quote with context, see https://www.sefaria.org/Yoma.71a.14?lang=bi
7. A Biblical commentator.

8.   There is a tradition that the man who brings the scapegoat to the desert on Yom Kippur is destined to die that year.

9.   The Raava'd, older than the Rambam wrote glosses on the Rambam 14-volume *Yad Hachazakah* [summary of the entire corpus of Jewish law] frequently differing with him strongly.

10.   I am unsure of this abbreviation. It does not seem to be a year (if it were, it would be 1852).

[Page 58]

My Rabbi, Yankeleh Moteleh's

by Yechiel Stern (Montreal, Canada)

A chapter from his research work, "Cheder un Besmedresh," YIVO New York, 1950

Translated by Moses Milstein

My Rabbi, Yankeleh Moteleh's, came from a family of *melamdim*[1], and sons of *melamdim*. Teaching in this family was transmitted by inheritance from generation to generation, from father to son, or father-in-law to son-in-law.

My rabbi therefore had all the qualities of generations-long tradition that regarded teaching as holy work, and looked down on the newer *melamdim* who took to teaching because they weren't fit to do anything else.

My rabbi did not mix into mundane matters. That he left to his wife. His rebbetsin even collected the tuition from the *balebatim*. She managed the whole house. All the family's worries were her responsibility. The rabbi devoted himself entirely to teaching. He was one of those Jews who was a stranger to money matters.

In spite of his complete ineptitude, he was really shrewd and could very well understand worldly matters, and his sayings were well known in the surrounding shtetls, not only by us in Tishevits. His little expressions were really well-wrought aphorisms with a deep meaning, and they always elicited laughter. He had a strong flair for humor. Especially profound were his sayings about study, teachers and students.

He used to say that there was no student who was not good at least at something, especially if it served himself as he understood it. His phrase for this was: "*Yeder shmoiger tzu zeinem toig er.*"[2] (*Shmoiger* is a simple soul, not the smartest).

[Page 59]

For a too clever student who shows off until he trips because of his own cleverness, he used to say, "*Klug un klug un banarisht sich.*[3]"

A local *maskil*[4] tried to catch him once, "Rebbe, you lecture us for being consumed with desire, but you yourself are so obsessed with snuff, truly like a real addict." My rebbe answered, "Devil, you are involved in all the lusts of the world, and that's okay, but if I have a little vice, as big as a sniff of tobacco, you can't begrudge me it?" This little joke of his later circulated through our whole region.

Although it was true that my rebbe was a passionate snuff consumer, he was at the same time a well-dressed person. His coat, tied with a camel hair belt, lay on his small frame perfectly. His velvet hat with its raffish little brim always fit him just right, his black little beard glistened with a festive nobility, and in general he gave off an air of a kind of spirituality.

He always began his classes in a happy mood, always saying, "*Oola hava patach bivdichut*[5]," accompanied by a strong sniff of tobacco.

Good-natured, he used to tell a joke, or sometimes even a funny story. The material for his stories he always took from daily life. He particularly made fun of the *shlimazl* in his jokes and anecdotes. Someone who "*Ken kein katz kein ek nisht tsubindn*,[6]" and brags about his family heritage, and won't do a certain work because it doesn't suit him. "*A Yid darf tzu alles toign*,[7]" he taught his students, one should not be ashamed to do any kind of work. "*Peshot neveilta bshuka ushkeil agera*."[8] As long as you practice your faith, every job is good. He would always laugh at the impractical speculative thinkers who always wanted to find out "*mah l'malah v'mah l'matah*"[9] but what's going on under their noses, they don't see. These philosophers, he used to say, always understand things literally, but the meaning of the thing, they don't get. At the same time, even though they want to figure everything out by themselves, they are always ready to believe the wildest stories anyone comes up with out of the blue. "*Petti yamin l'chol davar*,"[10] he used to always say whenever he came upon the topic of these thinkers. "These losers can destroy a world," he never tired of teaching his students.

As an example, he used to often tell the story of his father-in-law, Leibish Mayer, who was famous for his particular reasoning. This Leibish Mayer once went up to the attic to determine why people say, "*Boidem, boidem ois boidem*[11]."

[Page 60]

So he, Leibish Mayer that is, covered his eyes with his hand, and proceeded to walk backwards while repeating the words, "*boidem, boidem*", until he suddenly fell down the stairs, and then he shouted, "*Oy, ois boidem*!"[No more attic] He really discovered the secret of "*ois boidem*" when he broke his arm.

After telling a funny story, the rebbe used to take a sniff of tobacco, and with a Gemara melody, he would begin the lesson: "*The partner who wanted to make a partition...*" etc.

His little stories and jokes would also silence his wife who used to quite often–may she forgive me–respond with a sharp tongue. When Dineleh, the rebbetsin, would get carried away, the rebbe would say to us, "*Zie redt den, ihreh tsouris redn*[12]." Our rabbi was right. Great good fortune the vivacious Dineleh–who was known as a stalwart wife and was once considered a beauty–did not have with the rebbe. His entire home consisted of one room that served both as a bedroom and a kitchen, and a dining room, and a classroom for about ten students. Nevertheless, the room was always as clean as for the holidays. The rebbetsin was always busy, never idle for a minute, cooking, baking, cleaning, washing the floor, or the door and windows. If not, she was sewing, repairing or darning, knitting socks, and so on. In addition, she had the entire burden of earning a living on her head, because my rebbe did not mix into worldly things. His strength lay only in teaching. So she was embittered, the rebbe's earning not bringing in enough.

"*Groiser fardiner meiner, goldshpinner meiner*[13]," she used to say of the rabbi. "May you have an afterlife like the life I have with you here." Nevertheless, when the rebbe told a joke or an anecdote, she would listen and laugh along, and jokingly say, "You have a saying for everything. Maybe you have a saying so we can afford to make a Shabbes out of it, my big earner?"

To celebrate a proper Shabbes his little aphorisms were of no use, but to bond the students to him, so they would feel at home, and as adults, many years later, to remember him with affection, the rebbe's little witticisms did succeed in doing.

The entire skill however of Yankeleh Moteleh's was grounded in his power of persuasion. He was known as an expert interpreter even among the best *melamdim* in shtetl.

[Page 61]

He always explained things with an example, with a story, and the most difficult notions became easy and simple. How a teacher should introduce a student to an idea, my rebbe explained with an example like this: A melamed was teaching Hebrew to a *yeshuvnik*[14]'s son, but the boy could not grasp the material. So the melamed asked the boy, "Tell me now, Moishe, what's the deal with you knowing every goy in the village by name, you can even recognize him from a distance, but what a *kometz*[15] is, you don't know!" The boy replied, "Rebbe, that's not the same thing. The goy is so big, and the *kometz* is so small, and the goy is from my village, but the *kometz* is from an unfamiliar siddur." A melamed, my rebbe Yankeleh Moteleh's explained, must make the *kometz* in the siddur as familiar as the goy from his own village.

"First of all," my rebbe used to say, "you must first understand the matter well yourself. Then you can explain it to someone else. Whatever you're studying, you must see it with your eyes closed. If you can understand the matter with your head, and see it in your mind, it is a sign that you have understood it, otherwise you're just flapping your tongue, and it's all just words." He gave us these rules so that we could explain things to each other while going over the class, or while preparing a class reading, two or three to a class.

"Learning," the rebbe taught us, "is exactly like swimming, which can't be learned other than by swimming, and by always going deeper into the water. As long as you don't learn for yourself, you won't be able. A melamed who constantly teaches the children does them a disservice. He teaches them to not be able to study by themselves, and what will they do when they leave the cheder? A melamed, he further explained, just needs to be at the side, and be ready to give a nudge forward. When he sees that his student who is studying by himself has become confused and can't go any further, he must give him a push forward, explain things to him, make the matter easier to understand exactly like a father does when teaching a child to swim in the river. And when he sees the child stop in the middle, he gives him a push, but the child swims by himself." "*Eem ein ani li, mi li?*"[16] was his constant warning to his students. "If you don't study by yourself, you'll never learn."

"A rebbe," he would add, "must gradually make the material more difficult, but not all at once. Sometimes he must stop at a passage from Rashi, some *tosafot*, but slowly, increasing the difficulty.

[Page 62]

The rebbe must always remember that the goal is to make the children able to study on their own, and he is no more than an assistant. He is teaching swimming."

"*Dligmar insh v'hader lisbir*, translates as: First a student must teach himself to study the simpler Gemara, and afterwards he should get used to delving deeper into the contents. The way to do this should be taught to him by the melamed."

"The rebbe must see that he sharpens the minds of his students so that the good students, the capable ones, can later be better swimmers than he. The student on the rebbe's shoulders must be taller than the rebbe."

My rebbe would good-naturedly boast that he had students who later became rabbis, distinguished scholars, and some even became authors of religious books. He tried to influence our ambition so that we would try to be like these students. He used to tell us about his previous students, who we knew as well-known besmedresh young men with a reputation as scholars, and how they would get up very early and come to wake him up to study, and he used to go with them to the besmedresh to study with them at dawn. Many of us actually tried to copy those students.

While we were studying by ourselves, the rebbe would also be reading, or studying, in order to set an example. "*Kashot atsmecha techila*,"[17] was his constant refrain. "If you want someone to study, you must first study yourself." His eyes and ears were, however, directed at us. This way, he surreptitiously kept an eye on all those studying at the table so that no one would try to fool themselves.

If a group would start singing, "*Amar Rabi Yochanan: Shema manah telat*–from here three things follow," he would suddenly turn to this group, "What three things are implied?" First he asked the most capable student in the group, then the weaker one, and if someone didn't understand something, he would sit down with him and explain it over and over. Meanwhile, he tried to bring in all the students who were studying the same portion. Every one of the students had the opportunity to express his opinion, and the rabbi listened to everyone with great patience. Once he was certain that everyone had a good understanding of the matter, he returned to his work–reading for himself or helping another class that came asking for help. His extraordinary patience he exhibited not only by explaining something

[Page 63]

but also by tolerating his students and not punishing them excessively. Some parents used to come to the cheder to punish their children for past sins.

Our rebbe used to say," If the rebbe is a *ba'al zoiche*, the children do not sin, and there is no need for punishment. But you know," he would add, "today's generation, weak generation." But if my rebbe was forced to punish someone, he used to take the offending boy to a corner of the room near the door, and tear out a twig from the broom, and give a few lashes to the boy. He used to always sigh, "*Choshech shevto, soneh beno*," and angrily straighten the belt of his pants. After a situation like this, the rest of the class was without joy, somewhat depressed. The rebbe himself was downcast and tried to placate the punished child, paying him a lot of attention. And if the punished child did not want to make up, he would sigh, straightening the belt on his pants, "*Choshech shevto, soneh beno*," as if to say what can I do, it's written that you have to use punishment sometimes too. After the class, he would beg forgiveness from the punished child.

One thing scared him more than anything, that he was not up to "*Ma ani b'chinam, aff ata b'hinam.*" He would always defend himself before us that he is paid tuition only as a worker, because while teaching us he can't do anything else. But not being satisfied with this, he used to try to teach some students before classes started or afterwards. "For this," he used to say, "I certainly don't get paid." This saintly man, and loyal father to his students, was never sure if he was good enough in his holy work. For that reason, he was worthy that his students should always be satisfied with him, and that the rebbe should have no complaints against them, and as adults, revere him as a holy man. I can describe my rebbe with one word–he was a *yoreh-chet*[18] in the best sense of the word. May his merits be credited to us.

Thinking about all the little sayings and expressions of my rebbe, Yankeleh Moteleh's, I am convinced that there is a kind of oral Mishnah education that passed from generation to generation in the melamed families in the form of short aphorisms and anecdotes. As evidence that my rebbe was not an isolated case, it is worth mentioning another such melamed in our shtetl.

[Page 64]

We called him Pesach Melamed. He was an *iberzetz melamed*. This profession was passed on by inheritance in his family from generation to generation. When I knew him, he was already an old scholar, but he continued to carry on his teaching, and among his students, he gave the impression of being an older friend of theirs. Great respect for him his students did not have, but for this reason however, they loved him with sincere and devoted love. Pesach Melamed used to make sure that his students ate the breakfast that their mothers prepared for them to take with to cheder before classes. Every boy is required to eat every morning a bagel with butter, he used to say, so he should be able to study Torah, which smells like fresh baking. With his own hands, he used to whittle *knipkelach* (little knives with wooden handles) and flags for his students. Every Thursday when he would examine the class, he would pass out presents to the children who knew their Gemara, the abovementioned knives and flags. In summer, he would take his students downhill to the city river to bathe and he himself would teach them to swim in order to fulfill the quotation, "*Chayev adam lilmod et beno lischok b'nahar.*"[19] In the winter, he would stand at the edge of the frozen little river and watch as his nimble students flew across the ice.

While teaching the children the journeys of the Jews in the desert, he had a kind of paper sheet on which the names of the places where the Jews wandered, as well as the arrangement and forms where they rested according to the flags, were drawn. The whole drawing was called The Journeys. In studying the borders of Eretz Israel in the bible, he showed the students a sheet that was called The Borders–the border cities as well as the lands bordering Eretz Israel. The Mediterranean Sea was drawn in blue on the west side of Eretz Israel. It was a kind of map. The students had to copy it and color in these borders and journeys.

He also had a large model made of paper of the clothes of the High Priest; the breastplate and vest with the names of the twelve tribes written in boxes, and drawn in another color, the coat of arms of a given tribe. For Yehuda–a lion, for Dan–a snake, and so on. This was a way of representing the *urim-vetummim*[20]. Also a bonnet with a *tsits* of paper he showed to his students who used to copy and wear the garments of the High Priest.

He used to let his students fool around without restraint. "Let Jewish children have fun," he used to say, "They have plenty of time before they have to bear

[Page 65]

the yoke of the diaspora." If they got carried away, and he could not control them, he would wave his *kantchik* in the air over their heads. "Washing" their hair, he called it. His students were hardly frightened, because they knew he was pretending. Then he would fall upon his old proven method–telling a story. With this he was at home. The students would gather around him like lambs around a shepherd, and he would go on, and the children would listen with rapt attention. He would tell of *lamed-vovniks* who rescued Jews in need, about the Crusades, Spain, Chmelnitsky's times, about Rabeinu Gershom, Rashi, and the Maharam of Rotenburg, rabbi Amnon Chasid, and other great saints. "A melamed," Pesach used to say, "needs to know how to tell a lot of stories, because Jewish children love stories." His whole conduct as a melamed was only to please his Jewish children. It is no surprise that his students clung to him and loved him.

To the oral Mishnah we must add these general well-known melamdish sayings: "A good "zits" (meaning rear-end in plain language) is better than a good head," "A wanter is better than a knower," "All beginnings are difficult."

———

Footnotes:

1. Teachers
2. Every shmoiger is good at something
3. Smart, smart, yet makes a fool of himself
4. Adherer of the enlightenment
5. Oola began with a joke
6. Can't tie the tail of a cat
7. A Jew must be good at everything
8. Skin a carcass in the market and take payment
9. What's on top and what's on the bottom
10. The gullible will believe anything
11. Attic, attic, no more attic
12. Is it her talking? Her troubles are talking.
13. My big earner, my big money maker
14. Jew who lives in a rural Christian setting
15. A diacritic indicating a certain vowel sound
16. Pirkei Avot 1:14 He (Rabbi Hillel) used to say, "If I am not for myself, who will be? And if I am only for myself, what am I? And if not now, when?"
17. Harden yourself first
18. One who fears sin
19. A man must teach his son to swim in a river
20. Urim and Thummim, 12 precious stones with the names of the tribes on the breastplate worn by the High Priest

[Page 65]

Shloime Hersh Spodek's (Papier) Cheder[1]

by Berl Singer, Buenos Aires

Translated by Moses Milstein

When I remember Shloime Hersh Spodek's cheder now, a chill runs through me. At the same time, I am reminded of how strong our parents' conviction was that, by virtue of learning Torah, no harm would befall us.

The "cheder" on the dyke street was a multi-storied building, crooked on each side so that no matter from which angle you viewed it, it looked like it was about to fall down. Yet it remained standing for years and years, as if it was really only by virtue of the schoolchildren. In order to get to the entrance of the cheder, you first had to go through an alley that

[Page 66]

led from the dyke to a large courtyard that belonged to a lot of neighbors. The courtyard served as a garbage dump as well as a place where people did their business. Children would go wherever they felt like going. The adults to whom the courtyard belonged used to go where they would not be seen. They sat with their faces to the wall, and since they took care to cover themselves, you could never be sure if they were doing something, or whether they were trying to close up the mouse holes in the walls. In a corner of the court, there was a ladder that led to the cheder. Always exposed to rain and snow in the open court, the ladder was good and rotten. It was so slippery in winter that you took your life in your hands climbing up. In addition, the shaky ladder was missing a rail, so that you would have to climb up a few stairs first before grasping the rail, and, often, you ended up with bruised ribs after falling on the way up or down.

The cheder consisted of a large room containing a bed against one wall, and a bunk-bed on the other wall. In the middle, there was a long table with long benches on each side where the children sat. There was also a little room off to the side where the kitchen was found, and which also served as the bedroom for the rebbe's young daughter. I can't recall ever seeing a rebbetsin. The cheder also had two glass doors, one that led to a balcony overlooking the dyke street and was always nailed shut so that the children would not go out on the rotting balcony, and the other door, exactly opposite, led to the courtyard where the ladder was. None of the glass panels was intact. In summer, we had enough light. In winter, however, when all the gaps were stuffed with rags, it was not overly bright. As previously mentioned, people did their business in the yard, but the little kids didn't go down—the door that led to the ladder was opened and we stood on the little bit of balcony that was found there. Kids would go in groups, and a game developed over who had the dexterity to make a "bow-and-arrow" over the ladder. Whoever was able do it, was greatly admired, and everyone tried hard to do it. The smells going up were therefore not pleasant.

The kitchen was used mostly in winter to heat up the room, and rarely for cooking. The rebbe ate only bread and garlic most days.

[Page 67]

He could not afford anything better. It satisfied his hunger, and served as a remedy for toothache, which he always suffered from. That's why I remember him with a red flowered kerchief covering half his beard, and with a fat knot on the top of his head. He wore a big, tall velvet hat, and you never knew if it was originally green and was now blue, or vice versa. And because of this big, tall hat, he was known by the nickname, "Spodek."
He had a mild face covered with a grey beard. He was of average height, broad-shouldered, and with a significant belly. How he got such a belly, I don't know, because it seems he never had much to eat. In my time, he didn't use a *kanchik*[2] in the classroom. But he had his methods of punishment which involved pinching the soft spot on the bottom parts of the body. But I was always the lucky one who not only got pinched on the rear end, but also received

blue bruises all over my body. It happened like this: I used to like to write printed letters, or as it was called, *geksiveteh*[3] characters. So one time, while the rebbe was out davening, I printed on the table the words from the Chumash, "*Va'yidaber adonai el Moshe l'aimor.*"" *Adonai*," I wrote with all four letters like it is written in the Chumash. And when the rebbe came in and saw it, he was stunned, because it was forbidden to erase it. He made me a present of a few good pinches, and told the kids not to approach the table in case the word, God forbid, got accidentally erased. And he went off to the rabbi to ask for a solution. The rabbi and the *dayanim* decided that we had to saw out the whole phrase, and remove it it to the attic in the shul. And if it should not be possible to saw it out, then we would have to cover up the whole phrase with a piece of tin, and that's what was done.

All the Tishevitsers who studied with R' Shloime Hersh Spodek after me, will certainly remember the table with the tin nailed to it. But the blue bruises over my entire body I can still feel and see before my eyes.

Footnotes:

1. This was an "*Ibersetz cheder*" where the students generally came from the "*dirdikay cheders*" at 6-7 years old. See this topic in the book, *Cheder in Besmedresh*, by Yechiel Stern. Editor.
2. Small whip
3. Calligraphy in square Hebrew characters

[Page 68]

The Market

by Chanah Beech (Zwillich), Ramat Gan, Israel

Translated by Moses Milstein

It was a four-sided, large plaza. In truth, it was not as square as believed, because streets issued from there every which way. It only appeared like a square at first glance. This place, it seems, had been called "the market" for generations.

The strategic focus of this place was the pump in the middle of the market that served as a source of fresh water. In the old days, it was said that the mud was so great that a carriage and a pair of horses would get stuck for good. And at night, on moonlit nights I should say, the moon was reflected and shone so brightly on the mud, that it seemed there was no earth and no sky, but two skies, and two moons.

But that was in the old days, in our grandfathers' time. In our time, it already looked different. "*Pshekupkes*,"[1] were no longer sitting around, not even in the market. The muddy ground in the center had been paved. There were houses and shops with dry-goods, food, iron, and whatever you wanted, around the market. And from a corner, the red brick "*shkole*" that was built in the times of the Czar, peered. How beautiful it was. The market was opened every day by the water-carriers. They greeted each other with handshakes. The pump understood no other language. You simply gave the handle a pump and it responded with a full mouth, and everyone left happy. No one was insulted.

The men would hurry to shul early in the morning, most crossing and crisscrossing the market.

The first stores would open up. The storekeepers waited in anticipation of a "*pachontek*," (a first sale).

[Page 69]

This is how it used to be both summer and winter. In heat, or rain, or snow and cold, they would sit in their stores, warming themselves by a firepot, and wait for the first customer, and after that, a second, a third, and so on.

It wasn't always so sad. God gave a Wednesday in the middle of the week, and that was the market, the market day. Then the market awoke from its sleep, and became lively. It was packed with wagons, horses and goyim who came from the villages to sell their produce. The whole market seethed like a boiling kettle.

Human noise mixed with the cackling of hens and roosters, the quacking of ducks, and the shouts of children. It was a happy day. There were buyers and sellers, and people just looking around. All the stores were full. People like ants. But there was one thing, I couldn't stand—the pig slaughter. The smell would choke every Jew who passed by. This is how the noisy market day passed until night fell.

Then the market emptied of people and all the things that had been set up. It breathed easier. It was a market after all. It had to support everyone…The quiet night fell. Everything rested, including the market.

The dawn brought the first birds back to the market. And the old pump again satisfied anyone who stretched out a hand to its open mouth.

Footnote:

1.   Women street vendors

[Page 70]

What I Remember

by HaRav Abraham Moishe Brenner, AH
(Rav HaKollel in Lima, Peru, and rav in New York for several years)

Translated by Moses Milstein

Extract from a longer letter written July 4, 1968.

Regarding the plan for a *pinkas*, I can answer you with the little I remember of the following:

I, personally, was not a Tishivitser. I just married R' Nathan Dovid Zuker's daughter, Chanaleh, my rebbetsin. I boarded at my in-laws as a student for 7 whole years. However, I only knew several families–I can only remember a few friends like Shloime Kreiner, Moishe Itzchak Dorenfeld–your brothers Yechiel and Shloime Stern, Yekele Naster, Moishe Motl Shalier, etc. There were several people I liked to talk to and spend time with (although I was younger than them) like R' Binyomin Marder, R' Leib Ber Kalinberg, and last but not least, R' Abraham Stern, z"l. His name really suited him; he was truly a bright star, a "*Gadol b'Israel.*" It is truly unfortunate that this bright star was extinguished. When I was close to becoming ordained, I always consulted him, and he was like a father to me. Other than that, I did not know any local people. But in the Chasidic shul of Trisk-Kuzmir, where I prayed, along with my father-in-law, z"l, I knew the people very well, and I will mention a few, like R' Shabatil Hodes's (Ginsberg). I heard him recite the *musofim* and the *Shemoneh Esrei* full of heart and soul. I remember a certain R' Zalman Yasheh,

[Page 71]

dancing and clapping, and laughing for joy in the middle of the market, his blue, feline, eyes glinting when the Kielce rebbe was being led from the shul on Shabbes Kodesh. Also R' Izik Eng and his lively dances. R' Chaim Reiz and his loose coat-belt slipping down on Simchat Torah, dancing and singing in the market, and clapping his hands. R' Israel Leibish Grober shouting in his hoarse voice the *L'David Mizmor* until *Hirhur Tshuvah.* R' Hirshl Neimark and his sweet tenor that echoed like beautiful music. My father-in-law, R' Nathan David, z"l, who in the holy days was considered all soul. And similarly, many more from the Trisk-Kuzmir prayer hall. But other than those in the city, I knew very few. "For that reason, I can't describe any more of them."

I will take this opportunity to relate a part of my biography. I was rabbi in two small shtetlach, in Volhyn near Kovel for seven years. But I was a reader of Jewish newspapers especially " *Hatsfira*." Nachum Sokolow was once the editor. He and Dr. Yehoshua Ton from Krakow warned and lectured in their articles that Polish Jewry must pack up and get out of Poland, because very dark clouds were gathering, and would arrive in Europe, and fall hardest on the Jews of Poland. I was, luckily, a good student, and I was always attentive, and paid attention to the words of diplomatic prophecy from Nachum Sokolow. And luck was really with me. I thought about it and acted, and with God's help, I escaped with my family from the Nazi hell in good time. And after, being in South America, in Lima, Peru, in my modest rabbinical post, when we read and heard in the daily newspapers what kind of hell the German people unleashed on Europe, especially on the Jewish people, we were very sad, but we also reasoned that we, the survivors of the Nazi conflagration must be the ones to rebuild Jewish existence, and that we must join with the *She'erit Hapletah*[1] to weave once more the glorious "*Goldeneh Yiddishe Keit*[2] " that should, God forbid, not be severed again, and that we, the survivors, are responsible for its continuation, and must once again unravel the scrolls of Jewish culture, and continue an authentic life. This holy debt lies not only on the Jewish public alone, but on each individual. As our holy Kotsker grandfather, rebbe Mendl, z"tsl, said and warned, "Why does a person need two pockets in one coat? One pocket should be filled with "*V'anochi afar v'efer*[3], and the second pocket with "*Lo nivrah ha'olam eleh bishvili*,[4]" meaning that everyone is responsible for the survival of the world. I committed these words to memory, and will not forget them. And I took my three sons, may they live long...took them to work...and I was a father and a teacher to them. I was strongly committed, even though in America, to make of my children that which I had always dreamed about whether awake or in dreams, and by the grace of God, my sweet dreams came true. I have three sons of whom it can be said that they are *shlosha kinei menorah*, in a word, three jewels.

My oldest son, the biggest of all, is a Torah scholar, keeps the Sabbath, and leads a strictly kosher home. In addition, he is a medical doctor. Three years ago, he received from the American government in Washington a grant of $50,000 for searching for a cure for throat cancer. He was paid in three installments. His last installment has been paid in order for him to buy more appropriate instruments to be able to continue the medical mission he undertook.

My second son also became a rabbi with the title of doctor of history. He had a rabbinical position in New York for 7 years, and for the last two years as a rabbi in Los Angeles.

My third son also finished his rabbinical studies like the second one, and also at Yeshiva University and Columbia in New York, and is a rabbi in Queens, N.Y. for the last 10 years, the spiritual leader in his community, and they won't let him go. They're always giving him raises, and he is very respected by them. And because his doctorate is in mathematical statistics, he is also a professor at a university in Manhattan, N.Y. They are all married and have children. The oldest son, the doctor, is the son-in-law of a Hungarian rabbi, from Washington, Rabbi Weiss, *shlit"a*. And that is the fruit of my labor. My rebbetsin had a heart attack on July 9th of this year which she barely survived...The doctor [son] came for us when she started to feel better and took us to the States, and thank God, she is better.

If there is any cost to the memorial for the Tishevits martyrs you all will be making as many others have, I will also gladly contribute...

Footnotes:

1. The remnant of survivors
2. *The Golden Jewish Chain.* The uninterrupted transmission of Jewish tradition
3. I am but dust and ashes. Genesis XVIII, 27
4. The world was not created just for me

———

[Page 73]

My Grandfather Chaimtche Chazzan

by Hersh Ben Meir and Breine Zwillich, Lima, Peru

Translated by Moses Milstein

Who in Tishevits did not know my grandfather, Chaimtche Chazzan? His high forehead, his always disheveled beard and payess, his spattered coat, and his forever laughing eyes lent a special quality to the shtetl.

He was the city-cantor, and davened Saturdays and holidays in the cold synagogue. When he sang in the shul, the women in the women's section did not have to search through their siddurs or machzors. "Pearls flow from his mouth," Leah-Henig used to say to the women who were standing by the window grates wiping tears that fell like rain from their eyes.

I don't know if anyone in town knew my grandfather's family name. It was enough to say, Chaimtche. There were no other Chaimtches in Tishevits. That's why they called my father, *a"h*, Meir Chaimtche's, and I was called, Hersh Meir Chaimtche's, and when my oldest daughter began promenading on the sidewalk of the dyke, they called her Malkeleh Hersh Meir Chaimtche's. It seems my grandfather was a central figure, a creator of a dynasty. How old he was, no one knew. He was always the same. Hardly anyone knew him from his childhood. All the years I knew him, he was the same, his disheveled dark grey, but never white, beard. His voice was a lion's roar. He never walked bent over. At weddings he would do the Cossack dances, while shouting, "Hoo, ha," or " Let's have some more bitter water," (beer) so the whole house trembled.

During the Days of Awe, he would visit the cemetery and go around the moss-covered tombstones and chant *El Malei Rachamim* with eyes shut, knowing all the *Po Nitmans*. But his best was his weepy *Barchu*. The first Saturday night in Elul during Maariv, almost the whole city turned out to hear his tearful Barchu. It was the prologue to

[Page 74]

the approaching Days of Awe. He drew out the Barchu with various embellishments, and tears fell from all those gathered. The Barchu was a portent that the day of judgment was coming.

In the Days of Awe, he wore a patched, Turkish taliss, *kitl*, and white socks. He looked like a holy man, perhaps like the *Cohen Gadol* at work in the temple.

In his younger days, he was a shochet in the Radziner court. But something happened that made him leave them and come to Tishevits and join the Biskwitzer chasidim, and daven in the Ryewitzer shtibl. He travelled to see the rebbe R' Moishe Haimon, born in Tishevits, and brother of Henoch Sachaczewski. He never explained the reason he left Radzin, but in the last years of his life, he became closer to it, and even began again to wear *t'cheyles*.[1] He would spend hours in the shtibls telling stories from *Orchot Chaim,* or from *Mei HaShiloach*, about the land of Sicily where the snail was found,[2] and Shmuel Motl's with his blond beard would nod agreement.

My grandfather had five sons. The oldest, Moishe, was the only wealthy uncle in my family. He was already called Moshe Zwillich. He lived in Lodz. He was a big merchant with a groomed beard. His son, Mendl, had graduated from Krinsky's gymnasium in Warsaw. The other, Mordechai, also lived in Lodz, but was very poor. The third was my father, Meir. Meir Chaimtche's was already reading "*Heint*." He was a bookkeeper at Moishe Dutche Friedlender. He would read *Ahavat Zion* from *Mapo*, and was *dozor* in the community for many years, but Saturday mornings, he would study a page of Gemara with me. The fourth one was Shloime, the pursemaker, who lived in Laszczow and was poverty stricken. The youngest son, Yankele Zwillich, lived in Lodz, worked in a factory, and became a Socialist, took part in the attack on the governor-general of Lodz in 1905, and was shot by the Cossacks. It was whispered that that was the reason our grandfather was estranged from the Radziner.

When my grandfather neared his 80th year, he became a widower, but at he end of a year, he married a woman in her fifties. He used to go around with a sac and collect a few potatoes, kasha, and flour from the business owners, and his wife would cook it up for the homeless who used to come to the city. This, he used to say, he would take with him to the other world…Everyone in Tishevits liked him, but he had one enemy,

[Page 75]

and that was Yasheh, the shammes, because my grandfather would loudly claim that Yasheh Shammes could not be a mohel, because he was a gravedigger. Burying the dead, and circumcising children with the same hands was dangerous. The only time my grandfather combed his beard and cleaned his filthy kapoteh was when he was required to make a special ceremony and recite the *Hanoten Tshuah L'Malachim* for the Tsar or Pilsudski. At those times, the *voyt*, and the secretary of the gemineh would come to shul, and in their honor, he would get dressed up and give the *Hanoten Tshuah* his best efforts. At the end, the voyt, would shake his hand and shout, "*Niech Zie, Chaimtche*," and my grandfather would answer, " *Niecza, Nieczo*," the only 2 Polish words he knew.

1933, my last Shabbes in Tishevits before returning to Peru. It was the month of Elul. I felt, deep inside, that it was the last time I would see my shtetl. I wandered from one bridge to another—got a last glimpse of the besmedresh, the shul, the Husiatyn shtibl, the creek near the bath—to the meadows, and back to the market with its pump dripping drops of water, drop after drop. I passed the alley where Berl Gabil lived, caught a glimpse on the other side where Moishe Zalman, who sold soda water, lived, and farther down to Itzye Bombe's river to the *klentwes* where many cows were pastured. Then after, back up to the dyke where couples were walking. I met Moishe Motl Shalier biting his nails, and Raizel Nachman Yidl's dressed up in a white blouse. I began to make my farewells. I felt that everyone envied me for travelling out to the wider world. The truth is, I was envious of them for not having to travel to Peru, to be homeless.

Peretz Krant was standing on his balcony in his white shirtsleeves, combing his beard with his fingers. My father-in-law, Leibish Shtuden, was pacing nervously back and forth, lost in thought, and across the way, at the inn, the only accommodation in Tishevits, Miriam, Itzchak Yechiel's, her hair disheveled, was looking out the window with envy at the couples promenading by.

After havdalah, I went to say goodbye to my grandfather. He lived at Mordechai Itzieh's near the Radziner shtibl, in a room with a kitchen. He was sitting bare-armed, only in his *tallit-katan*, and reading a religious book. A naphtha lamp illuminated the filthy walls, and his wife

[Page 76]

was occupied in the kitchen, getting something ready for Melava Malka. "*Zayde, gut voch*," I said. "I have come to say goodbye, because I'm leaving at dawn." Where are you going, Hershl?" he asked me. "I'm going to Peru." "To Peru? Where is that? Overseas?" "Yes, zayde, overseas, far away in America." My grandfather closed his book, fingers in his beard, "So you're really travelling overseas, nu, and your wife? Your children? And is there even a rabbi there? A shoichet? A besmedresh? Well, maybe you younger people know better than me. Take my advice, Hershl. If you're in Warsaw, go to the Radziner rebbe and consult him. Maybe it's not worth it. God is everywhere. If God wills it, you can make a living in Tishevits. You see that Getzl Kuperstein, and Mendele Finger are wealthy here in Tishevits, and what about Leib Kolnberg who also lacks for nothing. Your father-in-law, Leibish Shtuden? Nu, if you're really going, eat Melave Malke with me." Grandmother set two plates of fresh grits on the table. The steam from the hot grits enveloped his beard, and drops of perspiration appeared on his wrinkled brow, but he did not eat. I saw tears starting in his eyes. "Travel safely, Hershl. You won't see me again. I'll tell you a secret. I'm almost 100. But what good did it do me? I had five sons. Two died young, three went away, now you, my only grandchild, are also leaving. How can one be alone?"

I left my grandfather's house and came out to a darkened street. Flickering lamps peered from the houses. A black cat was meowing on Mendele Finger's roof. At the pump, Yechiel Asher was filling a bucket of water. A sad singing was coming out of Ozer Blechervanik's floor where the library was. Itzye Chazer was singing *Slushei* by Ansky. Bright mantle light was issuing only from Peretz Krank's, and Perl was looking down from the balcony at the nighttime darkness.

After a year in Peru, I received a letter informing me my grandfather, Chaimtche, had died.

Footnotes:

1. Blue thread woven into tassels
2. Snail

[Page 77]

The Trisk-Kuzmir Shtibl

by Tuvieh Eng, Montreal, Canada

Translated by Moses Milstein

There were a lot of prayer houses in Tishevits. There was a city-shul that was over three hundred years old, where prayers were held mostly on Shabbes and holidays in the Ashkenazi style. There was also a large besmedresh where most of the city davened and studied the whole week long, and Chasidic shtibls where they davened in the Sephardic style. On the sides of the old shul, in the corridors, there were anterooms where bosses davened and held small feasts.

There was a Husiatyn shtibl, a Radziner, a Belzer, a Trisker-Kuzmirer, and once, also, a Biskewitz-Ryewitzer. These were shtibls where the congregants were affiliated with a rebbe's court. There was also a shtibl that had no connection to a rebbe's court. It was named after its founder and supporter, "Yankel Bashister's Shtibl." These were led by grandchildren of Chasidic courts who had no permanent Chasidic members. The members were mostly ordinary Jews who had not been able to find a place in the other shtibls. Later it became the shtibl for the Zhukover chasidim. There were also a number of private family minyans, and some from groups and organizations like Mizrachi and Shas.

In general, the arrival of a rebbe in town was a big deal not only for the shtibl, but also for the whole shtetl, especially if the rebbe had his own shtibl. On such a Saturday, people finished their davening and eating quickly in order to attend the "*tish*[1]" the rebbe held, usually in the besmedresh, because the shtibls could not accommodate such a large crowd. It was a special experience when a rebbe arrived. Even chasidim from other rebbes came to check it out and listen to some Torah. Chasidim from nearby shtetls and villages came and stayed with other chasidim. The rebbe's chasidim went around with shining faces as in Chol Hamoed, and stopped all other work.

[Page 78]

They were just busy with the rebbe: going out to greet him with a parade, providing a place for the rebbe and the gabais to stay, and receiving everyone who came to celebrate, or ask for a consultation. The result was little feasts with singing and dancing every day from morning until late at night

A lot could be written about each shtibl. I want to focus on memories of the Trisker-Kuzmirer shtibl in which I spent my young years, and from which I drew my spiritual and material gratification. My father, Izek Eng, a"h davened there. The Trisk-Kuzmir shtibl was renowned for its excellent prayer leaders, and good singers. For the Days of Awe, delegations came from the anterooms, besmedresh and minyans, even from the big shul to ask for prayer leaders to be sent to them. Usually they sent the younger ones. The older respected ones remained in the shtibl. The holidays were celebrated solemnly and happily. Rosh Hashanah for example, they would return from *Tashlich* singing, with youngsters leading the way and doing somersaults...Simchat Torah the whole shtetl came out to the *hakofes* in the

Trisker-Kuzmir shtibl. The dancing and singing at the hakofes was an extraordinary pleasure. Simchat Torah during the day was celebrated with a parade at the market with young and old dancing. Purim, they went from the shtibl out to the street dressed in the crazy clothes appropriate for Purim.

Rebbes from the Czarnobyl-Trisk lineage, all great singers and musicians, used to come to the Trisker-Kuzmirer shtibl. No one could listen unaffected to R' Nachumtche's tearful recitation of the "long *V'Hu Rachum*" on a Monday or Thursday. Their melodies were later sung everywhere. They used to come very often, and it was always a big event. Friday evening, since the rebbe went to daven at dusk, the tardy storekeepers stood on the thresholds of their stores in order to catch a glimpse of the rebbe, and immediately shut the store. Shabbes came to the whole shtetl. Friday evening and Shabbes, the rebbe held his "tish" in the besmedresh, and weekdays in the shtibl. He taught Torah and handed out the *shiraim*[2]. He did the honors himself, the gabai calling out the names loudly one after the other, the perennial musicians: Nathan David, Yehoshua Hodeses, Israel Leibish, and in the same tone: honor us with a song, with a *nign!* Thus we were also honored with the blessings, with the wine, the beer and with the start of the circle dance with hands on backs, some on tables and benches until it was good and dark, and time to daven Maariv, and Melava Malka until dawn. This happened almost every few weeks. All the daily worries

[Page 79]

disappeared.

Unfortunately, it has all disappeared. Hitler, the oppressor, may his name be erased, destroyed everything. It only lives on in the memory of those who survived, and who can never forget.

Footnotes:

1.   Literally, "table".
2.   Remnants of the rebbe's meal

[Page 80]

Reciter of Psalms

by Sholem Stern

Translated by Moses Milstein

A

Morning shines through my windows.
I sing the shepherd David's songs of praise.
The words murmur consolation and belief.
God, raise me up from the dust.
Prayerful songs in a dark diaspora
Accompanied us.
Pious, purified and stricken hearts arose
In Godfearing Jewish shtetlach in Poland:
Chtsos[1], the stars are burning
Over fearful, sinking houses.
Jews are reciting psalms.
All with one heart, one plea:
God, do not send help too late.
And I too pour out my prayer in streams of tears

For my despondent spirit, for my father's household,
For the entire frightened, holy community.
O', *me'ayin yavo ezri?*[2] Where to turn to?
Merciful God of the peaceful heavens pay heed.
The stars are singing.
A congregation of Jews shouts out against the evil decrees
Their hands reaching out from tongues of fire.

B

In all the sorrow, in all the distress, in all the disasters,
you ran to God with pleading psalms alone.

[Page 81]

All the fears in the valley of shadows fled.
The faithful, Jewish heart could by no one
Be broken.

Our psalms broke through the cold, sealed heavens.
God alone carried the words, the pleading melodyv into
the flask of tears.
King David, without a sword, without a crown,
An old, wandering Jew weeps over his psalms
In the sad evening, on the burning plain.
For Germany found us
Weak, bruised, dejected
In our fleeing, wandering way.
The murderer, the lurking neighbor
Captured us in the south, in the north.
And all the psalm singers under the trembling wings
Of the *Shechina*[3] call for revenge---

C

O tearful psalms, consoling and holy,
From all the broken Jewish hearts the purest weeping,
Lessen my sorrow, and through agonies purify my heart.
O psalms, your old pages whisper in grief,
The letters wash themselves in a sea of tears:
Yes, *me'ayin yavo ezri*? Where shall I go
Where to turn to and towards?
I see them now the singers, the reciters, the quiet murmurs:
Shmerl Balegoleh, Ephraim Shuster, Itchke Koval and
Gedalieh Shindler.
God, do not hide your face!
Take in the tearful words of the common, pious stutterer
Leibtche Blecher is hammering out his tin.
Ephraim Shuster makes squeaky stitches in the soles.
The sky above them–a deeper, bluish goblet.
The chimneys, the roofs sing psalms---

[Page 82]

D

Shabbes mornings.
The gardens, the orchards are blooming.
Bright tranquility veils the windows,
Father by the open window
Translates every hymn with a sad melody.
The pleading song trembles
On the weeping strings of the shepherd David's violin.
Childish, warm tears in morning's dawn.
Dewy-silver the skin of the leaves.
The singer David in Bethlehem valley.
On the golden sandy shore are
The fresh tracks of thirst-quenched lambs.

O, psalms consoling and holy,
Because all Israel has in you a share!

Footnotes:

1.   Midnight, custom of arising at midnight for study and prayer in memory of destruction of Jerusalem
2.   Psalm 121:1-8 *Shir LaMa'alot*, A Song of Ascents "(1) I will lift up mine eyes unto the mountain (2) From whence shall my help come?"
3.   The Divine Presence

———

In Elul Days

by Sholem Stern

Translated by Moses Milstein

Elul. Jews become quieter, more thoughtful, more pious.
Jews pour out their troubled feelings to the Creator.
In shtiblach, in besmedresh, in shul the shofar is blown.
Autumnal, pensive lonesome meadows.
In the orchards apple tress are shaken,
Secretive, family-close the shtetl becomes.
More serious, humbler become even Peisi Sherer, Berl Roifeh,
Avishal Trifniak and Hershke Kozak.
In fear, in trembling Shayele Zoifer slinks around.
Nachuml Soifer breaks out in tears at every dawn.
Quietly, in God-fearing piety
Every Jew pleads with God:
One year with no evil decrees, no pogroms,
For health and prosperity, and calm and peace.
Because grace is in the hands of the eternal judge–

[Page 83]

In white, cold dawns
The shtetl weeps during *sliches*.
Women weep engrossed over *tchines*[1]
In the gentile street, cows moo, dogs complain.
R' Abraham Shoichet sits absorbed in thought after *tvileh*[2].
His prayer must
Break through the gates of mercy.
From his black, dense beard and *payess*[3]
Drops of water drip.
The broken, tested spirit groans:
Jews need mercy.
Need a R' Levi Itzchak Berdichever[4]
Who knows how to stand before God and argue.
Who should have the innocence and the strength
To dictate to God.
And I myself have few chasidim,
I might heaven forbid give in to the *yeytser hore*[5]
And beg for pleasure and fine clothing:
I have to pray for all Israel,
For the entire holy community.
For myself, father in heaven, I therefore need
Something to exchange.
From your eyes nothing is refused
I don't beg for riches,
On silver spoons.
It is enough for me and my household
Rye bread and potatoes.
R'Avreml Shoichet stands before the congregation:
Father of mercy, your people Israel sanctified in suffering.
You alone know, how between nations,
We are persecuted for your name's sake.
Then why do you allow your favored son to be destroyed?!
And if I am poor and lowly in your eyes,
I am but a little screw in your Creation.
For our holy father's merit
For the people of Israel, open the gate of mercy!
Midat harachamim aleinu hitgalgali
U'vead ameich rachamim sha'ali[6]

[Page 84]

Woe the sobbing cries.
The face shines against the burning light:
Father in Heaven, you alone
Build Jerusalem, renew our days.
Sow compassion in the world!
The early morning, autumn surroundings are still.
The hay meadows spread quiet gloom.
The shtetl gapes in God-fearing piety.
Avreml Shoichet enveloped in his taliss glides to open gates…
And the *Shechina* pours hot tears on the spattered congregation.

Translator's footnotes:

1. Prayer in Yiddish used primarily by women
2. Ritual immersion
3. sidelocks
4. Famous chasidic master and rebbe
5. temptation
6. Divine Mercy, intercede for us, and on behalf of your people plead for compassion.

———————

[Page 84]

Memories of WWI

by Shmuel Knobl, Israel

To the memory of my dear mother, Freidl-Blumeh, z"l, killed by the Nazi murderers

Translated by Moses Milstein

I was still very young in the middle of WWI. I was studying in Moishe Mendl's, z"l, cheder. When the battles got closer to our shtetl, trade was interrupted, people stopped travelling to the villages, and we stopped going to cheder. I greeted this happily. No small matter being free of cheder...and to have the opportunity to hang out with other boys in the street, and watch the constant traffic of the army passing day and night without interruption. Or going out to the gentry's' fields, and bringing home things to eat that were not available because the farmers brought nothing into town to sell.

I accepted everything with a childish outlook, until things became scary. The Cossacks arrived. The men hid. The women smeared their faces with soot, and donned old torn clothes in order to look old and ugly. The Cossacks went around the houses looking for gold and women...At night, my mother would take us to the Christian neighbors.

Sitting on the ground, huddled together, we would spend the night there. The Christians would hang large crucifixes from the windows

[Page 85]

as a sign that Christians lived there. The Cossacks would avoid these houses. Father and the older brothers would hide in stalls or attics. When the Russian army began to leave and retreat, and we heard that the Germans were approaching, the military authority gave the order that all residents had to leave the city, and go over the bridge at the "courtyard," because they were going to burn down the bridge before the Germans arrived. The whole population of the city began to leave, some on foot, others with horses and wagons loaded with bedding and other necessities. I remember we also tied a cow to our wagon.

The whole population left the city and went across the bridge to the courtyard. Night fell. It became dark, and we, the children, fell asleep next to our mothers...Loud wailing cries interrupted our sleep. The Cossacks, under cover of darkness, surrounded the courtyard and wanted to abduct the women. I remember the first one to begin screaming, "Shema Israel!" And then the others began to scream without interruption, "Shema Israel!" This went on so long that the Cossacks started to run away. Whether they fled because of the cries of a whole shtetl, or whether they had to leave, my childish understanding couldn't determine...In the meantime, things quieted down, people calmed down a little, and soon an officer appeared to advise us to find a more secure place. The best option would be the forest. With half the night gone, we came to the forest exhausted, and scared, and some "occupied" a place in the darkness and went to sleep...When it became lighter, people began to move, make fires and cook food for the children.

Quiet reigned, and the people decided to send somebody to find out what was happening in town. A delegation went off, and returned before long, and happily informed us that we could return to the city. The Germans were there.

In memory of my father, Itzchak, z"l, killed by the Nazis

This took place in 1921. I was studying at my last cheder with Leizer Walkerman, z"l. One afternoon, when the rebbe

[Page 86]

was studying with us as usual, we suddenly saw through the window people running to their houses. The rebbe went outside to find out what was happening, and quickly returned with the news that the "Halterchikes" had entered town. They were beating Jews, cutting their beards off. He told us to go straight home. When we got out to the street, it was empty of people. Running by the pig stalls which led to my house, I saw signs of blood on the bridge. As I got closer to our house, I saw a lot of people gathered around our house. I understood that something had happened, because the trail of blood led to our house. I pushed through the mass of people, and entered the house that was also full of people. I saw my father lying in bed. Next to him was the city *feldsher*[1], and blood everywhere. After inquiring about what happened, I learned that a group of Jews had been standing in the city and talking. Suddenly, they were surrounded by a group of Hallerchiks with scissors in their hands, and began to cut the beards of those standing there. When they approached my father, he grabbed the scissors from one of them and threw it away. So they began to beat him with the butt of their rifles, and at the same time, cut away his beard with a piece of his flesh. My father fell covered in blood. Several Jews carried him home.

Translator's footnote:

1.   Unlicensed healer

Paiseh (Pesach) Sherer, a"h

by Ruth Sherer (Rita Pelz), Israel

Translated by Moses Milstein

There was a Jewish community in Tishevits, as there was in all the Polish cities and shtetls.

The community administrators (dozors) were elected by the Jewish population of the town. The representatives were elected from all the strata of society, and were also required to represent the interests of those who elected them. One of the representatives was the well-known figure of Paiseh (Pesach) Sherer.

For 14 years, that is until the last day of the existence of the Jewish community, until WWII, Paiseh Sherer fought for the handworkers of Tishevits.

[Page 87]

He fought like a lion for the interests of this poorer class, the artisans. He was known for his keen mind, his honesty, and his dedication to the welfare of the poorer classes of the shtetl.

Pesach Sherer and his wife Tsipeleh

His door was always open to whoever needed advice, or help. It was well known that he often suffered personally in earning a living because of his dedication to the struggle in his community. But it did not deter him, and he enthusiastically advanced his efforts to lighten the load of the artisans of Tishevits.

Thanks to him, the influence of the artisans' union in the Jewish community was strengthened, and during the last elections, four others from the handworkers union were added, 50% of the votes.

Paiseh Sherer the person was deeply embedded in the hearts of all Tishevitsers, not just the artisans for whose welfare he fought all his life, but also in his opponents, because of his integrity, objectivity and sharp intellect.

After the war, he came to Israel, and died here in 1962 in Haifa.

[Page 88]

In Memory of the Painter Adolphe Milich
a Native of Tyszowce

by Pinchas Landau – Israel

Translated by Sara Mages

I doubt if any of the former residents of Tyszowce who survived the Nazi holocaust know that in our city there was once a family from which there came a world-renowned artist named Adolphe Milich who lived and painted in Italy, Switzerland and France, and whose paintings once reached a price of half a million dollars.

It was only by chance that I got to know this painter two years before his death in 1965. As is well known, there is a painting school in Bat-Yam, Israel, under the patronage of the former mayor. As a painting enthusiast, he occasionally invited world-renowned painters to visit this school. Once, he invited the painter Adolphe Milich and hosted him at his home. When this painter visited the aforementioned school, my cousin (a descendant of the Ginzburg family and a native of the city of Lodz, Poland), who was the school's secretary, was present there. When he heard that this painter was a native of Poland, he dared to ask him from which city in Poland? When he told him that he was born in Tyszowce, he came and told me about it, and also arranged a meeting for me with the painter Adolphe Milich.

At this meeting, I saw before me a man who was semi-paralyzed and had difficulty speaking, so that I couldn't talk to him much, and yet, when I introduced myself as a native of Tyszowce, he hugged and kissed me. Tears of hoy flowed from his eyes and he called out – A Tishevitser – a Tishevitser! To his question: are there many Tishevitsers in Israel? I said about 250 people, and he asked me to arrange a meeting between him and all the Tishevitsers in Israel. He wanted to see them all. After his wife saw his excitement at meeting me, how he entered such a spiritual uplifting that he started singing Shabbat eve hymns, *Kol Meqadesh…* (that he still remembered from his childhood at his family home), she asked me not to arrange this meeting since it could harm his poor health. I understood that, and did not arrange the meeting.

As mentioned, I couldn't talk a lot with him because of his paralysis. With a stutter, he reminded me of a few places in Tyszowce that he still remembered, such as the synagogues, Beit HaMidrash to differentiate from the Council House, the Huczwa River *bombe* [bomb], the water mill and the steam mill, in his language - *die vasser miel un die pareh miel*. He did not remember people's names because he left Tyszowce in 1894 when he was still a young boy.

His wife, who managed his business, used to write down everything he said and told about himself, in a diary, even about the period before she met him in Paris. And she told me as follows:

When he was a young boy he started to draw all kinds of pictures. When he did not have a pencil and paper

[Page 89]

he painted on the walls of their apartment in Tyszowce with charcoal and coal. When they didn't let him "dirty" the apartment walls, he started to paint on the outside walls of the house, or on the walls of the houses close to his place of residence. When his parents saw that their child did not want to "study," only to paint, and couldn't tolerate the neighbors' complaints that their son was dirtying the walls of their houses, they decided to send him to his uncle (his father's brother) who lived in the city of Lodz, so that he would make a *mentsh* [man] out of him and teach him a profession, something they couldn't do then in Tyszowce. It didn't occur to his parents that they should teach him painting, that their son would one day be a world-renowned artist.

When his uncle in Lodz saw that the boy had a predilection for colors, he sent him to study the profession of house painting. After the great fire that broke out in Tyszowce in 1897, which destroyed all the Jewish homes in Tyszowce, his parents also moved to live in Lodz. They made a living from their son's work as a house painter and sign painter.

At the age of 18, he began to study painting. He studied in Warsaw, Italy, Germany, Switzerland (where he met his wife who accompanied him to the end of his life), until he came to Paris for the completion of his studies. More than once he suffered from hunger. Only thanks to his wife, who worked and supported him, was he able to continue his painting until he became known in the painting world.

In 1951, he fell ill with paralysis. His arms were mostly damaged, and he couldn't extend them to a distance of 20-30 centimeters, and yet I saw him painting (a picture he painted as a keepsake for his host, the mayor of Bat-Yam). He was sitting by the easel in a wheelchair and next to him stood an assistant who put into his hand the color he requested.

When I parted from him, he expressed his hope that on his next visit to Israel he would try to see all the natives of Tyszowce in Israel. He passed away in 1965 in Lugano, Switzerland.

Tel-Aviv, September 1966

The First Trade Union Strike

(In memory of my wife and child)

by Shmuel Knobl, Israel

Translated by Moses Milstein

After WWI and Polish freedom, various parties and libraries were established in Tishevits as in all other shtetls in Poland. But the greater part of the working youth remained outside the parties. They mostly came from poor families, and went to work at a very young age for the "old clothes" tailors. They could not read or write. There were also many construction workers,

[Page 90]

purse makers who were very backward in general knowledge.

At that time there was a group of us who came from petty bourgeois homes. After the war, we were quickly enrolled in private schools. Geniuses we were not. Nevertheless, we could read and write Yiddish and some Polish. We went on to learn trades. One became a boot-maker, another a carpenter, a third a tailor, or shoemaker. And since we had begun to think of ourselves as workers, we came up with the idea of organizing a trade union in Tishevits. We reached an understanding with the central committee in Warsaw and received all the information. In the beginning, we rented a locale in the "courtyard," and called for all young workers to a founding meeting. Thus the first trade union in Tishevits was founded.

We would get together every evening. We organized readings from the classics like Peretz, Sholom Aleichem, and others. It did not last long. There were some bosses who could not tolerate the idea that "workers could be seen as bettering themselves," and they applied pressure on the owner for so long that our locale was taken from us, and we were out on the street. So I asked my parents, and they agreed to give us the use of one of the unused rooms in our house. Here we really went to work. First, we initiated classes in reading and writing. We hired a teacher. He was called Shloimeleh, and many of us helped him. Classes were held each evening. We organized a choir, established various evenings where we dealt with different questions. Soon the Tishevits police became interested in us and began to demand various formalities for the *starostva* in Tomaszow. We were forced to hire a secretary with good Polish skills in order to carry out the correspondence properly. We used comrade Shmuel Erlich. He was a high school student then, and he carried out the correspondence for a modest fee.

I was then the elected secretary. I was involved with the Yiddish correspondence. In a very short time, we succeeded in eliminating illiteracy. Our young people started to visit the library, and became readers along with the rest of the city youth. Then the time came to improve our economic situation.

[Page 91]

At the time, the young people were held at work until late at night, and they were also used for house work. And the wages were inadequate. We decided to issue demands to the bosses, and if the demands were not met, to go on strike.

When they heard our demands, they laughed at us, and we declared a strike. We, the leaders of the strike, were young and without experience. We went out on strike with no money to help us during the strike. And from the very first days, mothers, really poor, came to me and yelled at my window, "What have you done to our children, getting them involved in a strike? You stuff yourself at your father's and they have nothing to eat."

I would like to mention an episode here. One evening, sitting at the union with Sh. Ehrlich, news came that there were workers sitting and working at Aharon Mashele's, a tailor. They were breaking the strike. I took with me two other workers. Sh. Ehrlich had a cane with a silver handle. So I took it along with me. The tailor lived in a new house with a high flight of stairs. I was the first to get to the top, and I entered with the stick in hand, and informed them that the workers have no right to be working, there is a strike. In the blink of an eye, the tailor pushed me up against the door, and threw us all down all the stairs. It was dark outside. We barely got out alive. The stick disappeared somewhere. When we got back, and Sh. Ehrlich saw the stick was gone he almost broke into tears, because his late father had left it to him.

The strike situation got worse from day to day. We were unable to continue to strike, but did not know how to end it. The bosses refused to talk to us. Then we turned to the older trade unions in Zamosc, and they sent us an older comrade, and we invited every tailor separately. They were willing to speak to this representative. And so we ended the unsuccessful strike with very small achievements. It appears that it was not yet the appropriate time to strike.

————

[Page 92]

The Artisans' *Gemiles Chasodim*[1] Bank in Tishevits

by Hershl Diamant, Israel

Translated by Moses Milstein

I was born in Tishevits. My father was Binyomin Diamant, mother, Breine. I worked at house construction from an early age. I served in the Tsarist army for seven and a half years until the end of WWI. I was a prisoner of the Germans for 10 months until the revolution. I was married in 1920, and lived the whole time in Tishevits employed in the building industry. From 18 years of age on, I became active in the community. I became a member of Chevra Kadisha, was gabai in the Husiatyn shtibl, and during that time, rebuilt the house. I was a member and one of the founders of the *gemiles chasodim* bank, and an active participant. I was elected as dozor to the Jewish community, one of the 4 artisan dozors. I was saved from death by fleeing to Soviet Russia. After the end of the war, I came to Poland with my family, and from there to Germany, and after quite a while, to Israel. I settled down, and here too I was elected gabai in the Netzach Israel synagogue in Haifa.

I want to describe the activities of the artisans' gemiles chasodim bank in Tishevits soon after WWI. The merchants union had its bank where merchants, as well as well-to-do artisans, could get loans. But the poorer artisans had nowhere to turn for help, and no one was concerned about them. I remember, at that time, going into the besmedresh and there were two melamdim there, Hena Melamed, and Kalman Dovid's son-in-law, Isrulik, and they asked me, "Why are they so determined not to let us found the bank? Are there no decent artisans who are in need, and who want to save themselves, and lend a few Zlotys?" I replied, "They will not succeed. The artisans have determined to found a bank, and they will do it." I was not alone in this view, all our comrade artisans believed this. It was not long after that all the artisans united, and we

[Page 93]

soon began to collect money for this goal. It's worth noting that the first to give the first 5 Zl was the poorest of all. He had practically nothing more. We got the first 150 Zl like that. After that, the Joint contributed two times as much — 300 Zl, and with this the bank was founded. Leading the whole initiative, and working on its behalf, was Paisey Ben Binyomin HaCohen Sherer, z"l. The first secretary, Moishe Bergman, who is now here in Israel, worked for a year or two, and after went to Warsaw. Also among the first managers were H' Pinchas Hershman, and Berl Hasser who also left for Warsaw. Others were then elected to take their place.

The managers up until the end — other than the chairman, Yechiel Asher Gelber, who died before the war — were the following: Yosef Mazer, tailor; Chaim Zuker, tailor; Paisey Sherer; Moti Pelz, tailor; Hershl Diamant, architect, the author of these lines; Elkanah Bitterman, architect; Israel Shalat, hatmaker; Abraham Pelz, tailor; Dovid-Leib Oifer, tailor; Yakov Moishe Gelber, kasha maker; Shloime Kreiner, secretary. Review commission: Gershon Shtuden, lumber merchant; Abish Firsht; Paisy Sherer who resigned from the management, but was convinced to join the review commission. There were also artisans co-opted to the management who were invited to special meetings. Abraham Loifer, baker; Moishe Chaim Kleiner, architect, Nuteh Loifer, tailor.

The first bank activities

The first loans were 25 Zl after 2 endorsers were found. But seeing that the loans were too small, and not of use to everyone, the management decided to give 2 loans to one home, including 25 Zl for the wife with 2 endorsers. If there was an exceptional circumstance, they loaned 75 Zl per house. Since the founding capital was so small, in order to provide loans for everyone, more capital was needed.

First a tea evening, and a small lottery were established, and took place Saturday night at Yantche Diamant's house. And so that you can have an idea of how faithfully, and dedicatedly people worked,

[Page 94]

here is an example. Chaim Zucker and Yoisef Mazer were not young men anymore. They went off to Moishe Lagrotzki Shliafrik and borrowed his large samovar. Chaim Zuker rolled up his long Sabbath kapoteh, got charcoal from the baker and brought it with joy. Then the samovar was set up and a pound of sugar purchased. Everyone was given a glass of tea and a sugar cube. And people donated whatever they could. And, with the lottery, 70 Zl were taken in that Saturday night. That same evening, it was discussed what methods to use to bring in more money for the fund. The following suggestions were submitted:

1.   To perform the play "*Mechirot Yosef*" in our shtetl and in Laszczow and Komarow.
2.   We should initiate a "plate," i.e., at every simcha in the shtetl, a "plate" for donations should be present.
3.   Purim evening, members of the board should go around seeking donations
4.   Approach the Joint for a larger loan.

All four suggestions were accepted. We began to prepare for the performance of *Mechirot Yosef*. We rehearsed and when we were ready, the whole board went to Laszczow. Even Raphael Shammas came along. There were no lack of mountains on the way to Laszczow. We were travelling with Tevl-Itche the baal hagoleh, and while descending a hill, one of the back wheels fell off, and the wagon overturned. No one was injured however. We just got to groan and get dirty.

A plate was acquired, and the words *gemiles chasodim* was painted on it, and for every simcha a member of the board brought the plate, and along with one of the guests they would gather the money, and at the end they would count the money, and record it on a piece of paper. Until the counting, the board member did not take part in the wedding. The money was then given to the cashier through the secretary.

Purim evening, the shtetl was divided into 4 quarters, and in each quarter, two chaverim from the board went door-to-door collecting donations.

A letter was sent to the Joint with a copy of the activity of the bank, and the signatures of all the board members and with the seal of

[Page 95]

the bank and a request for a larger sum for the bank. Based on the letter, we received a further 800 Zl from the Joint.

After receiving the 800 Zl from the Joint, we were able to increase the loans. Instead of 25 Zl, we gave out 50 Zl, and increased to 100 Zl for needy cases based on the evaluation of the board. But even after getting the 800 Zl and other sums, it was still extremely difficult to provide for everyone.

The loans were distributed like this: Every Saturday evening, there was a meeting of the board. There was a list of those requesting money, and they had to be approved. There were those who had to have it right away on Sunday, and others who needed it Wednesday evening after the market. After it was approved, and the secretary calculated the total amount needed for the neediest, and there was not enough in the bank, a couple of board members would get up and go to see some richer businessmen who used to help out, and get a loan for a week or two, a few hundred Zlotys, and then distributed to those in need. The following Saturday night, the scene was repeated. The first order of business was to pay back the freely given businessmen's loans. And the remainder was divided. This was how things had to be manipulated in order to satisfy everyone's needs.

Things advanced to where 150 and 200 Zl were given out per loan. Then small businessmen began to approach the bank with requests for loans. So it was decided to bring together members of the artisans. A meeting was held and it was decided to include small businesses in the loans.

Our own locale

At that time, the women's shul began to deteriorate on the side of Chanesh and Motl Presfer, and it had to be demolished. Since the rabbi said that it was forbidden to use the wood to build a private residence, it was decided to build a community house from the lumber on the place of the old rabbi, R' Shimsheleh, z"l. With the help of the rabbi we got the use of a large locale for the bank. From the bank, we gave them 1000 Zl and a loan. In return, we got a big place in the community building. When the bank moved over to the new building, it was decided that every Shabbes

[Page 96]

a minyan should be established there for the board to daven. Every week 5 or 6 businessmen were invited to the Shabbes minyan and they each gave as much as they wanted. These donations went to the fund.

Eventually, we came to the point where we could lend out 300 Zl. The hardest season was from Pesach until after the holidays when people came and asked for loans to lease orchards, and it was hard to provide for everyone. Aside from that, we had to give them a loan to buy a horse and wagon to transport the fruit to the city. The *sadovniks*[2] who had summer fruit were able to repay the loans earlier. But those who had winter fruits could not repay until after the holidays.

Here in Israel we know the meaning of "*protecsyeh*." In the shtetl, a certain measure of protecsyeh existed, but in a different manner. A man could come and ask for a loan of 200 Zl for another person. He wanted to use his protectsyeh because he had occasionally deposited money in the bank. He was told that, at the moment there was no money in the bank, but if he was so interested in getting a loan for the other person, he could give him a loan of 200 Zl for two months, then we could loan the money. If he agreed to that, the second person immediately got the money.

There were also cases like these: Certain retailers would get a loan of 300 Zl, and punctually pay installments every week, but under no circumstances could they pay off the entire loan. Instead, they would pay 150 Zl. They then went to an acquaintance and asked him for a loan of 150 Zl to pay off the entire loan, and get a new loan. Binyomtche Marder was a stable guarantor like this. On Friday, he would lend someone as much as he needed, and used to come to us for a loan for the other, because he had given him a loan in order for him to repay the 150 Zl and get a new loan and use only 150 Zl because he had to pay him back.

There were others like that who helped others. There were those who voluntarily deposited money in the bank for a given amount of time in order to allow more loans to be given out. These were: Mendeleh Finger, a wheat merchant; Motl Hersh Diker, a *shteper*[3]; Yankeleh Glick, a *shenker*[4]; Yankl Bashister; Paisy Bashister; Kalman Shteper. There were many

[Page 97]

others whose names I don't remember. Eliyahu Schwindler-Neuman was a frequent endorser for the carriage drivers of Tomaszow. He used to come every Monday-Tuesday to the bank and do many favors for the drivers.

With the passage of time, the activities of the bank were not just concerned with loans. We began to think about other ways to lighten the load of the handworkers. Flour for Pesach was purchased and sold cheaper to the artisans who needed a cheap *pood*[5] of flour. But every year, we had to deal with the *montchares* (flour sellers). There were many who were sympathetic to us, and bought flour for Pesach at the same price as at the montchares. They wanted to help us in our necessary work. If I had to describe all the difficulties everyone had for Pesach, there would not be enough paper. I will try just to describe events from 1938 onward. From this, you can get an idea of how things were in earlier years.

Before Pesach 1938, the flour sellers demanded that we should send a delegation, and they would reach an agreement with us. They would sell us the flour at the same price we sold it for, but with one condition, that we should not send anyone not a handworker, and deposit 100 Zl. as security, and the flour to be delivered 3 days before Purim. When the time came to receive the flour, and nothing was seen or heard, we went to them to find out what was happening. They replied, "Have patience, you'll get it." But seeing that they were stalling, we called a meeting, including members not on the board, and it was immediately decided to travel to Zamosc for flour. For several years, we used to buy flour from Fuchs. This year, when we came to Fuchs for flour, he said he didn't have any. After this, we found out that the mantcheres had asked the merchants in Zamosc, Tomaszow, and Hrubieszow not to sell us any flour.

We saw that the situation was bad, so we set out to find sources of flour. Suddenly we discovered that there was a merchant and farmer mill in the village of Madienec. There was a bookkeeper from Tishevits there, Ephraim Shlit (Asher Kuperstock's son-in-law). It was snowing and there was deep mud outside. One of the most loyal comrades, Mattis Gelber, spoke up and said that if one other person came along, he would go find out if there was flour there. I volunteered to be the second. I had my own horse and wagon,

[Page 98]

got some money and drove off. We got there in the evening. I went directly to Ephraim Shlit and asked him if he had any Pesach flour. He replied that two Jews from Hrubieszow had koshered the farmers' flour, and have some left, but he didn't know if it had been sold already. They were due at 8:00 o'clock in the morning. "If there is any, I will buy it for you." There was no place to spend the night, so we stayed in the stable. We guarded our money all night. We couldn't sleep and we waited impatiently for day. Ephraim told us not to hang around the courtyard. He would do the buying for us, if it had not been sold yet. At precisely 8:15, Ephraim comes to the stable and says, "Come in, *Yidden*, and let's see the money. I have bought the flour for you." I do not have the words to describe the joy we felt hearing that we had our flour. Frozen, we danced for joy. After paying the money, we harnessed 3 horses, loaded the flour and set off for home. Because of our elation, we forgot that we needed a *hechsher* for the flour. When we got home that evening, people were already going to hear the Megilla. They were waiting for us in the *polish*. On seeing us, joy broke out among all the chaverim in true Purim fashion. Men and women awaited our arrival. They even came out to the road to meet us. We quickly found a store at Naphtali Nuteh Hinde's, and still wearing their holiday clothing, the flour was unloaded. Everyone rejoiced.

When the flour had been stored, a tailor, Itche Zuker, "*Krumer Kop*" said, "Yidden, we have to assign two guards to guard the flour overnight, because the montchartes can sneak in and pour naphtha on the flour." So two men were assigned to guard the store all night.

But the joy only lasted until the morning. In the morning, the rabbi sent for me, Hershl Diamant, and Mattes Gelber, and asked us, "Did you get a hechsher for the flour for Pesach?" We replied that if Ephraim Shlit was the broker, then it must be kosher. But the rabbi required a written certificate, and we did not have one. We did not know the addresses of the two Jews we had bought it from. There were no telephones and phone books like today to search for names and addresses. Meanwhile, the montchares agitated and shouted, "What kind of flour did you bring for Pesach? There was never any Passover flour there."

[Page 99]

They also convinced some of our members who were saying, "What kind of flour did they bring?" So I had no choice but to drive to Hrubieszow, but no one wanted to accompany me because of the snow and mud. So we called on Abraham Moishenitzky and asked him to go to Hrubieszow for the hechsher. So he said, "How can anyone travel now? Who would want to set out now in such weather? You could lose your life." But he was nevertheless forced to go, and I had to go with him. We left in the morning, drove all day, and arrived in the evening, asked the way to the two Jews from the mill, and they immediately brought us the hechsher. Because the horses were very tired, and us as well, we stayed the night, and left the following morning. When we got home and the chaverim saw the hechsher, everyone cheered up, and we sold the flour for Pesach.

* * *

The bank also occupied itself with charitable issues. We brought in machinery to knit socks, and brought down an instructor to teach the work. The machines were installed in the bank locale, and the daughters of the artisans were called on to learn the work and help their parents earn a living. They took the work home and earned money. In order to have an idea of how popular and respected the handworkers' bank was, it is worthwhile remembering that in the elections for the Jewish community, for the first and second time, only one member of the handworkers was elected, Paisey Sherer. But by the third round, four handworkers were elected as dozor along with four from the town.

In concluding, I would like to add that in 1937 there was a meeting in town that included the secretary of the Joint. After he got a report on the work of the bank, he said that there were 660 such banks in Poland, "But your bank is in 6th place in terms of activity."

In 1939 we began to hear talk of war, and we called a meeting because people had stopped depositing money. A question was being discussed and argued: How to describe the activities and the balance of the bank. It was decided to prepare a report: 1. How much money the bank has. 2. What are the debts?

[Page 100]

3. How many voluntary loans are there? The report was to be made in several copies. The report was compiled and distributed to several members not on the board. There was no accumulation of cash, and it was decided that in the case of war, some floorboards in the bank should be removed, a hole dug, and all the documents should be buried there. This was done, but later events led to the destruction of everything.

At the beginning of the war, a German plane was seen flying around Aharon Berish Liak's mill. When the goyim in the mill went outside to look at the plane, a bomb fell and killed several people. A panic arose in town. At the same time, a unit of Russians and Germans engaged and shooting broke out. Mordechai Gottes's daughter was killed by a bullet entering her window. The panic grew. People had already buried their valuables. All the Jews locked up their houses and fled to the forest, hoping to return at night. That day, the goyim set the whole city on fire. They were seen pouring naphtha on the houses after they robbed them. When we got back from the forest, there was nothing left to save. Everything had burned, even our documents. The only things left were some copies in the hands of people who are no longer with us either.

I, the writer of these sentences, fled to Russia with my wife, Chaya, two sons, Binyomin, and Yakov, daughter Bronieh, father-in-law, Nuteh, z"l, and mother-in-law, Feige, who now lives with me.

My oldest brother, Yontche Diamant, who was one of the founders of the bank, died before the war. Killed by the Germans were his son-in-law and daughter, his son, Peretz and his wife, and three children, my older sister, Shaindl, and her husband and two children, my sister, Risheh, her husband and one child.

My dearest friends have disappeared, their lives tragically ended, and I am left alone and lonely. The lives of dear brothers and sisters, institutions and establishments are no more. Honor to their memory!

Footnotes:

1. Interest-free loans
2. Jews who rented orchards from the gentry
3. Cuts out and sews shoe leather
4. Tavern keeper
5. Russian unit of weight equal to 16.38 kg

[Page 101]

Remember Them Favorably

by Dr. Israel Stern (Montreal, Canada)

Translated by Moses Milstein

When it comes to remembering Tishevits, or my life in Poland in general, I suffer from partial amnesia. Whether this is a result of the effects of the catastrophe, or merely the passage of time, is hard for me to determine. By this I mean that I am not writing a history. I'm only trying to remember, and to mention some of the friends of my youth who were torn to shreds by wild beasts.

Tishevits, although naturally similar to other shtetls in Poland, and especially those of Lublin province, was nevertheless different. The rise of Poalei Zion in Tishevits took place in a different manner than elsewhere. There were no left wing Poalei Zion in the entire neighborhood. Only in Chelm, which had no contact with Tishevits, was there a large party organization. In Tishevits there was no Poalei Zion before the division. The right wing Poalei Zion was previously Tze'irei Zion. Therefore, the schism in Poalei Zion in 1920 could not have left any trace in Tishevits. Incidentally, around 1920 Tishevits had just begun to sample from the worldly tree of knowledge on a significant scale, openly. This worldly Tishevits, with its parties, locales, and unions, was initially a product of WWI. At the Tze'irei Zion locale you could find the earnest and honest Nuteh Rosenzweig, h"yd. He was unhappy with the Tze'irei Zion ideology, and took part in the founding of the Jewish people's library at the end of the 1920s, which was, at the beginning, in competition with the Tze'irei Zion association. The founders of the people's library with Mendl Singer, and Shmuel Ehrlich Brosh were Bundistish or Folkistish inclined. This put Nuteh outside the camp of Tze'irei Zion. How Nuteh became aware of and acquainted with the left Poalei Zion, I don't know. He was the founder and leader of the Tishevits left wing Poalei Zion until his departure from Poland in 1937.

[Page 102]

Nuteh was however in a certain sense an isolated individual, because, to our shame, it must be remembered that well-off and important people even in the worldly associations seldom mixed with the common people, the trades, the plebians. The Tze'irei Zion was founded by the "beautiful" young people and the well-off. And whoever came from such a home, or strived to have the "beautiful" friends, went there. Nuteh, the son of Itcheh and Chaneh Malicher came from a decent old family. The Malichers and the Kovales were a hearty family of *Tevye der Milchiker* type. At Tze'irei Zion there were few volunteers who left with him. Even those who went with him for a while, quickly regretted it and went back to the right wing Poalei Zion. So how does a leader get a following? The story is the following:

Aside from *Tevye der Milchiker*, there were also in Tishevits *Chaims* from Peretz's *Sholem Bayis*: common folk, tradesmen, who did not allow their bitterness to the "*yivatisheh,*" (well-off) to consume their "*chelek v'nahalah b'elohei Israel.*" There lived in Tishevits a Mecheleh Shuster, a real pauper. He also liked to read psalms, a chapter of Mishnah, a page of Ein Yakov, or a good story, in the shoemakers' section of the synagogue. While tacking shoes he also reflected on higher matters and needs. He was raising two sons from his first wife, Shifra. The oldest, Avrum Itcheh, and his brother, Mordechai Miller, hy"d.

Around 1926, a trade union opened in Tishevits with much drama. The majority of the common folk joined. There were better-off children in the leadership, but the masses were mostly the common people. The union was a cover, a transparent one, for the communist party. Abraham Itzchak Miller was one of the young members of the union and was drawn into the "Komyog.[1]" He was the chairman of the cell for a while. But he was bothered by the national question, especially the Jewish question. The assimilationist- Leninist program enraged and repelled him. At the same time, the glory of the October mythos enchanted him and attracted him. He was not aware of the leftist Poalei Zion and their calling themselves at that time, the Jewish Communist Party–Poalei Zion. I was then in my bar-mitzvah years, and by the notions of the time, old enough to be a party man. Social activities rarely continued after marriage so we had to get it in while we could. Communist inclined older boys would occasionally whisper secrets into my ears. But I

[Page 103]

hesitated. My sympathies for socialism drew me to their side, but from childhood on I was a big Jewish Chauvinist, and considered myself a Zionist. However, my sister, Shifra, sent me a children's newspaper from Vilna, "*Dos Freiyeh Kind*" (I think) put out by the left Poalei Zion. She, along with my brother, Yechiel, joined the left wing Poalei Zion in the Vilna teachers seminary. In that way I learned about left wing Poalei Zion Zionism, and the synthesis of Borochovian Marxism enthralled me and became sacred for me.

We were connected to Mendele Shuster's household partly because he repaired our boots and booties, and partly because our mother, Gitl, a"h, was mother to many lonely and broken souls. So I visited him not just to pick up a pair of repaired boots. We used to chat with Avrum Itcheh a lot and often, and when we discovered that we shared an ideology, we began to go on secret walks (of which, incidentally, both families were unhappy). Avrum Itche left the *Komyog* and took a lot of members from the trade union with him, and founded the Poalei Zion youth. This must have been around 1928. Those who remember the custom of those days to publish a declaration with grandiose phrases in the party newspaper columns–in this case, *Die Freiye Yugnt*,--will smile with irony and nostalgia at the same time. But for Avrum Itche and his friends the declaration "that we are leaving our underdog position of the "*yevsektsiyeh*,"[2] and joining the true revolutionary camp of Poalei Zion," was a deeply felt commitment. The name, Poalei Zion rang proudly and the dream was youthful and messianic.

Avrum Itcheh had influence. He actually split the working youth in half. And from then on until the war, the majority of the youth were the shoemakers, tailors, furriers, carpenters, hat makers, bakers, and leather workers, and plain common folk who were either communists or left Poalei Zion. The better-off youth had other unions. There were some better-off youth in the left Poalei Zion, but they were in the minority. After his wedding, Avrum Itcheh was less active in the movement, but his deeds will be remembered here for the good.

In this way, Nuteh became a leader of a mass organization. The details of combining the few older (in their early twenties) members around Nuteh with the younger working class youth, are not clear in my memory. The charm of it

[Page 104]

is not just what time has erased from my memory, but also that I, Abraham Shoichet's son, had occasion to steal through the back streets and byways like a Marrano, to our locale, because what a better-off kid could do publicly, a shoichet's child, eating kehilleh bread, could not.

Speaking of locales, they were not much more than one small cramped rented room. To get the rent money was a tall order. And to heat it in winter, we stole the wood. One location (the first one, I think) was rented from Avremeleh Baker, a garret in the house where, according to legend, the Tishevits Moshiach Ben-Yosef died. Other locations I remember were at the Ginsberg's "court," and the place at the Knobl's where I was active as one of the founders of the Tishevits *Yungbor* until I left for Vilna in 1931.

I remember names of surviving friends, among them Moishe Geyer, (party secretary in my time) and his wife, Risheh, today in the United States. His brother, Shloimeh, today in Israel, who was with us at the founding and left after a short time. Pinyeh Sherer, today in America, who seriously delved into

Party activists of the left wing Poalei Zion in Tishevits in 1931

[Page 105]

Borochovism, and came to the conclusion that the party must go into pioneering.

And those who died: The pretty Chayeh Rov; Munyeh Katz with the laughing eyes; Miriam Etl Kopl, the authentic proletarian with a big-city air; the dreamy Bas-Malke Chayeh Zuker; the tall smiling Elyeh Shleicher; the serious Abraham Ber Shafrach, our locally born director and reciter, and his sister, the proletarian intellectual, Rachel; Isralke Lev, and Shloime Shafer for whom the party was a personal redemption and more than a home. Yehoshua Stengl, the dedicated Poalei Zion and loyal personal friend whose room (years later) in Warsaw was the address for many hungry and homeless friends. From his mother's (*Rochel die Gendzlerkeh*) errand boy, *dorfgeyer*, and *yeridim forer*, he became a painter on the high, dizzying, scaffolds of Warsaw apartment houses. Hanging on outside on the highest floors was a terrible job, and therefore better paid. This was the secret of his relative prosperity during the hungry years of the thirties. He shared his earnings with the movement, and was the editor for many years (before the Polish authority) of the "*Arbeter Zeitung.*" Yehoshua died in the Warsaw ghetto, hy"d.

The Sacher family moved back into the city from a village. All the children of the house were members of Yungbor. Yosl, a"h, was a real go-getter, a true "*yat,*" in the vernacular of the time. He was also our "star" as actor at all the remembrance celebrations of the academies, and he shone. He passed away very young. But, may he live long, his older brother, Moishe, came from the village school smart and well-read. And he brought from his home the inheritance of his grandfather, Leibish Wassertreger, a manual laborer, and a *ba'al koreh*, a prototype of Yochanan the water carrier of Peretz. This naturally led him to eventually become the leader of the Tishevits left wing Poalei Zion, taking over Nuteh's place and role while he was serving in the Polish army. Incidentally, Nuteh could have gotten out of serving like many boys of his class, but military service was for him a preparation for the final liberation of the Jewish people and the working class. Whether he had a chance to fight against the German beast, I do not know.

He did, however, prepare himself…(let us remember that). Moishe remained the leader until the war. He, and his wife, Pesheh, (also one of the first Tishevits Poalei Zionist), and the surviving family in Israel, can remember and tell more.

[Page 106]

I won't go into any more detail about our activities. We carried out a broad cultural agenda. Even Feivish, the Communist, gave me sharp-edged compliments, that we were preparing them to be aware comrades. In truth, many learned to read and write Yiddish with us. Many were confronted with the Jewish and human problems of our time for the first time at our meetings, and they remained aware until today. The presentations, lectures, classes, discussions, trips in the forest, celebrations and performances are still warm memories. Our party was the only bit of light and celebration for a large part of our members and children.

I want to end with underlining that even though history mocked us, our dream was nonetheless honest and earnest. I remember only that when Nuteh came back from a Poalei Zion youth conference in Warsaw, in 1930, I think, and did not bring any plans for arming ourselves for the socialist revolution that we hoped and waited for in those days, it was a big disappointment for our *Yungtatses*, and Yungbors, especially as our *Komyog* friends arrogantly bragged about their hay-covered wagons of rifles smuggled into Ukrainian villages by itinerant "*gepeunikes*." It's possible that for our leaders in Warsaw or in other big cities, it was a game with fine phrases. We took it seriously, honestly…To us, it seemed like the road to Jewish and human redemption. But a brutal death, at the hands of the brown, German beast and its Polish, Ukrainian, and other murderous accomplices, may their name and memory be erased, and the cynical treachery of the Georgian despot, extinguished the flame.

Footnotes:

1. Communist youth in the USSR
2. Jewish section of the Communist party (1918-1930)

The Left Wing Poalei Zion Party

by Moshe Sachar, Israel

Translated by Moses Milstein

The left wing Poalei Zion party began operating around 1927. The organization actually existed earlier, possibly earlier than 1927, but not being permitted by the authorities,

[Page 107]

the first meetings took place in private houses illegally.

It wasn't until winter, 1928, that with great effort and difficulties, we succeeded in getting permission from the *staroste* for the name, "Society of Friends of the Workers of Palestine." Because the left wing Poalei Zion party was banned by the Polish authorities, activities took place under various names. Those responsible in the staroste in Tomaszow were the chaverim: Paise Shlafrok, Yoineh Mermlstein, Nuteh Rosenzweig, and Nachum Spritz.

The founding group of the left wing Poalei Zion in the year 1928

We immediately rented a locale, and began activities, first in the cultural domain, with literary readings, and *kestl-evenings.* Every Friday evening we held a press review of the week about actual political issues, and also political discussions with the participation of speakers from other groups. In time, a drama club was created which organized literary evenings with an artistic performance by the choir, readings, and one-act plays by Reisen, Leivick, Bergleson, and others. We even set ourselves the goal, because of our earlier success, of presenting a piece of social content, with the name of "*Gelt,*" performed for a large audience in the local "*Dom-Ludowy.*" This was the first public appearance of the drama club,

[Page 108]

and it received an enthusiastic reception in the city. We also organized trips to the forest every Saturday, mostly in the region of the Presper Forest. Yankele Kleks lived in that neighborhood. Incidentally, Zalman and Chaim Kleks were also members of the organization, which created a homier atmosphere. There we enjoyed various sports, or engaged in discussions. In the evening, we would return home singing. This activity became increasingly popular in the city, and more members kept joining, mostly from working class homes, who yearned for knowledge and social life. Most of the young people came from homes where the fathers were always busy with work in the workshops, or away working in the nearby villages for a whole week, or doing business, in order to support the family. The wives would stay home toiling to raise the children, preoccupied with cooking and washing, and in a free moment, plucking feathers, never staying idle.

Many families would rent orchards in the surrounding villages in the suburbs, and stay there the whole summer living in wagons surrounded by straw in perpetual fear of thieves, or the rains and summer storms. That's how they struggled through the summer just to feed their families. And if God helped, and they saved something for winter, they were happy and lucky.

With such a hard life, it was hard, really hard, for the youth of the above-mentioned class to benefit from a social-political upbringing. That's why it was such a great achievement for the founders — chaverim — who understood and responded to the situation by founding the organization. Yechiel Stern, Shifra Stern, Nuteh Rosenzweig, z"l, and others dedicated themselves to the organization. One marvels at the extraordinary will of these people to share their knowledge with others. The writer of these lines remembers the difficult conditions under which Yechiel gave his lectures on various political themes somewhere in a garret at Avremaleh Becker's, a"h. His scientific explanations about the "class interests in the national question" of Ber Borochov, read somewhere at Meir Shieh Shuster's, a"h. Those were unforgettable moments that will always remain in the memory of the survivors.

Nuteh Rosenzweig was the actual builder, organizer, and leader in all aspects of party life. He dedicated his entire work, efforts and energy to the organization.

[Page 109]

A separate and more important contribution was the work of Shifra Stern. Pouring her heart and soul into it, she organized the children's organization, *Yungbor*, (young Borochowists). She drew together the children of working class homes, from poor homes, and taught them to read and write first in Yiddish. Like a mother, she gave them an elementary upbringing, and later taught them the class distinctions in society, and to struggle for a better, more beautiful, life.

The passionate will and thirst for knowledge in the children and youth inspired the leadership in their dedicated work.

As a result of this fruitful work, new talented young people emerged among the chaverim themselves, and with time, they began to undertake the roles of the earlier leaders. After Shifra's immigration to Canada, Israel Stern took over the responsibility of the children's organization, and carried out the job with exactitude and faithfulness. His actual political discussions with the children were a pleasure to listen to, and were a font of wisdom. His frequent lectures and appearances were a great benefit for adults as well. He remained active and devoted up to the day of his departure.

With time, other chaverim stepped into youth leadership positions: Moishe Geyer, Pinieh Sherer, Shaul Klein, Yehoshua Shtengl, z"l, who fell heroically in the Warsaw ghetto, and Moishe Sacher who together with the above-mentioned chaverim worked and carried out the party activities until the outbreak of WWII.

There was also a group of party activists: Munieh Katz, Chayeh Rov, Ruchl Shafrach, Miriam Etl Kapel, Malkeh Zuker, Berl Shafrach, Yosl Sacher, Israel Lev,and Moishe Engelsberg. They all carried out their duties with complete devotion and discipline in whatever the party asked of them.

A part of the surviving erstwhile activists are now in Israel, or in other countries, and some of them continue to be active in various political or social movements: the chaverim Nachum Spritz, Abraham Reis, Pesheh Pelz, Gitl Gam, Chayeh Zuker, Rishe Laufer, and Menieh Kleiner. All the survivors certainly share a feeling of gratitude to all those who had helped to elevate the worker youth from our shtetl to a proper spiritual level.

The Betar Movement in Tishevits

by Moshe Zimri (Singer), Israel

Translated by Moses Milstein

In 1925, when the *Betar* movement was established in Poland and in other countries, Tishevits, like other cities and shtetls, also answered the call of Zev Jabotinsky and founded Betar. Most of the chaverim came to Betar from *Tzeirei Mizrachi*. The other parties, like *Poalei Zion*, right and left *Hechalutz, Freiheit, Mizrachi, Tzeirei Mizrachi, Bund*, and Communists, already had years of work behind them.

[Page 111]

When Betar first appeared on the "Jewish street," we didn't know what to make of them — were they *chalutzim*[1], or militarists. We used to make fun of their paper rifles, of the "fascists" as we called them because of their brown shirts and their uniforms, and the quasi-military aspect they had in Poland. The uniform was the main attraction for young people. The Jewish youth, especially in a small town like Tishevits, had no opportunities, neither in education, nor in employment, aside from the besmedresh or the shtibl, so the young people occupied themselves

Betar, Tyszowce, 1930-1931

with political parties, and discussions about socialism, Marxism, communism, Zionism, and revisionism. The youth consisted of children of storekeepers, and craftsmen. The greater part of the Tishevits population were paupers. As a result, the class differences were small. Young people frequented all the parties including Betar.

In a short time we established a strong revisionist Betar movement. We founded a library, and carried out Zionist and literary activities. We set up a mandolin orchestra under the direction of Yakov Reis. He is in Israel today.

[Page 112]

In the Betar locale, we opened a school where we taught Hebrew, Tanach, and the geography of Israel. The teachers were: Moishe Pietrishka, z"l — he was killed by the Nazi murderers, and chaver Henech Chavkin, who is in Israel now. We founded a *hachshara*[2] in Tishevits attended by Betar members from the region. Unfortunately, there was not a lot of work to do other than chopping wood and similar jobs.

In 1929, when the first Betar kibbutz was founded in Nadworna, Galicia, two chaverim from Tishevits attended: the writer of these lines, and Eliezer Lerner, who unfortunately did not make it to Israel but was killed by the Nazis. Ephraim Kuperstein, now in Israel, was sent to Warsaw to the first Betar instructor's course. On his return, he helped out a lot with various sports and military exercises. A lot of chaverim from Betar travelled to Israel with certificates, or with Aliyah Bet. It was called at the time, "excursions." A Betar member from Tishevits, Zvi Reifer, who came with Aliyah Bet, fell in the War of Independence at the Altalena ship skirmish.

I think it's worth remembering the fact that, when the Polish national holiday was celebrated on May 3rd, Betar was invited to march around the shtetl. With their brown shirts and white and blue flags they marched right up to the church, and waited outside until prayers were finished.

That's how low we had sunk in the diaspora in our desire to appear fine to the goyim. How proud we should be today in our country of Israel.

Footnotes:

      1.   Pioneers for Israel
      2.   Kibbutz training camp

———

[Page 113]

Memories of Days Gone By

by Dov Spiz (Israel)

Translated by Sara Mages

I know that there is someone from our townspeople who is more qualified than me to give expression to, and to devote time in writing, about the importance of the Freiheit-Dror[1] organization in our city Tyszowce in providing Zionist and socialist education to the youth. However, I find it appropriate from my perspective to bring up some drawings and figures that have been etched in my memory from that glorious era, the period of youth in which we spent the best of our young years, and absorbed into us the homeland atmosphere to which we longed to ascend in the course of time.

The Dror movement in Tyszowce

Yenta Zilberman z"l - I will never forget the first evening when I was at the home of the member Yenta for the first members' conversation at the branch. It was an evening full of experiences that ended with intense singing of songs in Hebrew and Yiddish of those days.

[Page 114]

The member, Yenta, contributed a lot to the design of the Freiheit-Dror organization patterns, and to the brave spirit she instilled in us when she explained the essence of our organization. Under her guidance and influence, a pioneering lifestyle full of social and cultural activity was created. The activity was expressed not only in evening conversations, but also in general activity, and we all joined her work and organized successful social performances that, over time, became the talk of the city.

Pesach Kreiner z"l - was my neighbor. I already knew him in my childhood when I came to play with my friend, Yankele Kreiner. Pesach's sister, Rivkaleh, was a noble and kindhearted person like no other, and both of them were always radiant and charming.

The Dror movement before the outbreak of the war in 1939

Pesach did a lot for the young people, who were called *skoiten* [scouts], and he was the one who administrated the oath of allegiance to us. I remember the successful play, "*The children of Ein Harod*[2]," that we presented under the energetic guidance of Pesach, and whose echo reached every Jewish home in Tyszowce. I also remember the meetings on Saturdays before dawn on the *krintzi*, and how much they were steeped in interest and great content. More than once, at the end of such a meeting, and after the end of the conversation, we had to run carefully and secretly back home so as not to be late for the Shabbat prayer with our parents. And later, when we grew up and were able to belong and to be integrated into the alumni organization of Freiheit, we were overwhelmed with pride that we were also privileged to join them. I remember well the graduate members who prepared for their *aliyah*[3] to Israel by training themselves

[Page 115]

for the hard work of lumberjacks, and various hard jobs at the sawmill, all this in order to adapt to a life of work in the longed-for homeland.

Moshe Motel Schler z"l - was one of leaders of Poalei Zion in our city, and we all drew and drank thirstily from the well of his knowledge and education. At every moment, and at every opportunity, he spoke words of taste and wisdom, and read and explained to us the folk tales of Y. L. Peretz and other writers. He sharpened our senses and organized public literary meetings with us that attracted the majority of the Jewish public in town. I also remember the experiences of the movement emissaries' visit to our city. In 1933, the member, Tzyvia Lubetkin, who was then a lively young girl full of energy and knowledge, visited us (later, her name became known in the ghettos as a partisan - she is now in Israel). How the years flowed and passed in extensive social activity, and pleasant dreams, to build a better and more just world. Oh, how much life content there was in the conversations we held from time to time in the Podbórner Forest, which were always accompanied by various games and social gatherings around a campfire. Who doesn't remember the Freiheit's" summer colonies" that were held in the Podbórner Forest.

And behold, suddenly everything has vanished and is gone. The wave of Hitlerism broke out and flooded every site throughout Poland, and the main victim was the Jewish people, and it didn't take long for these poisoned shards to reach our city, Tyszowce. Anti-Semitism bloomed and all the Poles raised their heads and started to harass the Jews.

This was especially noticeable every Wednesday of the week, during market hours. Polish hooligans walked around and prevented Poles from shopping and buying from Jews, under the well-known slogan, "Poland for the Poles."

In the meantime, livelihoods declined and the young people, together with the adults, began to search for possibilities and ways to leave Poland. In their hearts, they sensed and felt that a certain holocaust was hovering in the air, and that it was necessary to escape from it before it was too late. Some of the youth started to head to *Hachshara*[4] kibbutzim in order to prepare themselves for *aliyah* to Israel, and some also managed to leave as tourists to Israel, of course only a few.

That's how the Second World War found me when I was in *Hachshara* in Kibbutz Grochów near Warsaw.

At the time of the Tyszowce fire I was not in the city. At the outbreak of the war I, like others, started to walk from Grochów across the cities of Poland in order to get home and reunite with my family, and I saw the cities of Poland in their ruins, their convulsions and their destruction. Finally, on the holiday of Sukkot, I arrived home and saw the city burned and destroyed.

And suddenly, a rumor spread that the Germans were returning to the city, and terror fell on all the city's surviving Jews. By a miracle, our house didn't burn, because mostly Poles lived in this area by the river. And indeed, our whole family gathered in our apartment where they also prayed in public, because the Beit HaMidrash and all the shtibelach, which were used as a place of prayer, were destroyed to the ground.

All my friends fled across the Bug River, and some of them fled in the direction of the city of Ludmir. My parents didn't let me go because the wounds on my legs, from my walk from Grochów, had not yet healed. However, I could not come to terms with the situation because we received horrifying news about transports

[Page 116]

of Jews to Zbaszyn and other location from which they did not return. Later, the Poles finished the Germans' work and helped them eliminate the Jews. No wonder that Jews ran in every direction and every wind without knowing where, and no one wanted to help them. Also in Kibbutz Grochów the youth didn't know what the day would bring. And then, in this situation of the "sinking of the world," I decided to leave the city and to try to escape in order to be saved from this vale of tears. And on Thursday, it was on *Shemini Atzeret* of Sukkot... I left my hometown, Tyszowce, in which my family built its future, in which my cradle stood, and in which I wove the dreams of my youth, forever.

The Hebrew class group

Translator's footnotes:

1.   Freiheit-Dror (lit. "Freedom"), a Socialist Zionist youth movement founded before World War I in Russia, promoted national and Socialist values as well as Jewish culture.
2.   Ein Harod is a kibbutz in northern Israel.
3.   *Aliyah* (lit. "Ascent") is the immigration of Jews from the Diaspora to Eretz Israel.
4.   *Hakhshara* (lit. "Preparation") the term is used for training programs in agricultural centers in which Zionist youth learned vocational skills necessary for their emigration to Israel, and subsequent life in kibbutzim.

[Page 117]

The Hebrew School in Tyszowce

by S. Hechtman (Israel)

Translated by Sara Mages

Keren Keyemet Leisrael committee in Tyszowce

I was accepted as the principal and teacher of the first Hebrew school–and to our deep sorrow also the last one–in the 5669 (1929) school year. This school, which was as mentioned the first of its kind in the town, was opened after a lot of deliberations both on the part of the parents' committee, and on the part of the parents themselves, who in the early days refused to send their sons to the school for several reasons - apart from the reasoning that it was secular: -

1. The school was mixed, boys and girls together.
2. The pronunciation in which the subjects were taught was the Lithuanian pronunciation, or as we called it in Poland, the Ashkenazi (the parents didn't want to hear about the Sephardic pronunciation at all); and, especially, the teacher would be teaching bareheaded (I gave up on teaching bareheaded). In any case, it is understood that the struggle was not easy, but somehow we overcame all the obstacles and the school opened.

The building, including the furniture, in which I started my work didn't suit my purpose. The building was in Avraham HaShochat Alley, an alley full of mud and slush all days of the year, but I was determined to overcome all these "small" obstacles and to start working.

[Page 118]

The number of students doubled a month after the school's opening, and half a year later the number reached forty. Boys were taken out of the *cheders* and handed over to the school. There were cases where boys "went on strike" and demanded that their parents enroll them in the school instead of the *cheders* they attended. *Melamdim* [teachers] came to complain before the committee members about the loss of their

The Hebrew School in Tyszowce 1929, the teacher S. Hechtman

livelihood, and the number of students, especially the girls, increased day by day. Half a year later, the school managed to fortify its existence in all respects. This success was caused by the fine appearance of the students in the city (in special hats), the order and discipline in the school despite its poor location, and, above all, the success of the students in their studies.

In the second school year we moved to another building in "*Grabelia*" whose rooms were spacious and suitable for a school. New furniture and modern school equipment such as maps, paintings, etc. were brought in, and only then did the regular work begin.

The success in the second year was greater than expected, the children spoke fluent Hebrew, and many of them excelled in their studies. Balls and celebrations were held for the benefit of various founds. The emissary of *Keren Keyemet Leisrael* [Jewish National Fund] from Eretz Yisrael, who visited the school in the second year of its existence, expressed his enthusiasm for the fact that of the dozens of towns in the vicinity there was only one Hebrew school in Tyszowce. Over time, religious studies teachers were added at the request of some of the parents. I didn't

[Page 119]

object because the number of students was already large and diverse, and I found this arrangement necessary for the benefit of the school.

The school was quite well established from a budgetary point of view, since the distribution of the annual payments was progressive; the rich gave a lot, and those who didn't have the means gave a little. In addition to that, the parents' committee found a sympathetic ear at the office of the community committee headed by Mr. Schtrozer, a very kind Jew who extended his help to us. But, above all, I must mention three names of parents without whose help the school couldn't exist. They invested a lot of their energy and wealth and deserve to be remembered, and they are: Feivel Kupershtock the founder. He invited me and encouraged me in the first days, and thanks to him I didn't leave Tyszowce after my first failures. After him the Nuster brothers and, the last one, Mr. Gelber Leibush, all of whom will be remembered fondly, and May HaShem avenge their blood.

I found great satisfaction in my work at the school, but also outside the school's walls I found a wide field for cultural and educational work. Evening classes for the youth were opened. I lectured in the branches of Halutz Hatzair [Young Pioneers] and Freiheit, and also lectured at the library of the professional union, *HaAdom* [the Red].

The school in Tyszowce was my last place of work before I emigrated, and the truth must be told for this reason, as well as for other reasons, that this town remains not only in my memory, but also in my heart. I found in it a lively and active youth who devoted their time and energy to all the movements that existed in Poland at the time.

Many of these youth fulfilled the order of fulfillment and immigrated, and they were the pride of the city. And although many of them immigrated to other countries, they must be credited for saving the lives of their relatives from the hands of the oppressor.

A few figures from among the city's Jews remain etched in my memory, as if they are sculpted in stone. From them I especially remember R' Shlomo Landau z"l, a superlative scholar whose conversations with me gave me pleasure.

Here is R' Avraham the Slaughterer, a strong Jew who speaks little and studies the Torah a lot, one of Tyszowce's Jews who raised his sons for Torah and work, the preacher, Pinchas Ginzburg, who spices his talks with riddles and wit, and here's the old Kallenberg who loves to joke. I talked with all of them many times, and their conversation was very pleasant for me. I will carry their memory in my heart.

———

[Page 120]

Pages of a Diary

by Shifra Krishtalke, Montreal, Canada

Translated by Moses Milstein

ביה מסר תרבות בטישובצה כתה
לג בעמר תרצו.

Tarbut school in Tyszowce, Lag B'Omer class 1935-1936

It's been several months now since I arrived in Tishevits. After 5 years attending the Jewish pedagogic teachers seminary in Vilna under the direction of *Tsisho*[1], I have come home empty-handed, my life's journey derailed, miserable, a classless person.

Two days before the final exams, the education commission of the current Polish government, closed the Jewish seminary under the pretext that it was a Communist nest. And we, the 32 seminarians in our fifth year, were prevented from taking the final exams, and thus, the legal right to practice teaching in the Jewish day schools in Poland was taken from us. This is not an accidental act on the part of the government. It is a well-planned act to suppress, terrorize, and destroy the spiritual-cultural life of Jews in Poland in general, and the Jewish school system in particular.

[Page 121]

The justifications for shutting down the schools are not always the same. In one city or shtetl the school building is declared to be too old and unsafe by the education commission, and a danger for children to study there. In a second place, the health commission declares the school's hygiene to be in a too deplorable state for the children. Or, again and again, a Communist nest.

Jews are also methodically pushed out of economic positions, and ruined through the high taxes imposed on them. Our existence itself is in danger.

So I sit here now in Tishevits and am astonished at what Tishevitsers occupy themselves with. I can, under no circumstances, believe that what my senses tell me is actually real, is actually taking place. Is it possible that Tishevits has become like a congealed motionless body of water in the middle of a raging sea, and still occupies itself with trivialities?! When the earth is on fire beneath our feet.?! Is it possible that Tishevits is still stuck in the swamp of Mendele's "*Tuneyadevke*"?!

After the whole renaissance the shtetl underwent in the last years is it back in its sweet torpor?! No, it's impossible!

But I am now a living witness to a senseless quarrel, of a blind fanaticism, an unbounded hatred, simply savage, carried on by the majority of religious Jews in Tishevits. The Jews from the Chasidic shtibls, the besmedresh Jews, the shul Jews, the community leaders, leaders of the philanthropic organizations, and just regular Jews of the shtetl. Fathers and mothers who should be concerned about their security and the security of their children in the truly fearful days for our people.

A quarrel between the ritual slaughterers rages in the shtetl. The sides struggle stubbornly. The Chasidic shtiblach, each with its slaughterers, stand in "military positions." As if surrounded by fire. Each side bans the slaughter of the other side. The products of the slaughter of the opposing side are compared to carrion, as treyf as pork. The shtetl's daggers are drawn. Entire families are torn, at odds, blood enemies. Hatred devours them. Our own uncle Shmuel Reiz is on the opposing side and won't eat his father's slaughterings. And the tragi-comedy of it is that the poverty in his house is so great that the little scraps my mother gives to aunt Chaye from the slaughter that father brings home maintains the household of six children,

[Page 122]

literally keeping them alive. And now, Chaye is not allowed to take the scraps, because her husband is on the opposing side of the quarrel.

The greatest shame the shochets have to put up with is the women who come to the fowl house to slaughter their fowl. Each one of them lets the shochet from the other side know that his work is treyf. My uncle R' Nachum Helrubin, father's closest friend, presently in need, doesn't tire of scaring the women with *kores*[2] for humiliating the *talmid chocham*, R' Abraham Shochet. And some, following his advice, come in fright to our house in their socks begging father for forgiveness. In the meantime, the shochets aren't earning any money. There seems to be no end in sight for the quarrel.

The big strong Kielc and Trisk shtibls want to make it so that their two shochets should be paid more by the *kehile*[3] than the other shochets. My father, R' Abraham Shochet, and another shochet are on the weaker Chasidic side. That's why the common people stand behind my father. They come to my father with one argument, "R' Abraham, say the word and we will take care of these 'fine Jews.'" But my father doesn't want any revenge. He calms them down and sends them home to their wives and children.

It is hard for me to write about the sorrow and pain of my parents. Usually, cities and shtetls brag about their important people, about their intellectuals, hold them in respect.

But Tishevits is not able to. The Tishevits *balebatim*[4], particularly the unlearned, don't appreciate whom they have here. They are no experts. My farther, R' Abraham Stern, is a big *talmid chacham*, and with no exaggeration on my part, one of the *tzadikim* and *goanim* of our generation. So how does Tishevits support him?

As my uncle R' Nachum says, "*Rachman litzlan, Hashem yishmerenu.*[5]" Golden words. The Tishevits balebatim repay him and his household for as long as I can remember with animosity, envy, dishonor and shame.

* * *

I feel very constrained in the shtetl, like I'm suffocating. How long this darkness will endure is hard to say. I can't in any way come to terms with the fact that Tishevits is deaf and blind to everything happening in the country. That the shtetl Jews don't grasp their reality, or the reality of all Jews in present-day Poland.

It's not long, after all, since I came from Vilna, where I was witness to the daily hooligan excesses against Jews, and their possessions, led by the Endecja[6] fascist youth.

[Page 123]

Jewish students are forced to sit on separate benches for Jews only. The Jewish students in the medical faculty do not allow the ND students into the laboratories. Fights break out between the demonstrating students of the left and right.

The police show up every time the ND students find themselves in a dangerous situation and throw themselves with rage on the antifascist demonstrators, and on the spontaneously organized Jewish self-defense groups. The antisemitic hooliganism is directed from above, by the fascist Polish government.

It makes the blood run cold to hear about the goings-on in the "*prszitek*." The newspapers are full of news about the organized hooligan attacks across the country.

Jewish life is in chaos!

Tishevits, my shtetl, doesn't know what's going on in neighboring Germany where Hitler's gangs rampage openly and freely and sow destruction in everything that is human, cultural, liberal, democratic, to everything that is contrary to their bestiality, and most cogently, to our brothers and sisters! Hitler's agenda for conquest includes the total annihilation of our people. Our own government, with its own tradition of antisemitism and familiarity with Jew-hatred, receives their antisemitic hooliganisms with open arms. And here in the shtetl itself, I see patrols at the Jewish, almost empty stores, that prevent Christian customers from entering. "Each to his own." The stinging whip held over the wretched Jewish attempts to make a living. The heavy taxes are a very heavy burden for everyone here. There are no means to pay them. Little by little, furniture is taken away, bedding. What ever is possible, and whatever is still left. This week, they took my aunt Chaye's candlesticks for taxes.

The shtetl is poor. The shtetl is hungry. Some sneak out and go house to house begging for alms. But the shtetl Jews seems not to be occupied with these worries. They are preoccupied with "more worthy matters" — with quarrels — how is it possible?!

Is it only small-townness, or shortsightedness, or plain madness, or a distraction to evade the realities of the day? The country is in chaos: crises, unemployment, strikes, demonstrations, arrests. The ground is burning under everyone's feet, especially under the feet of us Jews. Does none of this have no relevance to Tishevits?!

What is the political orientation of the Jews in Tishevits? Is Tishevits really a shtetl unlike every other one on the map? Is everything here upside-down?

[Page 124]

It has been decades since Tishevits opened wide to the big city and the wider world. The shtetl is in constant direct contact with everything that occurs in the country and around the world. The merchants in the shtetl trade with other shtetls in the country. The working youth travel to find work. Young people travel to study in the big cities of the country and abroad. The youth in general strive to get out in the world. Newspapers published across the country come to the shtetl. Is the shtetl really reflective of the other cities and shtetls in the land?

But the youth are in tune with the times. There are active parties of all kinds — a trade union, the Bund, Zionist parties of all stripes. And all the parties engage in cultural work with their members. The young are taught to read and write Yiddish, become politically conscious, learn to read a literary work. They hold public lectures organized by their own efforts, and they bring in chaverim from the centers. There is a big library managed by the Bund, and the left Polei Zion, and smaller libraries run by the other parties. The Zionist parties study Hebrew with their members. Practically every party has an amateur drama club, and some have choirs as well.

The trade union, led by the left, defends the proletarian interests of the workers, against the bosses, neither of whom have the wherewithal to get though the day. But mainly, the trade union youth prepare for the proletarian revolution. And according to chaver Steinshreiber, the head theoretician here, the revolution is imminent. And according to his strategy, "The revolution will begin first here in Tishevits, and spread to Warsaw."

"What's the point?" He tells me that "this is because the leftist 'Selrobnikes' in our neighborhood are organizing the villages and are almost done, and we have to be ready." And the believing youth are getting ready. Motye Katz sleeps in his clothes "in order to be always ready, and not miss the proletarian revolution."

It's really impractical, small townish, but how many naively believe. Meanwhile, they are being sent off to prison or exiled to "Kartuz-Bereza."

The biggest influence on the young people of the shtetl are the Zionist parties, the Revisionists, and right and left Poalei Zion. The youngsters in the Zionist parties are preparing to make aliyah to Eretz Israel. They are ready to go this minute should the gates to Eretz Israel open. Meanwhile, everyone waits for his "lottery," his certificate,

[Page 125]

because the gates to our holy land are well guarded and prevent us from getting in to our own home! How tragically comic?! The Poles cry as if possessed, "Jews to Palestine!" And England forges an iron chain around the borders of tiny Eretz Israel that lies desolate since the destruction of the Second Temple.

The Jewish youth, unwanted by Poland, unneeded by England, locked out of the Americas, are desperate to go home to build the land of their forefathers — to remake themselves. They want to stop being superfluous to the world, save themselves from the abyss, become healthy, productive, normal. They must wait for the mercy of the Balfour Declaration. The younger grownup generation is aware of today's terrifying reality and is ready, everyone in his place and in his ranks.

A group of "Yungboristen" with the instructors before the departure of chaver Israel Stern to Vilna

[Page 126]

My shteteleh, Tishevits, has received the pleasant scent of the big city and processed it in its own characteristic way that has been felt here for years.

But for the quarreling Jews, to the clergy, it has no relevance. They, it seems, remained with their own specific scent.

March 5, 1932, Saturday night

I've just come from a meeting, a meeting that will write a very important chapter in the history of our shtetl.

A committee from the left Poalei Zion in Tishevits, under the leadership of Noteh Rosenzweig, negotiated with me the possibility of opening a Jewish school, a Jewish supplementary school. This will be a new type of school. All the other Tsisho schools in the country are full-time schools, where Jewish students receive Jewish instruction as well as general studies in their own schools with Yiddish as the language of instruction. The school we want to create would be a supplementary school to teach Yiddish and Jewish themes with Jewish children who get their general knowledge in the Polish schools, in "*szkola.*" A supplementary school can in time become a full-time Jewish school. And there has long been a need for such a school in Tishevits. Just as the Tarbut[7] schools have been successful.

Children for a Jewish school there are. Parents who would send their children to a Jewish school also exist here. The side streets of the tradesmen, workers, and poor storekeepers can be the foundation of the Jewish school. The main reason why we haven't had one yet is strictly one of means. We never had the funds to rent a suitable building, or to hire a teacher. The main difficulty is the building, because here we had to rely on the generosity of the government inspection commission trustees who discriminate openly against our school system. It seeks and finds ways to destroy our existing schools, much less to allow new schools to be built.

Today the obstacles disappear. A teacher is present — me. And a school building we also don't need. We can use our party locale. The supplementary school we legitimize as evening courses for children under the "social evening classes" of the left Poalei Zion. We function as an organisation under the same name. We carry on with "evening classes for adult" working boys and girls. We carry out educational work with our party members, "*Die Yugent*," and "*Yung-Bor*." We teach them to read and write Yiddish. We teach

[Page 127]

them our party platform. We read the newspapers and political journals with them. We teach them to enjoy artistic narratives and verse from our Jewish literature, and literature in general. We instill them with belief and courage as Jews and as people. Through example, we teach them how to be good, loyal chaverim. To help one another when in need.

The main leaders and teachers of Yugent, and Yung-Bor of the left Polaei Zion since its founding in Tishevits, are Noteh Rosenzweig, and my brother, Israel Stern. Until now, I was capable of working with and helping out only at Pesach and in summer when I come home from the seminary on school holidays. My brother, Yechiel Stern, also takes an active part when he comes to the shtetl. Now that I'm back home, we both carry on with the work, Noteh and I. Israel is in Vilna, studying in the Jewish polytechnic.

Yung-Bor was created by Israel Stern. His work with the youngsters was wonderful. His hard efforts and work produced and produce fruitful results. Israel created a choir of young people and small kids. The choir director is a young man who definitely has the talent to become a good conductor. The same with the drama club. The troupe is serious and devoted. Some of them are born talents. It's a pity that we don't have the means to send them to drama school.

A well-organized youth committee functions and comprehends the seriousness and responsibility of contributing to the holy work of their comrades and teachers. We are getting ready now for a performance. The cooperation of the youth and children is amazing. And if we take into account that these are young girls and boys, wage-earners who work all day, their evenings and Saturday their only free time that they give away to the organization, we can well appreciate the good work of their chaverim-teachers, as well as the readiness of our youth and children to learn.

March 13th, 1935

It's very late at night, and I am very tired. But I must quickly make a note while the impression is still fresh.

Our performance went well. And that is the best reward. The choir was a big hit. I studied the songs with them, but the director on the stage was our Abraham Shafrach. A pity, a pity, with proper training he could grow up to be a good conductor. The performance succeeded well. Real life was portrayed on the stage. Some displayed

[Page 128]

real talent. In general, all the participants really got into the drama from Y. L. Peretz, "*Amol is Geven a Melech.*[8]"

It was really crowded, both in the hall and on the stage. A stage of a couple of boards, and the play demanded space. The presentation and arrangements cost a lot sweat. But the rewards are there. The audience was enchanted. Our performances are always warmly received by the Tishevits audience. We always played to a full house. And today's performance as well ended in quite an exalted mood. The actors are beside themselves with joy, and are ready for me to start rehearsing with them a new play, and they are readying themselves for a new performance. But I need to take a break for a while.

Tomorrow I begin to teach in the supplementary school. With the evening classes for adults that I lead and teach in the evenings, I will have little time left for rehearsals. But *Chol-Hamoed Pesach* we will be ready to step out with a new production.

March 14th, 1932

I've just come in from my work at school. Today is a historic day for us. The inauguration of our Jewish supplementary school. And from a supplementary school to a fuller "Jewish school" like all the other Tsisho schools in the country.

The mood of the children is good and celebratory, radiant, with shining eyes like quicksilver from anticipation and excitement. Studying with them is so satisfying, simple and natural. Everything I did with them, they received with joy. They took part in the learning with fascination, faith, and curiosity not to miss or lose anything.

We have three groups of children. Classification is based on age. Shortly, we will have more groupings. I am already in correspondence with a girlfriend, a teacher from the Vilna teacher's seminary from the same course as me, to come and work with me at the school.

The classes start at three in the afternoon. Each group learns for one hour at the moment. We will certainly extend the class time when my friend arrives. In the meantime, it's impossible, because aside from the three groups at the school, I teach the adult evening classes from eight to ten at night, and I believe that for the kids as well it's better to begin like this. Let them slowly get used to the extra time they have to spend in the supplementary school after spending five, six hours in the Polish elementary school.

I get so much joy and satisfaction from teaching the children. So much contentment. I can work and work with the children with no rest, and

[Page 129]

not feel tired. I hope it lasts. Fear trembles in me, and my heart is heavy. Before I could even set foot in the school, I received a delegation of balebatim who came to warn my father, R' Abraham Shochet he should not allow me to become a teacher for the "Reds." That's what they call the school for the poor small children. "It's not appropriate," they say, "that the shochet's daughter should teach there." Secondly, they claim that I myself teach them to become Reds. I could not and should not put up with this. I really unmasked them, showed their true intentions. I pretended not to notice, and I began the school work today, and I will continue with all my strength.

I have all the odds of winning this war that the "fine Jews" and their hangers-on foisted on me since it became known in the shtetl that we were opening a Jewish school. The parents of the school kids are with us, and are ready to undertake the challenge. But I can't forget that I am a shochet's daughter and I am in the hands of the Tishevits big shots. What they can't do to me they will wreak on my father R' Abraham Shochet and take it out on him. Therefore, my hands are really tied. How good it would be if my friend were already here. Their main weapon would be useless. Not a shochet's daughter, and especially not Abraham Shochet's daughter. With no other shochets or shochet's children do the Jewish functionaries have as much concern as with my father, R' Abraham Shochet and his household.

* * *

Work at school is proceeding normally. New children are always coming. I know them well. The groups are well established.

The children learn with enthusiasm. They really like the school, and don't even want to go home after the classes are over. The parents are also happy. It turns out that some of them come to the school and stand outside in the hallway when I'm teaching the kids and listen in. Afterwards they go and defend me against those who plot against me saying

I am teaching godlessness to the kids. Ruchel, the poultry seller, is ready to swear that she heard me tell the children a story about Eliyahu Hanavi and always exclaiming, "*Raboinusheloilem.*"

An orgy of hatred is really directed at the school and at me. I go on with my work and don't pay it any attention. It's just a little hard for me not to have the materials I need for work. I have to set everything up and make it myself. Even books for the children. So I sit for hours in the library, and choose appropriate songs and stories from our poets and prose writers.

[Page 130]

I have to go to school soon. The kids are waiting for me already. After the antisemitic day school they really run to the Jewish school. They come here to lift up their depressed spirits. To improve their dejected mood. To feel like equals. They play here. They sing and dance here, not afraid to be children, and to act like children. Here they forget for a moment the poverty of their homes, and the Jew designation that the outside world foists on them at such a young age.

But dark forces in our own streets do not permit them a little joy. They obstruct, and do everything, and use any means, indiscriminately: provocation, lies and even denunciation, in order to take away from the very poor, reinvigorated Jewish children their only warm, bright corner, the Jewish school.

Their parents, tradesmen, workers, and poor storekeepers are saddened and embittered. They are ready for anything as long as they can protect the school and me. I have trouble keeping them calm. If I would permit it, they would have long ago already beaten up those who really deserved it. Because the "fine Jews" from the Radziner shtibl, who carry on vendettas against our school are not fussy about means. Betrayal is even kosher. And they help out the reactionaries in the shtetl, the big-shots, who are always on the lookout for opportunities to let loose.

Yesterday I had a guest in the middle of teaching. The policeman, Kotlicki. Kotlicki actually spoke Yiddish to me, as is his habit. He excused himself to me. He esteems me highly, because I am "the rabbi's daughter." He's referring to my father. He didn't have a problem telling me who sent him here. They say we are the real subversives. He can't help himself. He has to do what he has to do. I showed him what I do with the children. Showed him our permission for the school. With difficulty, I persuaded him we are all for Palestine. This saved me for the moment from being arrested and the school closed. He warned me that he was letting me go for now because of my father, "the rabbi." "He is a great man, but if your "*Yiddelach*" persist, I won't be able to help."

A delegation of parents went to the rabbi and demanded that he quiet down the plotting and the betrayals. Otherwise, blood will run. The rabbi promised to do so. But what can he do? I know the truth after all. Meanwhile, I am not surrendering. In school with the children, I forget about all the dangers that lie in wait for our new saplings that bloom and grow every day, and that have all the possibilities to grow further and develop into a full,

[Page 131]

thriving tree like all the other Jewish schools in the country. Aside from the children and their parents, my parents and my sister, Heneh, also give me strength to hold fast and continue with my work.

* * *

I'm not sure if I can continue to support the school much longer. Not because I am one of the frightened. If it were only up to me, they would have already lost.

My blood still boils over for my brothers who were tormented here by the same prominent city-balebatim. My ears still hear the slaps my brothers received from the Bentche-Hertzkes in the besmedresh while davening, while studying, because a shochet's children are unruly, and of course, of course, R' Abraham Shochet's children.

No, they can't break me. Five years of teacher seminary have steeled me for resistance. Five years I endured hunger in order to become a Jewish teacher. And I will be that. The love and devotion for the Jewish language and Jewish content that my teachers instilled in me, I will continue to try to instill in my young students. "Otherwise," my teacher Dr. Y. Biber used to say, "the wish of those who want to destroy us, the Jew-hatred everywhere and here in our country, will be fulfilled." If I have to give up, it will be because of my father. The opposition leaders have used up all their weapons to no avail. On the contrary, the school grows in popularity. Children from well-to-do families are registering.

So they have taken to going after my father now, R' Abraham Shochet alone. They abuse him, torment him. So much so that he doesn't daven in the besmedresh weekdays as was his wont. My uncle, R' Nachum Helrubin, always comes to scrutinize me, "Nu, nu, Shifra, how will it end? You are in the right, but have pity on your father."

My father is unrecognizable. He goes around stooped, saddened, but he says nothing. It seems that his silence is his way of waging a quiet struggle with those in the wrong. My father, R' Abraham Shochet is a great scholar, immensely devout, with an acute sense of worldly subjects. He understands very well the politics, and background of all the issues, and he certainly knows the truth that lies under the whole hullabaloo, why they won't let me teach in the school. Just like me, he understands that it has absolutely nothing to do with Reds, or Godlessness. The unadulterated truth is that the "Agudahniks" want to open a Bet Yakov school, and they see our school as a big competition. So they're looking for an excuse to get rid of us. And since all methods

[Page 132]

are kosher for them, they use this. And with all their libels and lies, they have recruited people like they themselves, and some simply from envy, begrudging me my teaching.

The Agudahniks know that without me the school could not exist. First financially, being from the shtetl I can teach for minimal pay. And then, my good reputation in Tishevits. It's not only the poor and the common people who bring their children, but also the well- off who would not bring their children if I were not the teacher. The Agudahniks know both of these things, the material needs of the school and its founders, and the reputation of the teacher. Therefore, they want to get rid of me. In me, they have a good target. I am in their hands. They could not have drawn a better card.

In reality, I should give up soon. I can't, under any circumstances, risk the health of my father. However, I'm young. And young blood boils and revolts, and does not want, under any circumstances, to give up.

So I go on with the work, look into my father's eyes, and am afraid for the verdict coming. Only my father can stop me from my school work. I may not expose him to this temptation, but I can't help myself. On my own, I won't quit the school work. I alone can't, under any circumstances, close the school.

March 20, 1932

It's twelve noon. I've just come from the library. I worked there from eight in the morning. I've chosen and put together enough material for a whole month, that means until Pesach. I created a detailed teaching plan for all the groups in school, and for the adult evening classes. Coming into the house, I immediately saw that I wouldn't be using my new material and work plans in our school.

From the agitated discussion between my mother and my sister on one side, and my father on the other side, everything was clear to me. The Agudahniks, and the whole gang, are threatening to take away his shochet trade. They made it more pointed: Me or my father. My mother, Gitl the *shoicheteh*, and my sister, Heneh, insist that he should not agree. "They didn't make him a shochet, and they can't make him an ex-shochet." "Once and for all, he should stick up for his honor, and the honor of his family." And similar valid arguments. Both are very rebellious

[Page 133]

and ready to fight. How grateful I am to them. Father knows all this. Maybe he also wants this. He has become old and grey from all the Tishevits work. All his sons have been driven far away. But he can't help himself. He's not a fighter. He doesn't have the physical or spiritual strength. Peace is his nature. He is so sick and tired of all this.

Today it seems I must give up my school work. There's no helping it. I have to bear witness to the destruction of a holy building, the Jewish school. A pity the children, a pity their parents.

It's late at night. Today I bade farewell to my little kids. I told the truth to the third class. The children burst into tears. I was angry, the pain fresh, and I also cried. We all cried. Finally, I mustered my courage, quieted down the children. I read Sholom Aleichem's "*Tzvei Shalach Mones*," and distracted them from their sorrow. They really identified with the story, laughing and crying from pleasure. As we were parting, I had to promise them that I would come back tomorrow. "You won't abandon us, *chaverte* Shifra, right?" they pleaded with me for assurance.

The first class, I taught as usual. I danced with them, sang with them, told them a story in honor of Purim. I couldn't tell them it was the last lecture. And this was the way with the second class too. How many broken little hearts can I see? The evening groups were more grown up. They already knew the news. As soon as I walked in, they began to cry. "What do you mean, they're taking our school, our home, away from us?"

I sat with them, tried to sing with them, tried to read them something, tell stories, play, but it didn't work. The children did not stop crying. "We have nothing again." How can I help them? A deep sadness weeps in me as well.

Footnotes:

1. Acronym for Tsentrale Yiddishe Shul-Organizatsye (Central Yiddish School Organization). Secular Jewish schools under socialist auspices.
2. Divine retribution
3. Jewish community. Shochets were engaged by the community officers and paid from community funds.
4. Bosses, businessmen, proprietors, or regular folks
5. May the All-Merciful protect us, may God protect us
6. The Narodowa Democracja party (ND) was a fascist pre-war political party promoting boycotting of Jewish businesses.
7. Secular schools teaching in Hebrew
8. "Once there was a king."

[Page 134]

Saved From a Pogrom by a Miracle

by Pinchas Landau (Israel)

Translated by Moses Milstein

This happened before WWI. A Jewish girl (around 20 years of age) ran away from the village of Niewirkow a few kilometers from Tishevits. It was said that either the local priest convinced her to convert, or she had fallen in love with a Christian from the village and because of him she converted. The latter was correct.

One can imagine what kind of impression that made on the Tishevits Jews of that time! The family of the girl was frantic to get her back. The Niewirkower father was well off. He used to, as it is said, "spread money in the streets." He paid a lot of money to all the priests in the area who promised him they would find his daughter. He also travelled to pious Jews, gave significant amounts of money, but his daughter could not be found. It was as if she had vanished into the earth. It was rumored that she was in the convent in Terkowicz, a village near Niewirkow, but no one could get in there. The parents of the girl hung around the convent for weeks on end, hoping for a miracle, hoping to see their daughter. But they had no sign at all that their daughter was in the convent.

After several months of searching with no success, the parents tore their clothing in mourning, and sat shiva for their daughter exactly as if she were dead, and if she had converted, she was no longer alive to them anyway.

Late in the summer, after harvest time, on a Saturday, a wagon drove into town in which a nun was seated and next to her a young girl of about the same age as the lost Jewish girl. They drove over to the administrative office (in Polish, Gmina).

As they were getting down from the wagon to go into the offices, a passerby recognized the girl as the one missing from the village. Tishevits Jews began to congregate at the offices, men, women, a few hundred people. They wanted to forcibly detain the girl. The writer (secretary) and the *voit*[1] seeing

[Page 135]

the agitation of the Tishevits Jews, locked the doors of the offices. The mob was ready to break down the doors. But one of the mob, a more reasonable person, suggested, "Since we are not 100 percent certain she is the Niewirkow girl, we should run and get her father. If he were to identify her as his daughter, then we will see what has to be done." But how can we get the father if he lives outside our area? From Tishevits to Niewirkow was a distance of 7-8 km. There were no telephones in Tishevits yet. There were no "*samachods*" either (cars in Russian). The only method of communication was by horse and rider. But what to do? It was Shabbes. They went off to the rabbi, rav Shemeshele, who gave permission for a rider to go and bring back the father from Niewirkow.

At the same time as the rider went off to bring the father of the daughter, another rider, that the Tishevits Jews knew nothing about, was riding off on another road. The writer and the *voit*, saw that the mob was ready to break down the doors and take the girl, and knew that they could do nothing in the face of the mob even if they brought in the police to help. There were at the time 3 policemen in Tishevits (*strazhnikes* they were called). They sent an assistant secretary out the back door, and he went off to Prespa, a village near Tishevits, but in another direction, the same distance from Tishevits as Niewirkow. At that time there was a company of Cossacks there on summer maneuvers. The assistant was carrying a letter to the Cossack company commander, asking them to come help them against the Jewish attack.

You can imagine what would happen if the Cossacks came to Tishevits and encountered several hundred Jews attacking the offices. But a miracle occurred. The rider to Niewirkow rode a lot faster that the rider to Prespa, and he brought the girl's father. He maintained that it was not his daughter. (It was said that the father, upon seeing with what chutzpa his daughter, a cross hanging from her neck, looked at him through the window, did not want to recognize her).

Meanwhile, it was time for Mincha, and the crowd dispersed. Later when the Cossacks arrived, there was hardly anyone left at the offices. Thus, we were saved from a certain pogrom.

The more pious Jews of Tishevits later said that the Jewish rider who rode off in the cause of a mitzvah was endowed with "*kfitses-haderech*,"[2]

[Page 136]

and by virtue of the Jews going off collectively to daven Mincha, we avoided a great calamity.

Tel Aviv, August, 1965

Footnotes:

1. Village mayor, justice of the peace
2. Supernatural ability to transport oneself instantly to a distant place.

The Burned Post

by Pinchas Landau (Israel)

Translated by Moses Milstein

It happened in 1907. That year winter lasted long. There were severe blizzards on Pesach. Soon after Pesach, spring arrived with huge rains. Days and weeks went by without a ray of sun penetrating the heavy, black clouds. My grandfather, R' Yakov Ginsberg (the author of the book, *Zichron Yakov*, a commentary on fruits in the *Yoreh De'Ah*, salting laws, meat, and milk, and mixtures), died then.

Grandfather died on a Thursday afternoon. His two sons, R' Pinchas Ginsberg, and Moishe Ginsberg, were not in Tishevits. R' Pinchas, the *magid*[1], was on the road, and the other one lived in Lodz. When they were informed of the death of their father, they telegrammed that they would come to his burial. Because of that, the burial was postponed to Friday morning.

Friday morning the preparations for the burial began. The deceased was purified according to law, but due to the rains, the two sons were delayed a little, and when they finally arrived, the burial was further delayed because the rains had flooded the streets.

I remember that awful day! The washing of the corpse took place in our house by lamplight. It was so dark in the house, the street, and in our hearts. A crowd gathered in our house. We waited for the rain to let up a little so we could get on with the funeral. In the meantime we studied *mishnayes*. Among the crowd, was also R' Shmuel Sofer, a"h. Affected by the depression caused by the death, and the rain, he found a *nutrikn*[2] from the year 5667[3], in Polish, "This year is only full of bad."

The rain stopped at about 2:00 o'clock in the afternoon. We began to hurry to the burial. It was, however, Friday, and from us to the cemetery was a great distance. By 4:00 o'clock the grave had been filled in,

[Page 137]

and at that moment, the sun broke through the clouds. Everyone standing near the grave was stunned to see that in a corner of the fresh mound of earth the shadow of a cross appeared!

It happened like this: not far from the cemetery there was a Christian house, and near the house, a wooden cross maybe 8 meters high. In the evening, at sunset, when the shadows lengthened, the shadow of the crucifix reached grandfather's grave. It lasted only a few minutes because the sun was setting further and faster. Nevertheless, you can imagine the impression the shadow made on everyone, and especially the Bnei Yakov.

The whole crowd went home very upset. Saturday night, the cross was burned down. As mentioned, the cross was 8 meters high, and right next to it was a farmhouse 3 meters high. The cross burned only from the top of the house and higher. The Tishevits Jews saw this as a sign from heaven. Those who are expert in crucifix law said that according to "their" laws, you can't erect a wooden cross in the place where there had been one already. You could build a new one from bricks, or pour one from concrete, but such a cross could only be 4 meters high maximum. The shadow of such a crucifix would not reach the grave. Turns out the "experts" were right. When I left Tishevits to make aliyah to Israel, in the year 5693[4], that is 26 years after this incident, the burned-out pillar was still standing unrepaired. Later, during the war, the Nazis, may their name be erased, destroyed the cemetery. They used the tombstones to pave sidewalks, and ploughed up the ground, so that the old Tishevits cemetery, with the grave of Moshiach Ben Yosef, no longer exists, like the cross, so that from everything, no trace remains.

When I was older, I asked my parents, and in general everyone who had a connection to our family, how did the cross catch on fire? Who in our family had done this? How much did it cost to do this bit of work? But I came to the conclusion that nobody in our family had done this or had helped do this, and it has remained a mystery until today.

It's worth adding that from the work mentioned earlier, *Zichron Yakov*, only the first part, *Halachot Mlichah*, was published. The other two parts, *Basar V'chalav*, and *Ta'arovet* which were much bigger than the first part, grandfather, a"h, was unable to get printed while he was alive. The section, *Basar v'chalav*, I reworked (from my grandfather's manuscript) when I

[Page 138]

made Aliyah to Israel, which I left with my brother, Itzchak, a"h. The portion, *Ta'arovet*, was with my uncle in Lodz, R' Moishe Ginsberg, z"l, who also prepared it for printing. During the war it was destroyed along with my family. Of the 10 thousand copies of *Halachot Mlicha* printed, all of which were sold, only one copy remained with our family which my father-in-law and uncle, R' Pinchas Ginsberg, brought with him to Israel. The copy is now in the library of Hebrew University in Jerusalem.

Grandfather, a"h, had his diploma for the rabbinate. He did not use it to become a rabbi, but he always took part with the rav in delivering a judgment, as well as in questions of kashrut and treyf.

I have a judgment from my grandfather, a"h, in his handwriting (understandably in *loshen koidesh*)[5] that he delivered as sole arbiter in 1884 in a *din-Torah* between R' Dovid Kuperstock, a"h, (Henich Kuperstock's father) the "prosecutor," and R' Eliyahu Milich, a"h, (the father of the famous painter, Adolph Milich) as defendant.

In Tishevits grandfather was "*a mefitz Torah b'rabim*[6]." In the Trisker shtibl, he used to give lessons in Talmud and Jewish law to anyone who wanted to come. I still remember a lot of the scholars in Tishevits who used to come to our place to hear a lesson in Talmud from my grandfather.

There is no picture of my grandfather, because he never allowed himself to be photographed.

Footnotes:

1. Itinerant preacher.
2. Mystical technique whereby the letters of a Hebrew word are interpreted as initials of other words.
3. 1906-1907
4. 1932/1933
5. Hebrew
6. Spreader of Torah

Section translated by Sara Mages

This letter is a court ruling of my grandfather, R' Yakov Ginzburg. My grandfather wrote down his every judgment and here is its content: -

"Then, came before me the men, and they are, the community leader, our teacher and rabbi, R' David Kupersztok, and the community leader, our teacher and rabbi, R' Eliyahu Milich, from here (Tyszowce), and the aforementioned R' David sued the aforementioned R' Eliyahu with the authorization (power of attorney) of his grandfather, R' Shmuel Zwillich, how when the aforementioned R' Shmuel sat and lived at the home of the aforementioned R' Eliyahu, the customs officers found and took the "Peasch vodka" (kosher vodka for Passover) (in Tsarist Russia, all vodka production was under the sole control of the government, a special license was needed to sell vodka and, whoever sold vodka without a license, was liable to punishment and imprisonment) that R' Eliyahu hid at the aforementioned R' Shmuel's, and so that R' Shmuel would not say and place the blame on R' Eliyahu, R' Eliyahu immediately gave him ten rubles and also promised him that if a financial fine would be imposed on him according to the state law, the aforementioned R' Eliyahu will pay everything out of his own pocket and, God forbid, no harm or loss from this would come to R' Shmuel, and now the aforementioned R' David showed a receipt how his grandfather, R' Shmuel, was forced to pay eighteen rubles and forty eight kopecks according to the judgment of the Magistrate's Court, and now he is suing the aforementioned R' Eliyahu to pay him the balance, that is, the sum of eight rubles and forty eight kopecks (a kopeck was a 100th

[Page 139]

part of a ruble) and R' Eliyahu replied against him with some claims of his own, and that of his son R' Moshe Milich, what is due to him from R' Shmuel and, apart from that, he claimed that R' Shmuel once promised him two lumber wagons worth three rubles as a commission and brokerage fee, so that he would try to lend a total of two hundred rubles to the master (Polish landowner), and R' Eliyahu has done so, and tried with

[Page 140]

great efforts until he obtained the aforementioned sum of money, and after a while, when the master returned the aforementioned amount, he did not give R' Eliyahu anything for his trouble, and now R' Eliyahu is demanding from R' Shmuel the sum of three rubles for all those who came and asked him to tell them his opinion, a decisive opinion according to Jewish law, and they also agreed to approve and comply with everything that came out of his mouth without any change at all, to both the law and the compromise. After hearing all their claims, without exception and also fraud, everything in the balance of justice, I have decided that a sum of three rubles would be deducted for R' Eliyahu from the aforementioned amount that Shmuel is demanding from him, and if so, R' Eliyahu owes R' Shmuel, or R' David who came with his authorization, the amount of five rubles and forty eight kopecks. Regarding the claim that R' Eliyahu is demanding a fee of three rubles from him for professional services and R' Shmuel denies it, when R' Eliyahu will give a handshake that I will honor, he will deduct the three rubles, and then two rubles and forty eight kopecks will come from him, and if he doesn't want to give a handshake about it, then the aforementioned debt of a total of five rubles and forty eight kopecks is as before, and R' Eliyahu is obliged to pay it without any claim at all - and to prove all the above, I signed today (Monday, 7) Nisan 5645 (1885) here in Tyszowce, the words of Yakov Ginzburg."

To the former residents of Tyszowce I will describe who are the litigants mentioned in the above letter. David Kupersztok was the father of Hanoch Kupersztok who was called Davidtche Tatele's in Tyszowce, and Shmuel Zwillich was the grandfather of the aforementioned David on his mother's side.

Eliyahu Milich, who was called Eli Walfzitz in Tyszowce, was the father of the well known painter Adolphe Milich, and Moshe Milich was the brother of the aforementioned painter.

Tel Aviv, Marcheshvan 5729 (1968)

[Page 141]

Ten Synagogue Jews Write a Sefer Torah

by Yakov Zwillich

Translated by Moses Milstein

The congregants at the shul, where services were held just on Shabbes, were only the common people. Among them was my father, a"h, and his friends who had been davening there for years.

Zachariah Zwillich, z"l

My father, and Moishe-Laizer Hasser, were the *gabaim*. The custom was to have the kiddush at the home of one of the group. Once, when the kiddush was at our house and a kugel was served made by my aunt, Shprintze, who was a specialist at it, my father addressed the group: "Well, everything is really good and fine. But I would propose that all of us here should create something for our children so they will remember us. I suggest we write a sefer Torah."

[Page 142]

It was decided to call Rav Shmuel Sofer as soon as Saturday evening. My father, a"h, gave the first 10 sheets of parchment, i.e, calfhide. *Motsi Shabbes*, everybody came together again at our house, and discussed all the details with the *sofer*[1]. The people who participated were the following: Eitl, Israel Aharon Bicher, Zalman Garber, Shimon Hammer, Moishe-Laizer; Treasurer–Meir, Yoineleh's Zegmen, Berl Zwillich, Zachariah Kopel, Binyomin Kopel, Laizer Shtengel, Itzik. Helping out was Raphael, Shemesh without whom nothing was done. All those who davened in the shul also looked on this holy work, that their comrades were carrying out, with enthusiasm.

When the work of writing the sefer Torah was coming to an end, the group sent two members to Warsaw to buy a nice *keser -Torah*[2], and two silver plates upon which the names of the contributors were engraved. This, of course, cost a lot of money, but everyone lived with the faith that God would repay them everything. When the discussion turned to whose house we would lead the Torah from, it was decided to hold an auction, and whoever gave the most would have the honor. We started with 10 Zlotys. This was bid by Israel Aaron Eitl, until it was raised to 35 Zlotys. Then Itzik Stengl bid 50 Zlotys. Then my father, a"h, said, " I bid 100 Zlotys, and I'll provide the meat for the whole feast." The others had no response and all sat as if frozen. My father lived with profound faith, and it came to pass.

In the morning, my mother, Shprintze, invited all the neighbors, told them about what was happening, and asked for their help, that is, the accommodation for the guests who would come. Everyone received the request with joy. Uncle Yakov, and aunt Iteh fixed up their house holiday style. The same with uncle Melech, and aunt Ruchel, Moishe Yaniwer, and Oizer Bicher. We hosted guests from Hrubieszow, my grandmother, Sureh-Braneh, z"l, and uncle Yoshele Pachter, and others. The sefer procession was a real holiday in the shtetl. I believe that all the survivors will remember the celebration.

A little while later, my father, a"h, and Avremele (Beker) Loifer were again elected as *gabaim*. They made the wonderful door for the shul which I can still see before my eyes. They also made the beautiful menorah by the *omed*. This was all made by the efforts of ordinary people with limited resources.

[Page 143]

Carried out the Bequest

by Sender Gelber (Israel)

Translated by Moses Milstein

This happened in the winter of 1928. It was winter when the decree to close the old cemetery came out. Another place was not yet available, so the Jewish community got together and decided to buy a new field. But what do you do before you can use the new field? And suddenly, R' Aharon Borik died at the age of 80. So the Chevra Kadisha got together with other Tishevits Jews to bury him in the old cemetery. These were Herzke Spiz, Kahat Friedlender, Moishe Chaim Kleiner, Moishe Hershl, and Moishe Gelber.

At night, in the freezing cold, the field covered with snow, they began the work by starlight. They worked energetically, and from time to time took a swig of whiskey, until the grave was completed. What to do next? They hatched a plan–they decided that everyone should remain at the graveside and Moishe Gelber (glazer) should get his horse and wagon and put a box of glass on it and the deceased on it and bring him to the field.

Moishe Gelber accepted the task even though it could mean jail because Aharon Borik was a Belzer chasid as was Moishe Gelber. Before his death, R' Aharon Borik had asked Moishe Gelber to bury him in the old cemetery. His request was carried out. Moishe Gelber took his horse and wagon, put the deceased on it and drove off. On his way out, he came upon the police standing there, but he was not afraid. He told the police he was driving to the village, and he drove to the old cemetery where the Chevra Kadisha were waiting. That is how R' Aharon Borik came to be buried in the old cemetery.

[Page 144]

The Corpse Calls Him to an Accounting

by Berl Singer (Buenos Aires–Argentina)

Translated by Moses Milstein

I must state at the very beginning that this story was told to me by our fellow townsman, my friend, Yehuda Zlototsiste.

This took place in the 1920s when in the shtetls of Poland Jewish communities were organized with elected "*dozors*." Our Tishevits already had elected *dozors* and a Jewish community. Among all the big and little things the community had to institute and to carry out was the cemetery. Until then, the *Chevra "Moloches"–Chevra Kedusha*, ruled over the cemetery, and they distributed the burial places, and if someone from the family asked for a nicer place, it was possible only with a large bottle of whisky for the "Moloches." In those days, the Chevra Kedusha was located at the family of Leizer Isiks along with the Garber family (well-known families in the shtetl and not always in a complimentary way…) And it was these people that the kehilla had to restrain and discipline, something not easy to do. The kehilla chose a *gabai* from the Chevra Kedusha, Shmuel Glatter. In the shtetl, he was called Shmuel Abraham-Itche Yaechnik's because they dealt with eggs. He was a respectable young man, a Chasid from the Kuzmir shtibl, who took his duties very seriously, and had quite the job to discipline the Moloches.

At the time, however, a big tragedy occurred to the Leizer Isiks. Benimileh's much loved son-in-law died suddenly. He was a nice young man, a student, a good *baal tefillah* and a very good *baal koreh* in shul. His name was Sholem, and the shtetl greatly regretted the big loss.

The Leizer Isiks organized things without the knowledge of the kehilla, and without the knowledge of the *gabai*, and went off to the cemetery to dig a grave that they

[Page 145]

alone had decided on. But when the *gabai*, Shmuel Glatter, found out, he, with the authority of the kehilla, stopped the digging of the grave, and gave them another place. And here begins the second part of the tragedy. A short time after this incident, the *gabai*, Shmuel Glatter, fell ill. One night he dreamt that Sholem Benimeleh's son-in-law was calling him to account before God and his ministering angels, because he shamed him when he stopped the digging of his grave. When he awoke, he remembered the dream well, but he paid no attention to it. But when he dreamed the same dream the following night, he told it the same day to a group of Kuzmir chasidim who had come to visit him. Among them were his friends Isaac Eng, and R' Yakov Dovid Shoichet. The chasidim and friends heard him out and said they would send a letter and a "*kvittl*" to the rabbi who was living in Zamosc at the time. They did indeed do that but no answer was returned. When the dream reoccurred for the third time, they went to see the shtetl rabbi, and the rabbi and the other dayanim directed the sick *gabai* to go to the cemetery and beg forgiveness from the deceased. Unfortunately, it did not help. Several days later, the *gabai*, Shmuel Glatter, died.

The shtetl had lots to talk about after this for a long time, and to mourn, because both deceased were young men. The chasidim from the Kuzmir stibl saw a magic portent in the rabbi's not answering. That he had foreseen the bad outcome, and for that reason, had not replied.

———

In Memory of Distinguished Personalities from Tyszowce

by Pinchas Landau

Translated by Sara Mages

Who can count the personalities who lived in Tyszowce even though this town was small (only 800 Jewish families), but there was a vibrant Jewish life in this town. There were those who studied the Torah for the sake of the *mitzvah* and not for personal gain. I've heard their names and also knew some of them personally. I also knew the common people who, even though they didn't study Torah, did a lot to ease the lives of the town poor. They founded *Kupat Gemilut Hasadim*[1], the society of *Linat Tzedek*[2] and *Bikur Cholim*[3], and were always ready to sacrifice themselves for the sanctification of God's name.

After the First World War, when the state of Poland was resurrected, the

[Page 146]

gentiles from the surrounding villages came every year to enlist in the army and started to beat the town's Jews. Who were the ones who risked their lives and drove out these rioters from the town? Who were "The People of Shklov[4]" of Tyszowce? They were the common people who lived from the labor of their hands, and in the days of fear of riots they didn't go to work, and guarded the town day and night.

I knew these and those, my memory is very poor to remember their names, and I cannot list what they did for the benefit of the Jews of this town without expectation of a reward. These words will be a monument to their memory in the Yizkor Book for the martyrs of Tyszowce.

In this book I will mention two of these personalities who were very close to me: the first, my honored father, R' Shlomo Landau, z"l, and the second, my uncle and father-in-law, R' Pinchas Ginzburg, z"l.

The family of Shlomo Landau

Translator's footnotes:

1. *Kupat Gemilut Hasadim* -Interest Free Loan Fund.
2. *Linat Tzedek* (lit. "Righteousness lodged") refers to a hostel or boarding house to serve the poor sick or poor passers-by needing temporary lodging for free.
3. *Bikur Cholim* (lit."Visiting the sick") refers to the *mitzvah* of visiting and extending aid to the sick.
4. Zalman Shneour describes in his book, *Anshei Shklov* ("The People of Shklov"), the life of the common people in his hometown, Shklov.

In Memory of my father R' Shlomo Landau Segel

by Pinchas Landau

Translated by Sara Mages

Since my father was humble and didn't like to stand out, there is no native of Tyszowce (of those who remained alive after the Holocaust) who can testify that he knew my father, z"l. Therefore, I will write the memory of R' Shlomo Landau in the Yizkor Book for the city of Tyszowce among the personalities from our city.

[Page 147]

My father was a descendant of Yehezkel Landau Segel, z"l, the author of the book *Noda BiYhudah* [Known in Judah]. In his youth he studied in the Beit HaMidrash in his hometown, then at various yeshivot until he received his rabbinic ordination.

My grandfather, R' Yakov Ginzburg, z"l, author of the book *Zichron Ya'akov* and a rabbi in our city, traveled to yeshivot to choose a groom for his modest daughter Rachel, my mother, z"l. In her name he chose Landau, z"l as fitting to be his son-in-law and his daughter's husband.

He was twenty years old when he got married and at the age of twenty-one he had to report to the army. He was not released because he was a perfectly healthy young man without any physical defect. This matter was to my grandfather's dissatisfaction. My grandfather traveled with his son-in-law to the capital city of Warsaw to arrange for him a deformity in his body that would release him from the army. They went to a doctor who dealt with creating body defects. When my father was waiting for his turn to see the doctor, he saw how young healthy men went in to see this doctor and came out sick and weak. He refused to go to this doctor and didn't do any *feler* [defect] (as it was called). In 1891 he entered the service in the Russian army of that time, and because of this my grandfather forbade him to ever serve as a rabbi.

Father served in the army for four years and eight months in the city of Petrograd, and during all this time he didn't taste army food. In the first six months he existed only on bread and water. After that, when the officers saw that they would not be able to make a proper soldier out of him, he received, after lobbying and bribery, the position of a drummer in the army and was given a drum that he never drummed on. After that, he was able to leave the camp and started to eat at the home of the Rabbi of Petrograd in exchange for educating his children in Judaism, the Torah, *Shas*[1] and the Bible.

When my father returned from the army, my grandfather accepted him as a partner in his earthenware factory, and in this manner he became a merchant.

Years later, after my grandfather got old and his eyesight weakened, when they came to him to rule in matters of *kashrut*[2], or when the city rabbi sent his *shammes* [beadle] to call grandfather to consult with him on a certain judgment, my grandfather used to say - go to my Shlomo, he will advise you and rule according to Jewish law.

That's how they started flocking to my father, at first only from our family (which was quite large), and then from all over the city for two reasons: a) my father didn't get paid for the judgments. b) my father was known in the city to be not so strict in matters of *kashrut*. I testify under oath that my father, z"l, observed light commandments as if they were severe ones, but when they came to him with questions in the matters of *kashrut*, he took into consideration "great loss," time of distress "and "preservation of human life," that all the arbiters took into account, and he thought and researched thoroughly until he gave his verdict. There were cases in many questions that the city rabbi ruled *treyf*,[3] and then they came to my father, without telling him that they had already visited the city rabbi who ruled *treyf*, and that my father ruled *kosher*. Those told their neighbors, and the neighbors to the neighbors, etc., and everyone came with their questions to my father, z"l. There were also honest people who said, after father ruled *kosher* what the rabbi ruled *treyf*, R' Shlomo, "we were at the rabbi and he prohibited," as is well known, "if one sage prohibited the second cannot permit without the consent of the first." Then, father had to go to the rabbi

[Page 148]

to prove to him that it is possible to permit what he had previously prohibited, "because when a *kosher* item is declared *treyf* it is possible to give judgment in the future."

There were dozens of such cases that I remember very well. Two of them have been etched in my memory more than the others: a) it was on the eve of the holiday of Rosh Hashanah when father went to the rabbi (by the way, I accompanied him). We returned after midnight, and only then did we eat the holiday night meal. b) that brought my father to the conclusion that he should no longer rule in matters of *kashrut* due to the honor of the city rabbi. The possessor of the question gave a lot of publicity to this judgment and shamed the city rabbi in public.

As mentioned, my father was a busy man, and yet he gave lessons in the Talmud (without payment) in the Detrisk *shtiebel* where he prayed. Many young men studied in these classes. Several years later, when my grandfather passed away and father managed the business alone, he stopped those lessons, but in his spare time he studied a lot of Talmud, *Shas* and *Poskim*[4]. He always wrote his own innovations on many issues from the Talmud, and recorded them for eternity inside the volumes of our *Shas*. Those who have seen our *Shas* must have read the aforementioned innovations, and, with God's help, there are those who are still alive and saw our *Shas*. When I grew up and left the *cheder*, father started to study with me at home. In order for me to have a study partner, he chose a young man of my age to study together, and so it was with my brothers, Yitzchak and Yaakov, z"l. All of these "friends," who are still alive, remember my father well and surely saw his innovations on the Talmud.

More than once, father expressed his opinion that it would be better to collect all of these innovations in one volume, and maybe also to publish them, "There are many thoughts in a man's heart[5]" etc. In 1933 I immigrated to Israel, and I intended to return to Tyszowce a few years later to liquidate my possessions (I had a shop and a house that I built some time before immigrating to Israel), and I would bring all our books (that father promised to give me). I would gather all the innovations on the Talmud that father, z"l, invested a lot of thought in, and immortalize them by printing them in one book. I planned to travel to Tyszowce in 1940. As is well known, the war broke out in 1939, and of course I didn't travel and everything was destroyed by the Nazis, may their names be blotted out.

My father, z"l, passed away on the 8th of Av 5698 [5 August 1938]. About a year before the war I was informed of his passing. Even before I left Tyszowce my father became "*Saggi Nehor*[6]" and couldn't write to me, and my brothers who wrote to me didn't inform me of his passing. When the war broke out I didn't get any letters, not even from my brothers. Only when the first survivors from Tyszowce came via Russia did I learn about the day of the death of my father, z"l. I also learned that of our large family only two daughters and one son survived of my older sister Esther, z"l. This son immigrated to Israel in 1949, and he told me that a few days before the outbreak of the war that my brother Yitzchak had sent me a letter in which he informed me of my father's passing and his last words to me. I didn't receive this letter because of the war. I have nothing left from my father except for a letter he wrote in Hebrew in 5651 [1890/91] when he was serving in the army, and also a photo of the tombstone on my father's grave in Tyszowce that my sister's son gave me when he immigrated to Israel. Also this tombstone no longer exists because the Nazis, together with the Poles,

[Page 149]

destroyed the cemetery in Tyszowce. May these words that I have written here in the Yizkor book for the martyrs of Tyszowce be a tombstone in memory of my father R' Shlomo Landau Segel, z"l.

May his soul be bound up in the bond of eternal life.

Tishrei 5729 (1968) Tel-Aviv, Israel

This is the monument of Shlomo Landau Segel, z"l
Standing right: Itzchak Landau, z"l
Left: Shimon Reichenberg–a grandson

Translator's footnotes:

1. *Shas* - the Six Orders of the Mishnah and Talmud.
2. *Kashrut* is a set of dietary laws dealing with the foods that Jewish people are permitted to eat, and how those foods must be prepared according to Jewish law.
3. *Treyf* is a Yiddish word that refers to any food that is deemed not *kosher* (i.e. forbidden under Jewish law).
4. *Posek* (pl. *poskim*,) a legal scholar who determines the application of *halakha*, the Jewish religious laws derived from the written and Oral Torah.
5. There are many thoughts in a man's heart, but God's plan-that shall stand. (Proverbs 19:21)
6. The Aramaic epithet, *Saggi Nehor* means "of Much Light" in the sense of having excellent eyesight, an ironic euphemism for being blind.

[Page 150]

In Memory of my father R' Shlomo Landau Segel

by Pinchas Landau

Translated by Sara Mages

I think that all the natives of Tyszowce, even the young ones who didn't personally know my uncle and father-in-law, R' Pinchas Ginzburg, z"l, must have heard his name, because he always appeared in public. He was an excellent *magid* [preacher] even though he spent all his days traveling outside Tyszowce. But,

The family of Pinchas Ginzburg

when he came home to rest, he appeared in public and preached in the Beit HaMidrash, at Zionist meetings and conferences, and all the townspeople, young and old, came to hear the "sermon" of R' Pinchas Ginzburg, z"l. (Our townsman, the writer Ya'akov Zipper, mentions R' Pinchas Ginzburg, z"l, in his book *Tsvishen Teykhen un Vassern* ["*Between Rivers and Waters*"] under the name R' Baruch der Magid).

R' Pinchas Ginzburg, z"l, son of R' Yaakov Ginzburg, z"l, (my grandfather), was the author of the book, *Zichron Ya'akov* [Ya'akov Memory], an essay about *Yoreh De'ah*[1] and *Pri Megadim*[2]. My grandfather worked on this essay for twenty years until it was ready for printing, but he didn't have the means

[Page 151]

to print the aforementioned essay. Therefore, he tasked his son, R' Pinchas, z"l, to go out into the wide world to collect subscriptions for this essay in order to finance the printing. It was at the beginning of this century when visas were not needed to travel from country to country. R' Pinchas, z"l, traveled all over Europe and collected subscriptions and consent from rabbis and great Torah scholars for the aforementioned essay, and they committed themselves to buying this book and distributing it widely. In every place that my uncle, z"l, arrived, he advertised that the *maggid*, R'

Pinchas, would preach in a certain Beit Midrash. Before he announced the purpose of his arrival he gave a short sermon on biblical laws that he was very good at, and that's how he became famous as a world renowned *maggid*.

My uncle managed to amass five thousand subscribers. The first part of the book *Zichron Ya'akov* (the essay had three parts: a) salting laws; b) meat and milk; c) mixtures. It was printed in ten thousand copies, and by 1913 almost all the books had been sold. Then, they started to prepare the second part, "meat and milk," for printing, but in 1914 the First World War broke out which lasted until the 1920s. The last two parts were not printed, and in this way the work that my grandfather invested dozens of years in was lost.

In the 1920s, R' Pinchas, z"l, began to raise support for *Keren Hayesod*[3]. He was sent on behalf of *Keren Hayesod* center in Warsaw, Poland, to such places in which the Zionist label was considered to be heretical, mostly in Eastern Galicia. There were towns where a clean-shaven lecturer (without a beard) risked his life if he dared to come there on behalf of *Keren Hayesod*. But R' Pinchas Ginzburg, z"l, was warmly welcomed because he was a man with a very long beard. He seasoned his sermons with words from the Torah and also managed to attract these fanatics to *Keren Hayesod*.

It is worth mentioning here one case that my uncle, z"l, once told me about, in order to understand the nature of these places he arrived in to turn them into Zionists.

Once, my uncle, z"l, came to a town in Galicia and that same week the Rebbe, whose Hassidim made up the entire Jewish community in this town, also arrived. In order to travel to meet the Rebbe on the road before his entry into this town, they took from the landowner, *pritz*,[4] (in Galicia there were also Jewish landowners) a handsome carriage with a pair of the best horses that this *pritz* raised and only used for trips. The Hassidim loaded this carriage with more people than it could hold, and also sped up and galloped the horses. One horse overheated, fell ill and died. This horse was of a special breed and the Hassidim had to pay the *pritz* a thousand zloty for the carcass. At that time one thousand zloty was a very large sum.

My uncle, z"l, who this time failed to do something for *Keren Hayesod*, when he got on stage in the Beit HaMidrash to preach his sermon, said: "In this town there is money only for horses, but there is no money for *Keren Hayesod*."

On that occasion they wanted to beat him, and that evening he had to flee the town for another town that was a two-hour train ride away. The Hassidim, who knew where my uncle was travelling to, called there so that they would not allow this heretic, R' Pinchas, z"l, to enter a Jewish home.

When my uncle arrived in this town he turned to a hotel to sleep overnight. He was turned away because there was no place

[Page 152]

[Page 153]

for him. He walked to another hotel, and also there encountered the same thing, "No vacancy," and also in the third and the fourth. Then he understood what was going on and went to the Beit HaMidrash to sleep there on a bench. Immediately, children with *payot* [sidelocks] gathered around him and began to study the Talmud in a loud voice so that he would not be able to sleep, and from time to time they approached him to pester him with questions about issues in the Talmud. When he refused to answer, they started to beat him. He was forced to flee from the Beit HaMidrash, went to the police of this town and asked for help.

In 1926 my uncle was in Warsaw, and on that very day they celebrated the birthday of Marshal Józef Piłsudski. That evening, when my uncle spoke at the convention on behalf of *Keren Hayesod*, he mentioned the name of Marshal Józef Piłsudski and blessed him on his birthday. The next day this blessing was printed in a well-known Polish newspaper, and Marshal Piłsudski sent my uncle a letter of thanks for this blessing that was signed with his signature.

This letter helped my uncle many times when he had to arrange something with the authorities, for example, a permit to speak at a meeting, etc. This letter also helped him this time at the police station in this town. They arranged a place for him to spend the night and the next morning they brought him to the train and sent him on from there. He never returned to the vicinity of this town.

R' Pinchas Ginzburg composed many sermons. Some of them he collected and printed in a book called *The Gefen* [the grapevine] the [Hebrew] initials of, Ginzburg, Pinchas, Netta. He worked on behalf of *Keren Hayesod* until his immigration to Israel in 1934. Here, in Israel, he was a lecturer on behalf of Mizrahi for a while, but due to his poor health, he stopped all his activities for *Keren Hayesod*.

He passed away on Lag BaOmer 1939 and was buried in Nahalat Yitzhak Cemetery near Tel Aviv.

May his soul be bound up in the bond of eternal life

Tishrei 5729 (1968)

Translator's footnotes:

1. *Yoreh De'ah* (lit. "It Teaches Understanding") is the second of the four volumes of the *Shulchan Aruch* ("Set Table"), the compendium of Jewish Law applicable today.
2. *Pri Megadim* by Yosef ben Meir Teomim is a super-commentary on some of the major commentators on *Shulchan Aruch*.
3. *Keren Hayesod* (lit. "The Foundation Fund"), a fund raising organization that was established in London in 1920 to provide the Zionist movement with resources needed to establish a Jewish homeland in Palestine.
4. *Paritz* is a landowner in Poland.

[Page 154]

Rabbi Avraham Stern of blessed memory, the Shochet and Rabbinical Teacher from Tyszowce

by Shalom Krishtalka, Montreal, Canada

Translated by Jerrold Landau

(Head of a literary family)

A number of family members are known within Yiddish literature as people who enriched Yiddish literature with their literary creations in one or two generations. From among the better known ones in our time there are the Zeitlin families: the father Hillel Zeitlin, may G-d avenge his blood, and his two sons Elchanan and Aharon Zeitlin; the Bergner family, the mother Hinde, may G-d avenge her blood, and her sons Melech Ravitsh and Hertz Bergner; Y. Y. [Yisrael Yehoshua] Singer, I. Bashevis, and their sister Esther Kreitman; the brothers: Vladek and Charni Neiger; the Reyzen family: Avraham Reyzen, Zalman Reyzen, and their sister Sara Reyzen; the Olitski and Imber brothers, and others.

The Stern family from Tyszowce, currently in Montreal, spans three generations of Yiddish writers and educators: The father, Rabbi Avraham Stern, may he live long Amen; the children: Yaakov Zipper, Yechiel Stern, Shalom Stern,

Dr. Yisrael Stern, Shifra Krishtalka, Hene Marder; the grandchildren Aharon Krishtalka, Leibel Krishtalka, the sons of Shifra and Shalom Krishtalka, Eidel Stern, the daughter of Dr. Yisrael, and Amalia Stern.

I did not take it upon myself to write a monograph about the latter part of those three generations of writers and their contribution to Yiddish literature, pedagogy, and education (this would be a very interesting and important work). My modest task is only to note bibliographically the works of the head of the family, Rabbi Avraham Stern.

In its monthly journal, "Congress Bulletin" of July 1949, number 1, page 10, the Canadian Jewish Congress published a large, biographical-critical work titled: "A Jewish Literary Family." The author, David Romm, examines the creative role of four members of the Stern family: The father Rabbi Avraham Stern, Yaakov Zipper, Yechiel Stern, and Shalom Stern. That article portrays the creative personality of each of them and their literary contributions to Yiddish literature in

[Page 155]

the realms of prose, poetry, and criticism, their contributions to educational endeavors, and the important position that each played in their participation in Jewish cultural life in Montreal in general, and in education in particular.

It is also worthwhile to stress that in the year 1951, the Canadian Jewish Congress, in collaboration with the Jewish Public Library in Montreal, organized a Canadian Yiddish book and poetry exhibition, which lasted for two weeks. At that exhibition, everything that had been written by Jews and about Jews, and had been published in Canada in Yiddish, Hebrew, English, and French was collected.

At that exhibition, a special table was set up with the works of the Stern family. The books of Rabbi Avraham Stern may he live long, of blessed memory[1], Yaakov Zipper, Yechiel Stern, Shalom Stern, and excerpts from Aharon Krishtalka's poems of those ten years that were published in the press.

In that way, the Montreal Jewish society gave honor to the gifted family of writers – Stern-Zipper.

The Book of Testimonies in Israel

Rabbi Avraham Stern, the father of the Stern family, lived in Tyszowce for most of his years. He also lived for a time in Szczebrzeszyn [Shebreshin]. He came with his wife to Montreal in 1938 from Tyszowce, Poland, where he was a rabbinical judge, a rabbinical teacher, and *shochet*. He was known and held in esteem not only in Tyszowce, but also in the surrounding area where his name was quite well known. He was involved in Torah and Divine service all his life. While he was learning, he would point out certain notes, interpretations, and novel ideas, and sought to find an answer to questions that great scholars and rabbis also sought and tried to answer. He also studied with a number of students, mainly friends of his children with whom he himself studied.

When he arrived in Montreal, they convinced their father that his novel ideas and glosses should be published.

That treasury of novel ideas found its proper manifestation in the book entitled *Edut BeYisrael* [Testimony in Israel], novellae on the Babylonian Talmud and his commentaries in *halacha* and *Aggadah* [lore], as well as a bit on the Jerusalem Talmud, the Rambam and his commentaries, and the *Shulchan Aruch* [Code of Jewish Law], which the Good G-d has graced me , the lowly in the troops of Yissachar, Avraham the son of Reb Yissachar of blessed memory Stern.

He was previously a *shochet* and teacher of righteousness in the city of Tyszowce, Lublin Region, in the State of Poland. Now he is a *shochet* of fowl, and he studies with attentive friends in the Tzeirei Dat VaDaat [Youth of Religion and Knowledge], and Yavneh *Beis Midrashes* here in Montreal. Montreal, Canada, Marcheshvan 5704 – 1943. 328 pages (A quote from the title page).

[Page 156]

From the name of the book, one can already see the broad scope of the novellae with which the prominent author deals. The book *Edut BeYisrael* received great acclaim in the entire rabbinical and scholarly world immediately after its publication, both through the announcements in the press as well as through the personal letters of gratitude and appreciation from the prominent great ones of the generation from all the Jewish communities of the world.

Due to shortage of space, I will only cite a few excerpts from an article in the *Kanader Adler* from April 5, 1944, by Rabbi Pinchas Hirschsprung, the spiritual leader of Yeshivat Chachmei Lublin, rabbi of the Adas Yeshurun Synagogue, and currently rabbi, head of the rabbinical court of the rabbinical council in Montreal.

"A new treasury has arrived in the treasury of commentaries and novellae in *halacha* and *Aggadah*. Talmudic literature has been enriched with another composition that bears the name *Edut BeYisrael*. The author of that valuable book is the great scholar, Rabbi Avraham Stern, may he live long, Amen, who has acquired a name for himself in all parts of Montreal, both for his learning, as well for his fine renditions of Hassidic stories.

"Even though we have economic worries during these times, and each of us has a 'sighing soul' due to the events in Europe, and we are far from comfortable, in spite of this, the important author told me that he decided to publish his book *Edut BeYisrael*, of which approximately ninety percent is commentaries on *halacha*, Talmudic didactics, Talmud, Rambam, the four sections of the Code of Jewish Law, etc." After that, the important rabbi cites a few novellae from the book *Edut BeYisrael*, and he ends with his assertion, "The newly published book, which is without doubt an important contribution to our Talmudic literature, should be reckoned among the treasury of books. It is worthwhile that every appreciator of books enrich his bookshelf with the Code of Jewish Law and the like."

The *Kvutzat Kitvei Aggadah* Book

It is like the second part of *Edut BeYisrael*, that the good G-d has already granted me the merit of publishing to the light of the world, and to distribute in Jacob and Israel, anthologized with the help of G-d, may he be blessed,

Avraham the son of Yissachar Stern of blessed memory,

Formerly, the *shochet* and teacher of righteousness in the State of Poland, region of Lublin, district of Tomaszów, city of Tyszowce; currently in the county of Canada, here in Montreal, where he studies with attentive comrades in the Tzeirei Dat VaDaat Beis Midrash and in the Yavneh and Chevra Shas synagogues of the aforementioned city. This book is divided into three sections, two in Hebrew and one, the first part, in Yiddish. Montreal, Canada Elul

[Page 157]

5707 – 1945. (Excerpted from the title page), 52 pages, 494 in Hebrew , 96 in Yiddish, and 12 pages of content with explanation. This is an anthology of letters that the author wrote to his children throughout the duration of 22 years.

In the letters, the father shares with his children [ideas regarding] current events, political and economic, from the timeframe when the letter was written. He also discusses the weekly Torah portion, a fine teaching about a Talmudic passage, or an answer to a question asked by a child. The children saved the letters.

And when the author arrived in Canada, the children collected the letters and brought them to the father. This resulted in the letter collection that the author anthologized and compiled into a large, important work. It can be called an anthology book, if one can say such, in which the readers and teachers can find questions and answers on *halacha*, *Aggadah*, *Zohar*, and Kabbalah. The author demonstrates his wonderful expertise and analytical skills. It is also full of folklore material of great value. As with the first book, the book Anthology of *Aggadaic* Writings has received great acclaim in the scholarly world.

I will only cite a few excerpts from the remarks of Rabbi Yehoshua HaLevi Hirshorn of blessed memory, the head of the rabbinical court of the city at that time.

Following that, Rabbi Hirschorn gives the definition of the uniqueness of diligence and expertise that demonstrates the level or style of each scholar (*Kanader Adler*, February 20, 1948). He writes:

"… The author was a rabbinical judge, rabbinical teacher, and *shochet* in a shtetl in Poland. When he came to Montreal, he came to the realization that, not taking into account his great learning and expertise in all aspects of Torah, it would not be appropriate for him to seek a rabbinical position in the city when he will be. Who knows about the president and assessors, from whom he would probably suffer the spiritual suffering that our rabbis and Torah scholars suffer from… The author earns his livelihood from the income of his holy work, which he receives with great honor. However, the scholar and Torah great within him did not slumber. Rather, he sits with excitement and produces his novelle in *halacha* and *Aggadah*…" And… Anyone who looks into his book will not be satisfied by merely perusing what he said, as one does with all books of exegesis. One cannot grasp anything by reading quickly. One must delve deeply and also look into the cited sources in order to grasp the intended idea. The book was written in the style of *halacha*, with a wonderful level of expertise that is rich and well considered. It is obvious that the author wished to transmit everything with great influence. Since he possesses a great level of breadth of knowledge,

[Page 158]

the book is full and overflowing. It is often a pleasure to see that the author had fine sources at his hand for his thesis in *Aggadah*…"

And the important rabbi concludes… "The author also has a great mastery and knowledge of books of Kabbalah. He deals with terminology from Kabbalah and *gematria* together with *halacha* and *Aggadah* in a fine fashion. He also brings down very many statements of famous *Admorim*, and at the same time interjects a thought that has a connection with *halacha*…"

… "The portion of the book written in Yiddish also contains very fine ideas. However, I believe that every reader will realize this without me pointing it out."

… "The book makes a very fine impression with its breadth, in Gemara, in the literature of the revealed Torah, and also in the literature of the hidden Torah [i.e., Kabbalah]. It is excellent, and can and must be well supported in all Torah and rabbinical sources."

Sefer *Chutim Hameshulashim* [The Book of the Threefold Threads]

Containing three opened books

a. Hassidic stories. b. *Sarei BeYissachar*. c. *Orein Tlitai*.

Authored by (the author of the books *Edut BeYisrael* and *Kevutzat Kitvei Aggadah*)

Avraham the son of Reb Yissachar of blessed memory Stern

He was formerly the *shochet* and teacher of righteousness in Tyszowce, district of Tomaszów region of Lublin, State of Poland. Currently in Montreal, Canada.

Montreal, Canada, Kislev 5614 – 1953 (cited according to the title page).

This book consists of three parts. The first part contains 32 stories in Yiddish about the Baal Shem Tov and his students – 100 pages.

The second and third parts – collected novellae about the Talmud and responsa – 103 pages.

The author was an artistic storyteller of Hassidic stories. His audience would be raised up spiritually when they heard Rabbi Stern tell a story about the Baal Shem Tov.

Each story in the book is full of Torah [thoughts], *notarikon*[2], and lessons about how one should conduct oneself. In general, they are replete with love of one's fellow Jew. Telling over a story was like the oral Torah for the important author. For the most part, the stories in the book include the sources from which Rabbi Stern had heard the story.

This demonstrates how careful and reliable the author was to the verse: if one says

[Page 159]

something in the name of the person who stated it, etc.[3]. He told almost all the stories at the Sabbath table when the children came for kiddush or other occasions, and also to his students during the third Sabbath meal in Tzeirei Dat Va Da'at. The book *Chutim Hameshulashim* has received great recognition, just like his previous two books.

In *Tag* from April 21, 1955, Menashe Unger writes, among other things: "The most important thing is when one turns the oral Torah into the written Torah from the stories that elderly Hassidim told at their table celebrations, at the third sabbath meal, at *Melave Malka* [the post Sabbath meal], or at a yahrzeit of a Rebbe that are then recorded. Rabbi Stern, who was a Husiatyner Hassid, recorded Hassidic stories that he himself had heard. Thus, one can state about this endeavor that he was a unique person in his generation, the one and only in our generation."

Sh. Ernst – Tel Aviv, under the chapter "Hassidic Stories from Primary Sources," *Kanader Adler* August 13, 1956, Montreal, writes amongst other things: "It is the fine trait of the stories of Rabbi Stern, who had the opportunity to live amongst Hassidim, and did not restrict himself to merely literary pursuits, for he portrayed the legendary lives of good Jews, thanks to his personal experiences and sharp observations. From the 32 stories that he published in the book *Chutim Hameshulashim*, it is difficult to find a story that was previously known in the large, rich body of Hassidic folk literature. If one can find such a story, it would be in a different fashion.

"Being a Hassid himself, Rabbi Stern wrote his stories with great sincerity. For him, every story is full of love, infused with faith and warmheartedness. This is the true style of Hassidim. The light of faith and belief – is the illuminated Stern, who emulated the good Jews in the way of their lives.

"One can cite from almost every story and demonstrate that those stories have poetic and literary value. This is a rare phenomenon in old-style rabbinical literature."

In Israel, some publisher has republished the Yiddish section of *Chutim Hameshulashim* – i.e., the 32 stories – in a separate book called *Hassidic Stories from Avraham the son of Yissachar Stern*, Tel Aviv, 1960, without the knowledge of the Stern family. The publisher did not include the name of a publishing house. When he found out that the family was still inquiring about this, it was suddenly removed from the market. The Orthodox booksellers were silent when they were asked form where they had obtained it.

When the Montreal students and appreciators of Rabbi Avraham Stern found out that their rabbi was publishing a book, they were overtaken

[Page 160]

with great joy. They subscribed to it, and helped raise the necessary funds to cover the expenses.

They did the same with the second and third books. Several hundred copies of the book were sent for free to all the Yeshivot in Israel, and to places where they were able to obtain an address of a Jewish community.

Rabbi Avraham Stern died on 8 Adar I 5715 – 1955 in Montreal after a brief illness.

Jewish Montreal accompanied their rabbi [at his funeral] with great honor and respect. Almost all the rabbis of Montreal eulogized the rabbi.

A. Perlman, who writes under the name "The smallest of his mourning students" in *Tag* of April 21, 1955, writes in a letter to Menashe Unger: "When one found oneself in his environment, one felt elevated. He was one of the few Hassidic scholars who was also clear in worldly matters, like a Mishnaic scholar before his time. We treated him with great honor, like a true Tzadik. The entire local community is in sorrow. May his memory be blessed."

* * *

N. B. A brief bibliography excerpted from the work of the second and third of the Stern family is included in this book under the section: "Supplementary Material on the history of Tyszowce – Authors and Writers."

Editor

Translator's footnotes:

1.   Both abbreviations, one for the living and one for the deceased, are used here. Obviously, one is superfluous. He died in 1955. I suspect that the z"l was a later addition to the original article.

2.   See https://en.wikipedia.org/wiki/Notarikon#:~:text=Notarikon%20is%20one%20of%20the,was%20also%20used%20in%20alchemy.

3.   This is not a biblical verse, but rather a Mishnah from *Pirkei Avot* 6:6: And who says a thing in the name of him who said it. Thus you have learned: everyone who says a thing in the name of him who said it, brings deliverance into the world, as it is said: "And Esther told the king in Mordecai's name" (Esther 2:22). [translation from Sefaria].

[Page 161]

Gitl the Shoichetke[1]

by M. Fisher (Montreal, Canada)

Translated by Moses Milstein

In memory of Gitl Stern, a"h, from someone from the back streets.

She was called "*Gitl die shoichetke*" in town, but for us kids from the backstreets, she was "*die Miemeh Giteleh.*"[2] We had mixed feelings for the Miemeh Giteleh. We liked her and of course had immense respect for her, but nevertheless we trembled, and anxiety befell us when we sprained an arm or a leg at play, and our mothers took us by the hand and said, "Let's go to Miemeh Giteleh."

The Miemeh Giteleh was not at all to blame for our sprained hands or legs. But try to reason with a little heart that flutters from fear. We all knew what she would do. First she would rub alcohol or vinegar on the injured limb. She would do it very, very gently so that you could barely feel it. Then she would put back in place the hand or foot. But no matter how easily or slowly she did it, it would still hurt. Even though she would keep blowing on the painful spot and tell us, "Now, now, soon, soon, it's back to normal already."

Through tears of pain we looked at her with a heavy, constricted heart, full of resentment, almost hate. It was even worse when R ' Abraham Shoichet was home and helped out. Our cries could be heard ten streets away. "What are you doing to the child?!" "Don't squeeze so hard!" "Are you dealing with an adult?|!" The kid is in agony!" "Good, take over again." "Can't you see you need to use more force?" "You've been poking around for almost an hour already, and nothing's happening." They argued as if not with each other, but with us, resenting the fact that they are causing us pain. But as soon as the Miemeh Gitleh bandaged our hands or feet, and told us under no circumstances to move the hand or the foot, and often ordered us to keep the arm suspended with a kerchief, so all at once,

[Page 162]

our tearful eyes gleamed with love and respect for our Miemeh Giteleh.

We ate with delight, a sweet cookie, a *vikeleh*, a piece of *komish broit* dipped in syrup she gave us to *derkvikken sich dem hartz*.

Gitl Stern a"h

She would also come to our homes if we were ill. We looked forward to her coming. She always brought something for us that we liked, a candy, a good cookie, an apple, and a spoonful of raspberry juice to drink with a glass of tea. That was the best

[Page 163]

prescription. But, when she saw that tea with raspberry juice and staying in bed would not be enough, she would advise calling in the doctor.

She was also called to see adults. She brought them raspberry juice as well, and gave the same advice: to lie in bed and drink a lot of hot tea and raspberry juice.

Often she also brought blackberry juice. But this was only helpful for diarrhea. She also applied "*bankes*[3]" for shoulder or back pain. And if none of this helped, she advised calling the doctor. And if they couldn't afford a doctor, she made sure they got one. She first gave from her own purse, and then went around the shops. Soon there was enough for a doctor, and also for a chicken to make a little broth for the patient.

Our Miemeh Giteleh knew about all the suffering souls. Not because she was, God forbid, a gossip. No, every one in town knew that her advice was priceless. All those with heavy hearts came to her for advice, to get things off their chest, in complete confidence. "Speaking to Gitl the shoichetke is like a stone in the water." She spoke softly, slowly, more with a wink than with words.

And this was also the way she walked, hugging the walls, slinking off to the side in order not to be noticed. Thin and small, dressed plainly but clean. And her big dark eyes expressed sadness, rarely, rarely did they display a smile. Everyone knew that she had suffered a great loss.

Her oldest son, Issachar, perished in the first World War. He was killed in his own home by a Russian bomb that was aimed at the German arsenal in town. She was not even there at the time. She was in a nearby shtetl with the other children. Upon arriving home she was greeted by her husband, grown grey from the great tragedy, standing by their ruined house, and Issachar in his grave in the cemetery.

From that time on, she removed her wig, and put on a kerchief. She hung up all her holiday dresses never to be seen again. She avoided looking at Issachar's friends, the light gone out of her eyes, in order not to pass on, God forbid, the evil eye. And they, missing him, sought rather her closeness, to sooth the longing in their hearts.

First, R' Abraham reasoned with his Gitl, "Don't sin. God gave, and God took. It is his. We were granted him only for a while. Have pity on yourself, on me, on the children."

[Page 164]

So she shut everything within herself, and in this way, continued on with her household, raised her children, took care of her husband, and devoted herself to the forlorn and poor of the shtetl.

She ignored her own poverty to lessen the poverty and hunger of the surrounding backstreets. She literally shared her food with them. The few scraps R' Abraham Shoichet brought in twice a week she distributed to others. Other shoichetkes sold their scraps and got a few Zlotys which were always helpful in a shoichet's meager earnings. But not Gitl the shoichetke. No matter how many scraps R' Abraham brought home after sharing with the other shoichets, it was not enough to distribute to everyone.

Among the poor, she had several types. There were those who insisted "they don't want it for nothing." So she took whatever they could afford. "As long as it goes well."

To the needy that came for a piece of intestine, or a piece of fat, a piece of liver, spleen, and were too ashamed of the watching eyes nearby, she would say with a smile, "You can pay me later." And the woman went away with her bit of scraps, with joy, and a blessing for Gitl the shoichetke, R' Abraham, and their children. She would hurry home to kosher the food and cook supper. And before her eyes danced the avid little flames in the eyes of her hungry children at supper that night.

Gitl also had secretive, hidden paupers. Those who died from starvation quietly in their houses, not wanting anyone to know about their poverty. For them, she brought the scraps herself to their houses. And when her children were grown, she sent them to help the paupers. She knew she could trust her children.

Her children observed and learned from their father and mother. In later years, when she would travel in the summer to the dacha of a relative of hers to help her poor health a little, she would give the task to her grown daughter.

In giving away the scraps, she had little left for herself, for her own household and a little something for her relatives.

Poverty in the shtetl was widespread. There were only a few wealthy or well-off families. The majority of the population slaved to get enough to eat. And good people with God in their hearts,

[Page 165]

shared what little they had. Otherwise they would have died from hunger and cold.

Thus on frigid mornings you could see Gitl the shoichetke with an armful of wood on her way to a poor neighbor, or a closeted pauper. At daybreak, so no one would know, she would carry the pieces of wood to the frozen houses, and only after that, would she heat her own house. She and R' Abraham brought to bear all their knowledge about heating so that it would be warm at home, and still have enough to share the wood, because winters were harsh, and the accumulated wood must be enough "both for us, and for the needy."

There was always sickness in the shtetl, some died from their bitter ailments.

Gitl the shoichetke, for whom "time had healed" the great longing for her son, Issachar, weak, and exhausted, did not dwell on her feeble strength, but went wherever she was called. And when she saw that the sick person was at death's door, and needed immediate succor, and getting a few Zlotys here and there would not be enough, that greater help was needed, she went home, put on better clothes, and went off to the shops to her better-off, close friends, to get bigger donations. When she showed up at their door, they received her with great respect, and gave generously, and expressed the wish that "they would be protected by her worthiness, and that the patient should have a speedy and complete recovery."

She only went to particular people for donations. To those who gave wholeheartedly, to those who also went themselves seeking donations, and helping the needy. When she was seen among the shops, the shopkeepers knew that Gilt was coming after a very significant donation again, and everyone waited and hoped that their shop would not be missed.

She taught her children early on to follow in the footsteps of their parents, to help as much as they were able, to share whatever they had, to treat their friends equally. Not with words but with deeds. From early on, she made her children helpers in the great mitzvah of charity, especially with regard to the embarrassed. From their earliest days, she sent them around to the poor with whatever help she could provide, and whatever help she could get from others.

Friday evening, as son as the blessings for the candles was done, she sent out her two little daughters, to gather challah from the homes for the poor. And in the morning, Saturday, she helped them make portions from the pieces of challah, and take them where needed.

[Page 166]

When they were older she sent them to the "*ladess*" to help out making matzes for Pesach, so that the others could take a break for a few hours, or have a nap. The "*lad*" was working constantly, day and night. To be kosher, so the matzes should not become *treyf*, everything had to be done quickly.

The dough kneading, the rolling, the hole-making, and the baking, all had to be done quickly. The supervision by the rabbi and the dayan was strict. And the "lad"-makers also wanted to bake as many matzes as they could. They waited all year with anticipation for the earnings of those two weeks of work. Gitl's daughters helped out mostly with the rolling of the dough. The older one was also allowed to do the hole-making. Her children grew up with poverty, their own and others' around them, and became one with her. Gitl the shoichetke was busy from early to late at night.

In spite of the fact her children eased the load for her, spared her weakness, it was difficult for her to carry out her daily activities, to provide meals with little money, especially since she always had to be ready to feed dinner to an unexpected guest. She also had to worry about her relatives coming from shtetls near and far to "eat their full," and to even leave with a few zlotys in their pockets.

Like her secretive paupers, she also did not want anyone in town to know about her own poverty, about the way she had to piece together, calculate, finagle, the few Zlotys her Abraham brought home and gave over to her management, for some food, clothes for a child, and for the needy. The other three shoichets in town were considered to be poor. But not R' Abraham. "By R' Abraham Shoichet you live comfortably." An open door for beggars to eat, spend the night. Their own children slept doubled up in the narrow bunk beds. And the guests slept on straw mattresses on bench boards.

That Gitl gives up her own food, and her own children leave the table hungry, no one in town could imagine. The secret of his "wealth" that the shtetl believed in, R' Abraham warmly proposed, was his Gitl, the *eyshet chayal*, the *berye niflo'e* , and every Friday evening, coming home with his boys from davening, he would stride cheerfully across the big room, and loudly sing Shalom Aleichem, and invite the "*malachei hasharet, malachei elion* to their Sabbath home. With fervor he sang "*Eyshet chayal mi nimtzah*" to his Gitl, his eyshet chayal, and with love his eyes went from Gitl to

[Page 167]

the children, from the children to Gitl. And Gitl, bent over the candles, occupied with Maariv, glowed and blushed. The Sabbath gave her strength for the whole week. The *zmires* from her Abraham and the children at the Sabbath table melt her, caress her not-healed wound, the gnawing longing for her boy struck down in his youth.

This Sabbath day, Gitl gives up completely the Sabbath. Saturday mornings she goes to daven in the shul or the Husiatyn shtibl where Abraham davens. Like her Abraham, she believes deeply in the old Husiatyn rebbe, long may he live. Once a year she travels with Abraham to the rebbe to celebrate. During the davening, she gathers the women around her, shows them what part of the davening they're at. They know that if you're next to Gitl you daven and don't talk. After eating, and during the Shabbes naptime, she reads the *Tseneh Reneh*.[4] Winter, *peyrek*, and summer, *barchi nafshi*. In the hot, long Shabbes afternoons, she liked to read with her older daughter on the sidewalk, at the front of the house. The women neighbors from the streets around occupied the whole sidewalk and listened in eagerly and with great enjoyment.

Shabbes, she also visited her good friends, or invited them to her place. With the end of prayers, with a sad melody "God of Abraham," Gitl lit a candle for the new week of toil and worry with the great plea, "To God, blessed is He, our father, he should shield and protect all his children, and her lonely child, her Yankl, away from home, among them."

An empty spot remained in the house. And a fresh wound in her wounded heart since her Yankl had to leave for foreign places. She remembers his studying, his sweet music, her heart constricting, unable to find comfort. She gets ready to go and travel to Volhyn where he is living.

She brings all manner of good things. Preserves, dried fruit, stuffed, baked tripe. All his favorite foods. "May he feel a little bit like home."

And no matter how long she spent with her beloved son, and no matter how much joy they experienced in each other's company, "she left him away from home, wandering like Yosef Hatsadik from his home." So it continued until Yankl travelled to Canada.

* * *

Gitl the shoichetke aged a lot before her time. Not by her years. Really terrible times arose for everyone, especially for Jews. The youth were restless. The shtetl was too small for them. They left for the wider world, for the big cities looking for work.

[Page 168]

To change the world, to push through a crack to Eretz Israel, to study in high schools, and teacher seminaries. Gitl sees one child after the other leaving for foreign places. Even overseas to Canada, or for the time being, to Vilna.

And each time when she and Abraham return home they look at each other with dumb sorrow in their eyes, and a new longing takes root in their hearts. Now they live only through the letters and photographs of their children. She becomes a grandmother through the letters. Through the letters she becomes a mother-in-law.

And she, the hard tested mother, provides consolation to other mothers with broken hearts. Her home is often happily restored for weeks and months at a time when the children come for Pesach, or during summer holidays, from Vilna. And Abraham goes into debt up to his eyeballs so the kids can come. He can't look on as Gitl declines. She eats less and less each day. And he too can't find a place for himself. He misses his children at the studying, the davening, at the table, during meals. To have a chat about world events, abut the bitter Jewish events. R' Abraham is proud of his children. He derives strength from their letters, and studies with them through the letters he writes to them.

The noose tightens more and more. The Polish earth burned beneath every Jew's foot. Everyone was looking for a way to save themselves. Not particular, as long as they escaped this hell. Gitl the shoichetke, and Abraham, saw that God had performed a great kindness for them, truly a miracle. So they wrote to their two sons in Canada that they should not rest, and bring the other children to Canada. And if God were willing, and with the rebbe's blessing, to bring them over as well. Their sons truly did not rest. So Gitl the shoichetke began again to see her children off, to part with "who knows if we shall see each other again." And with each child her "soul separated from her body." First the oldest daughter and her husband, three days after the wedding. After them, the youngest daughter, and after her, the son and the daughter-in-law and grandchild, and then the youngest son.

Gitl was left with Abraham like a petrified stone. The only thing that kept her going was her daily work for the sick and hungry in the shtetl. Her preoccupation with the needy eased somewhat her great longing for her children.

And when God helped her, and the time came for her to be reunited with her children in Canada, she distributed all her

[Page 169]

goods to the needy, and some things to her relations and friends. She left very little for herself, mainly just as a remembrance.

When the time came to leave the shtetl, she felt as if she was leaving a part of herself. The shtetl remained in chaos, danger. She must save as much as she could. She told herself, and them, that she would not rest until she saved them from the great danger which was approaching them and all Jews.

The whole shtetl accompanied them far along the sandy road. All "Miemeh Giteleh's children" who were still in the shtetl came. Even the Christian neighbors came.

R'Abraham had to wrest her away from her near and dear ones, her shtetl.

He had to force her into the carriage that took them to the nearby train station. The cries and shrieks carried to the skies. A lamentation followed the disappearing carriage, "Gitl, how can you leave us?!"

* * *

"The rebbetsin," as the students of R' Abraham Stern, z"l, called her here, died Erev Rosh Hashanah, 5716.

Translator's footnotes:

1. Feminine form of shoichet, ritual slaughterer
2. Aunt Gitl
3. Cupping, a form of moxibustion
4. Religious texts in Yiddish for women

————

[Page 170]

Memories and Reflections on the Town

by Zvi Zwilich – Israel

Translated by Sara Mages

In the early 1920s, our great writers, who often depicted Jewish life in the "town" of Russia and Poland, did a favor to our people.

In their wildest imagination they never imagined that these works would also be the "swan song of the town." After the Holocaust of the Second World War of 1939-1945, their authentic work was also the tombstone for the glorious Jewish town - in Poland and most of the European Diaspora.

The writers of our history, through all the years of our exile in the Diaspora, knew how to commemorate heroes, and acts of heroism, that were displayed among the people in time of calamities. From the Babylonian exile through the Maccabean wars to the present. To this day, thirty years from the beginning of the Second World War, a national poet has not yet arisen who can encompass the magnitude of the Holocaust, and the horror of the greatest destruction in the brutality of war that the world has known so far.

The burden will be too heavy for the historian who will want to discover from the ruins of the towns and ghettos their unknown heroes, because there are many. Many are the characters who experienced hellish torments before dying in the Nazi furnaces, and left no remnant behind for their family. Only a few were left from each town, as the poet said: two from a city and one from a family. And a sacred duty rests on those left to perpetuate their names lest their memory be forgotten forever. Because it is only by chance that this was their bitter fate, and we were privileged to be among the founders and builders of our longed-for homeland.

In referring to the map of Great Poland - Tyszowce was maybe a small dot of no importance from a strategic and economic point of view. In terms of the history of Poland, the town is mentioned during the time of General Stefan Czarniecki, and the agreement that was signed after the war of that time under the name "Confederation-Tyszowce." For me, in the early 1920s, Tyszowce was the whole wide world. This muddy town, in an area of streams, was located in an environment of forests and pastures, fields and gardens. In most months of the year, the mud reached up to your knees. There were still no roads in the town, transportation with the immediate surroundings was conducted by horse and wagon services, and the train passed about seven kilometers from the town.

Here, inside small, and incredibly clean wooden houses with no electricity, water, and minimal sanitary arrangements - a traditional Jewish life was conducted for many generations. Our great poet, Y. L. Peretz, came here at the beginning of the 20th century to commemorate his heroes, the common Jews who woke up before sunrise to worship God. By the light

[Page 171]

of a kerosene lantern, they walked slowly to the first *minyan* in Beit HaMidrash and from there to their daily work, someone to the store, someone to the small industry, or somebody to the neighboring village with his merchandise.

There were no wealthy men in the town, but there was no lack of scholars, learned men, and rabbis. Beit HaMidrash was not only a place of prayer and the study of a page of Gemara, but also a meeting place for every public activity in the town. Here was the parliament and the shaping of public opinion for every public and local event. Here the public activists fought for their influence with all the tools at their disposal. A famous rabbi came here to inspire his Hassidim and to sit with them. And on another day of the week a famous cantor arrived. The town's synagogue was known for its beauty throughout the area and served as a public center for the Jewish way of life in the town. This is how Jewish life went on in peace and harmony for many years.

The shocks that befell the Jewish world after *Meora'ot Tarpat*[1] and the rise of anti-Semitism in Poland didn't skip Tyszowce. The feeling of financial insecurity and the many question marks - what next? remained unanswered. The mature youth began to seek their own way. A number of youth left for the big city to learn a trade. A small number began to study trades in Tyszowce that were in demand in the town, and a large number, who finished school or part of it, didn't find a job at all. The echoes of the Hebron and Safed riots in Israel directed the attention of the boys and girls to a new direction - Eretz Yisrael.

As on the waves of a fierce storm, the magic word, Eretz Yisrael, appeared in every remote Jewish town. A great wave of Jewish youth movements, in every town and city rebelled against conventions, and it seemed that the time was ripe for a revolution. In place of Beit HaMidrash appeared the club that gave an outlet to the energy that had accumulated within the youth. The [older] Jews didn't easily accept this phenomenon of boys and girls walking together without a head covering, the walks on Saturdays in the great outdoors, the departure for summer camps and more. However, many, deep in their hearts, gave a blessing to their children who might, one day, pave a road for themselves.

The club of Poalei Zion Right "Freiheit" attracted, as if by a magic wand, masses of boys and girls into the walls of a shack to frame the movement "Freiheit- Skoiten" ["The Free Scouts"]. Here, within the walls of the shack, they spent most of their free time learning the basics of the movement, Hebrew, and information about Israel. Here the boys and girls absorbed the atmosphere of Eretz Yisrael, and here they held public trials on various subjects. Here dramatic talents were discovered, which manifested themselves in independent performances within the walls of the movement and in our celebrations, and the choir was well known in the town. The library also grew. On Saturday nights the branch was noisy like a beehive. The echoes of the singing and the dancing of the *hora* echoed from one end of the town to the other. Here in the shack, the youth discovered themselves, and the movement gave them a purpose in life.

Tyszowce was blessed by the number of movement activists, who devoted their time and energy to this sacred work, among them many who are no longer alive, such as: M. M. Schaler, Yitzhak Landau, Aharon Ang, Eliezer Klenberg, Tuvia Wachsbaum and others. And may they live long, Pinchas Landau, Hersh Kizel, Shlomo Roth and others, and among the young generation: Pesach Kreiner, Yechiel Haser and others.

With maturity many groups moved to the HeHalutz[2] framework in order to leave for *Hakhshara*[3] and fulfillment. In the *Hakhshara* kibbutzim, the Tishevitsers were a united group. Small Tyszowce of that time, which was poor in famous personalities, who

[Page 172]

didn't appear in newspapers headlines, was blessed with good youth who found their place in each social and public circle. It was a melting pot for us, a rooted movement for human values in society. This Tyszowce no longer exists. Gentile Tyszowce harassed its sons, its Jewish builders, for hundreds of years and in active partnership with the Nazi oppressor, it vomited them.

We will not weep for its destruction, only for the desecration of human dignity. We will condemn the young lives that were deprived through no fault of their own, and the loved ones who were sacrificed in the Holocaust and died for the sanctification of God's name.

We will repeat and remember to the last generation - Remember! what Amalek did to you!

And this is a crime that will be remembered forever.

The committee of Poalei Zion United and the Zionist-Socialist Party in Tyszowce

Translator's footnotes:

1.   *Meora'ot Tarpat* (lit. Events of 5689) was a series of demonstrations and riots in late August 1929 in which a longstanding dispute between Muslims and Jews over access to the Western Wall in Jerusalem escalated into violence

2.   HeHalutz (lit. "The Pioneer") was a Jewish youth movement that trained young people for agricultural settlement in Eretz Yisrael.

3.   *Hakhshara* (lit. "Preparation") the term is used for training programs in agricultural centers in which Zionist youth learned vocational skills necessary for their emigration to Israel.

[Page 173]

The Purim Ball that did not Happen

by Menya Goldman (Borg) (Israel)

Translated by Moses Milstein

The membership card of the Y. L. Peretz library that was found, with the signatures of the chairman and secretary, Mendl Singer, and Yosl Shtengl, z"l, and the date of January 1938,was hidden until now by Shmelke Kizl as a souvenir. It reminds me of certain moments that I can see as clearly as if they were living occurrences, but unfortunately, are a deadly reality of our destroyed shtetl, and cultural institutions such as the Y. L. Peretz library.

Externally, the house where the library was located was no different from the other houses in the city other than having big arc lamps whose light spilled out into the street. But as soon as you went through the door,

[Page 174]

you could see at once that this was a library, and on coming in, you felt that you were in a cultural institution. The atmosphere here was more serious than in other party locales. In the first room, a bookcase full of Yiddish, Hebrew, and Polish books. All the works of the classics of Yiddish literature like Mendele, Sholem Aleichem, Peretz, and others. Books of a literary nature, and books about science. It had everything.

In the second big room–a reading hall. On the tables all the daily newspapers, weeklies, and journals. There were also two big catalogues. And most importantly it was always packed full of readers, regular readers and occasional. One of the regular readers was Hershl Hantz, z"l. He would always be found sitting at the same spot bent over a book or a newspaper.

The library also had a radio which was a rare thing in the shtetl. The radio was purchased with the fees that the members levied on themselves in 1936. In the heat of the Spanish civil war you could find the membership director, Wolf Getz, z"l, next to the radio. He was responsible for taking care of the radio, and turning it on at exactly the time for the daily news. (*Djenik*).

Some times the radio did not do its job because of some problem. But the devoted listeners would still sit around it even thought it was silent…The accounts of the library were always in a deficit, because the membership fees of 30 groshen a month were not enough to cover all the expenses, especially in winter when the library had to be heated and everything was so expensive.

So the board had to wrestle with the deficit and find ways to carry on, and cover the deficit. The only method was to organize events like, for example, a Purim ball, and invite a lot of guests with the calculation that it would bring in a certain amount of money.

In January 1938, it was decided to organize a Purim ball. They voted in a special committee with Mendl Singer Brush as chairman. Among the youngest on the committee were the writer of these lines, and my friend, Zisl Worzl, z"l. Our job was to write invitations from a prepared list. We were very happy with our task, and fulfilled it with complete accuracy. The frequent assemblies, meetings, discussions, votes, interested us greatly until the ball was accepted.

The invitations were sent via a courier, because we wanted to avoid paying postage, and also for the security of knowing that everyone received their invitation.

[Page 175]

All the invited members and sympathizers were also asked to bring a present to the ball, aside from the admission price. Certain designated people were selected for this. One of them, I remember, was Feige Pelz, z"l.

Everything was going along very smoothly. We, the young, experienced the feeling of satisfaction that we could accomplish something, and that we would be part of such a thing as a Purim ball. One evening, the hall already decorated, and the last preparations underway for the ball, a policeman showed up and told us that the administration had to go see the commandant at the police station. Everyone present froze in that moment. Some of the members said that it was nothing, probably only to clear up some matters to do with the ball. There were others, however, who held that the matter was not so simple, and there was a danger that the ball would not take place, and even worse…knowing that the commandant, Radiszewski, was capable of anything. The scoundrel was well known to the Jewish population in the city, always living at the expense of the Jews. He used to buy things, eat and drink, and demand that it be pout on his account, which he never paid.

And when he was approached for help for a Jew who had been assaulted by a hooligan in the middle of the street, this same commandant would ask with a smile, "Beaten, or killed?" If merely beaten, it must have been by a certain drunk. This according to him was a natural event. From such a personage, we could expect the worst.

The police commandant informed the board that two weeks from then, the library must no longer exist, for the reason that communist activities were taking place there.

In an oppressive mood, full of sorrow and pain all the gathered presents were returned, and the long-awaited ball did not take place.

The books and the inventory were given to the Poalei Zion party, and one evening the police came and sealed the doors of the library, which was actually non-partisan.

The arc lights were extinguished together with the cultural center, the Y. L. Peretz library in Tishevits.

The reading hall was in darkness, like an omen of a portending darkness, and the coming devastation and destruction of the entire shtetl set on fire by the Poles, and burned to the last Jewish house after the entry of the Germans.

Only the sad memories remain, and a silent witness–the surviving membership card.

———————

[Page 176]

A Charming Town
(Reflections)

In memory of my grandfather
R' Shraga Feivel and his dear family members

by Michael Drori (Finger)

Translated by Sara Mages

I often debated how, and in what manner, to give adequate expression to the feelings in my heart, to the feelings in my emotions, for the charming town that once was and is no more…

This town was typical of many towns in Poland before the Second World War. Nevertheless, it seems to me that there was something special in Tyszowce, so typical of the special virtues of its inhabitants…

Although I am not a native of this place, I visited it many times during my beautiful and pleasant childhood years. I visited it and spent days and hours there that, in no small part, had a decisive influence on the course of my life. This is not just a matter of nostalgia, because I am often attacked by deep longings for the grandeur, supremacy and grace, which remained etched in my memory (although quite a few years have passed since then)…

Sometimes, for many reasons, we tended to describe the town (any town) as a place of poverty, degeneration and compassion. We also often told our children about the lives of sorrow and deprivation, the fate of the residents at that time - irregular livelihoods, idle life, lack of content and future - in one word: nothing!

However, for the sake of the historical truth that we are commanded to instill in our children and future generations, we do an injustice to ourselves, and to Jewish towns in the Diaspora, if we describe the town and its natural and human landscape in this way.

It seems to me that I am unable to describe a sincere and true description of that good, pure human spirit, in which the residents of this town lived, grew up and were educated in. The social life of this town was based on several charitable institutions: *Gemilut Hasadim, Linat Tzedek, Bikur Cholim, Hachnasat Kalla*, etc.

Love of mankind, honest love, real and thorough - these, and many more, are the exalted and beautiful qualities that were found in this town. How much magic could be felt in its narrow streets, and its low houses, with the setting of the sun when the Shabbat atmosphere was felt in every corner… Its inhabitants, who most days were concerned with their livelihood, were filled with sorrow and grief from their gentile neighbors who placed a real heavy burden on their lives, and yet, at the beginning of Shabbat, or on the eve of the holidays, you could really feel the holiness…

[Page 177]

Serenity was felt in the air. Jews, among them quite a few, struggled hard to earn a little money to provide food for their family members. Jews on whose foreheads were seen deep wrinkles, young Jews whose hair had turned prematurely white - all of them knew how to raise and live a human Jewish life, full of content, full of inner happiness, and belief in the redemption of man and the Jews.

These are just reflections from that beautiful town, charming and beautiful, where my grandfather and grandmother, may they rest in peace, had lived.

I remember the Hasidic melodies that emerged from the *shtiblach* on weekdays, like on Holy Days, or the special melodies that accompanied the study of the Gemara in *Oi,amar Rava* [Thus, Rava said] *Oi,amar Hanina* [Thus, Hanina said]… How pleasant it was to stand behind the wall of the Beit HaMidrash and listen to the special melody that penetrated the depths of the heart, and reached the roots of the roots, and the depth of the soul…

Shaul Tschernihovski, the greatest Jewish poet, emphasizes in a wonderful way the years of childhood that absorb into them the events whose influence is sometimes decisive in man's path.

Man is but…

> "Man is but the soil of a small country,
> Man is but the imprint of his native landscape,
> Only what his ear picked up is still fresh,
> Only what his eye has absorbed is not yet sated to see,
> Everything that a child encountered on a dewey path,
> Hesitating, tripping over every lump and heap of earth,
> While secretly in his soul and without his knowledge, an altar

Is set, on it he will burn incense each and every day
To the Queen of Heaven, to the star and zodiac;
But with the passage of time, and in a war of self-existence,
And the scroll of his life is interpreted-
And they came one by one, and he will discover the meaning
Each letter and letter and symbol and symbol all that follows,
Which were engraved on her at the beginning of her covenant -
Man is but the imprint of his native landscape."

And again: I cannot free myself from that home saturated with warmth, the joy of life, manners, and a family bond that united such a beautiful framework, like the home of my grandfather, Rabbi Feivel, may he rest in peace.

Shabbat eve at my grandfather's house, the special Shabbat atmosphere, the Kiddush, the varied and special food and the songs, oh, the Shabbat songs, the very same wonderful melodies that are still playing in my heart…

And today, now that I have grown up and look back, again and again, I feel that in my approach to modern Israeli life, in search of my path after an educational orientation in intergenerational education, I take inspiration, among others, from those good days that are gone…

The chain has not yet been severed- it goes on and on, from then until today.

———

[Page 178]

The Funeral of the Young Yosl Sachar

by Moshe

Translated by Moses Milstein

If you could describe someone as energetic, high-spirited, and a go-getter, it would be Yosl.

His activities in the Poalei-Zion organization as member of the youth committee, and his taking part in the drama circle was a natural thing for him.

Part of the funeral for Yosl Sachar, z"l, in 1937

He was at first interested in the Yiddish program of the organisation. Something was not entirely clear to him. He was not satisfied because the youth of the left wing Poalei Zion and the communist youth were practically saying the same things. That's why there were times when he met with the communist youth in their illegal meetings, *massovkes*[1]. His open discussions with folks in the street reached the police, and they suspected him of belonging to the illegal communist organization. There were times when the police would come to the family home and conduct searches, especially on May 1st, looking for illegal literature.

Ultimately, Yosl came to the conclusion that the theories of Ber Borochow were the most correct and one had to fight for the realization of proletarian Zionism.

He felt too constrained in the shtetl. Looking for broader horizons, he went off to Rawa-Ruska. He worked as a tailor there. Later he fell ill. Being certain of his strong constitution, he, unfortunately, did not follow his doctor's orders. He returned to Tishevits terribly sick. In a very short time, he, a young man, passed away.

The whole shtetl attended his funeral. Everyone mourned, young and old, religious and secular. Everyone rued his untimely death at 21 years of age.

Footnote:

1.   Collective gatherings in former USSR

[Page 179]

The Tishevits Klezmers

by Moshe

Translated by Moses Milstein

The Tishevits klezmers were not merely a randomly created group, but really a family.

Maybe that's why their music was so full of charm. Their playing at Jewish weddings, at wedding processions to the shul–where it was established–was a happy event in the shtetl.

Their delightful melodies were also heard at Sefer Torah processions, and Purim evenings where they used to go around playing at people's houses.

The social institutions also used to get the klezmer to play at the special events they would organize. Even the Christians treated them with respect and used to laud them: "The Buruches are the best klezmers," and used to hire the klezmer for their special national celebrations.

[Page 180]

The joy of their music is gone…

Everything has been silenced, The Tishevits klezmers are no more.

The Tishevits klezmers

[Page 181]

Yakov Szpiz z"l

by Dov Spiz

Translated by Sara Mages

Yakov Szpiz z"l was born in 1922 in Tyszowce to his parents, Arye and Rachel. He studied in *cheders*, in a Polish school, and also in a yeshiva in Ludmir. When he was fourteen he joined the "Dror" movement, and at the age of fifteen joined the *Hakhshara*[1] in Grochów near Warsaw.

Yakov Szpiz z"l

After two of his fingers were amputated in a work accident, he left the kibbutz for Warsaw where he worked as a furrier and continued his activities in the movement.

At the beginning of the Second World War, he escaped to the Russian occupation zone, and from there he was sent to work in the Northern Steppes. He was released after the Stalin Sikorski agreement and moved to Turkestan. He suffered greatly from the alienation of the Polish representatives to the surviving Jews, the citizens of their country, and from all the hardships of the war. He tried twice to cross the border from Russia to Persia in order to emigrate from there to Israel, but was returned to Russia.

After the war he joined the ranks of the Jewish refugees in Tashkent, and arrived in Poland with them. He immediately rejoined the "Dror" movement. For two years he worked in the Bericha Movement[2] and showed his abilities in difficult situations with the knowledge and unique qualities he acquired in Russia.

[Page 182]

In July 1946 he immigrated to Israel on the *Ha'apala*[3] ship "Biriah."

In Israel, he was among the first to volunteer for the Israel Defence Forces despite the defect in his hand. His notes on life in the army are vibrant with healthy humor. He participated in the conquest of Neve Ya'ar, Bethlehem, Zvulun, and the German Colonies in Lower Galilee. He attended the first artillery course in the Israel Defence Forces, graduated and was sent to the defense of the Jordan Valley.

He defended Kibbutz Degania Alef and Kibbutz Degania Bet. On May 18, 1948, 11 Iyar, he was wounded in the leg and abdomen defending the police station near Zemach. He ran to the Jordan River and continued by swimming. He was picked up by a military boat, was brought to a hospital in Tiberias, and died on May 22, 1948.

He was buried in Tiberias and in 1950 was transferred to eternal rest in the Nahalat Yitzhak Cemetery.

May his memory be blessed.

Translator's footnotes:

1.   *Hakhshara* (lit. "Preparation") the term is used for training programs in agricultural centers in which Zionist youth learned vocational skills necessary for their emigration to Israel.
2.   The Bericha (lit. "Escape") Movement was the underground organized effort that helped Jewish Holocaust survivors escape post–World War II Europe to the British Mandate for Palestine in violation of the White Paper of 1939.
3.   *Ha'apala* (lit. "Ascension") was the clandestine organized immigration of Jews, most of whom were refugees escaping from Nazi Germany, and later Holocaust survivors, to Mandatory Palestine between 1920 and 1948. It is also commonly called *Aliya Bet*, "Bet" being the first letter of the word *bilti-legalit* which means "illegal."

Rucheleh Vakerman z"l

by Pesheh Sachar

Translated by Moses Milstein

Who did not now Rucheleh Vakerman (Fleese). She was quiet by nature, yet everyone knew and valued her, and she was loved by everyone.

Those who knew her well emphasized her active participation in the social work of Poalei-Zion.

In Israel she was always involved with Tishevits people. When Tishevitsers arrived on Aliyah, she would seek them out. Unfortunately, death took her from us in her youth. Honor to her memory!

[Page 183]

Rajfer Zvi, Arye Klenberg z"l, Yosef Sarar z"l

Rajfer Zvi

The soldier Zvi
Son of Yosef and Miriam
Born on 10 Heshvan 5668
(5.11.1927)
Fell on 14 Sivan 5708 (21.6.1948)
Buried in Nahalat Yitzhak
Cemetery

Yosef Sarar z"l

Was a member of our organization's audit committee. He passed away on Saturday 22.11.1969 at the age of 46.

Arye Klenberg z"l

Arik was born in Kiryat Haim on 13.4.1942. Served in the army in the Navy on the ship "Haifa," sent for reserve service on the ship "Eilat" on which he lost his life in an Egyptian missile attack on 17 Tishrei 5728, 21 October 1967.

[Page 186]

In the Days of Horror

Tears

by Sholom Stern Montreal, Canada

Translated by Moses Milstein

In Poland the country
In Jewish cities and shtetlach
The Shechina[1] rested.
The river turned blue–a transparent mirror.
Green was the footpath, the open plain
And the serene grassy hill.
Yearning, cozy hometowns nestled in the
forest.
In spring, the lilac branches caressed
like warm fingers.
Affectionate joy shone on the meadows
Around the shepherd's tent.
From pure Jewish hearts, from students and
friends
Light and love, courage and faith welled up.

Now, the sun in smoke–a glowing brick.
The Jews lie murdered on their doorsteps.
Signs of horror: a bloodied child's cradle,
Rusty bolts, shredded East drawings[2].
And the Shechina flutters with broken
wings,
Sobs over the holy sacrifice.
And my tears flow over the great
devastation.

Translator's footnotes:

1.   The Divine Presence
2.   A hand drawn sign posted to indicate east, the direction of prayer, in the house

[Page 187]

Woe is Me

by Sholom Stern Montreal, Canada

Translated by Moses Milstein

The shtetl incinerated.
Pieces, holy parchment–
Frozen, Jewish hands.
A drunk Nazi dances in Moishe Shmuel's *kitl*[1],
He covers a bloody fleck with the statute board
Of the Jewish worker's library.

The decree fell on me too,
To be annihilated by the Nazi murderers.
No one should know of my body.
At my head there must not be
Any tombstone.
Who then annulled
The evil decree for me?
From whose merit?
For what reward?
Maybe I was not worthy at all,
For the same to happen to me?
God, woe is me
For such mercy
For such protection!

Footnote:

1.   White linen coat worn on holidays

———

[Page 188]

Watchman, What of the Night?

by Ish Ya'ir[1] Montreal, Canada

Translated by Moses Milstein

Magic, magic, magician;
Fog, froth, from goblets.
Demons crow on the chimneys;
The whirlwind weeps in hovels.

The moon spins a silvery net,
And sleeps on foggy down.
The devil dances a minuet
With a Jewish child's skeleton.

Ghetto-Poland writhes in fever.
The goy drunk with hate.
He goes to the plain
The nobleman on a hunt–
A Jew fleeing from the flame.

Watchman of the night of horror,
How can you bear it?
God rocks Yankele in his cradle
The baby carriage bloodied.

Rolling wagon;
Wheel on clods
The whip cracks
A curse
From the hut there blinks
A frightened eye–
A corpse–the *balagoleh*[2]

What do you mean, Poland,
False snake,
We abandoned you?
My blonde beard,
Your corn in the field;
In the wind
My voice protests.

Watchman, watchman on the watch
Do you also hear the protests?
God beweeps Yankeleh
In horrible dawns.

From the well–
My brother's eye;
Your river
My blood floods over.
My fear chokes
Your blue night,
Until god pries open
The graves…

Watchman, watchman of the night,
What can you tell us?
--God cuddles Yankeleh;
day is already rising.

Translator's footnotes:

1. Pseudonym of Dr. Israel Stern
2. Carriage driver

———

[Page 190]

These I Shall Remember

by Avi Goel – Montreal (Canada) (Hene Shtern-Marder)

Translated by Jerrold Landau

Blood, my blood, do not cool ! ! !
Do not silence the nights of horrors –

Carry the blind away to dream's darkness–
To light and evil, to Greece, Rome, and the
bonfire ! ! !

A desolate plague on the plains of Poland,
That destroyed my home and child ! ! !
A conflagration before the Germans, the vile
ones,
Who devoured my life and soul !!!

Accursed be the nations,
Who burnt my steps in vain,
Who want to wipe out my name,
My holy home is destroyed and desolate ! ! !

In the name of the race of the slaughterers –
I render an accounting for the violence –
For the shame of generations and murder –
For disgrace in the conflagration of the exile !!!
– – –

———

[Page 191]

Destruction of Tishevits

by Berish Finger (Israel)

Translated by Moses Milstein

On September 1, 1939, the dark clouds descending on Jews everywhere, especially on the Jews of Poland, quickly enveloped the Jews of Tishevits. Every Tishevits Jew was consumed with deathly fear by the question:

Berish Finger and his tragically murdered wife

Where to run to? On that day, many Polish cities were sadistically bombed, among them also Tomaszow. Several Jews were killed, and some wounded. Among them, Moishe Frieder and (Oizer Bicher's son-in-law). The panic became

[Page 192]

unbearable. In fear of being bombed, the whole shtetl fled to the farmers on the outskirts leaving everything behind unguarded. It was the second day of Rosh Hashanah. The next day, a squadron of airplanes appeared over Tishevits, and dropped several bombs on the police station. The result was that 13 Christians were killed but not one Jew, even though the whole Ben Zvi Adler family was nearby. This apparently did not please the Tishevits antisemites, and early the following day, i.e. Rosh Hashanah[1], 9:00 o'clock in the morning, about 20 Christians with bottles of benzene in their hands set the whole shtetl on fire from one end to the other, so that only 10-15 Jewish homes were left standing. Even the courtyard beyond the bridge, where Shloime Landau and others lived, was partly burned. It was an indescribable blow to everyone. From all their possessions they were left with only what they had managed to carry away when they fled to the Christians; everything else was burned. Having no other choice, every Jew had to arrange accommodations with Christians, paying large sums for rent. For one small room with no comforts, they had to pay 50 Zlotys per month (10 dollars a month)! It's hard to imagine how the poorer people made out, not having the means to pay such high prices. In addition, winter was approaching. Understandably, food was also a problem. Slowly, they began to feel the sting of hunger. Two days later, the Nazi murderers entered Tishevits. When they were told the reason for the fire, they said, "Pity that all the Jews were not destroyed with the houses." No Jews were to be seen anymore in the streets. Everyone hid. Suddenly, several days later, came the news that the Germans were leaving and the Russians were coming. The news alone was enough for the Jews to come out of their hiding places. And when the news was confirmed, quiet evening meetings took place, and the joy was boundless. The Germans left Yom Kippur Eve. The Polish military arrived via the Hrubieszow road, in an exhausted state. On Yom Kippur the Polish army fled any way they could, and at 2:00 AM the Soviets arrived.

The Jews went out into the streets. Joy like this had not been felt in a long time. But unfortunately, the joy did not last long. Not even three whole weeks. As soon as we heard the terrible news

[Page 193]

that the Soviets were pulling back to the river Bug, and the Germans were returning to Tishevits, the panicked frenzy returned. Whoever knew someone on the other side of the Bug fled immediately. The majority remained in Tishevits reasoning that if they had to die, it was better to do so at home, because at that time there was a great flight of Jews to the other side of the Bug, and nobody would let you into their house. There were also a lot of epidemics caused by the mass of homeless.

The Germans entered Tishevits for the second time after the holidays. After a few days, they left again, abandoning the shtetl, so that the Jews could again go freely about their business. Trade and movement picked up again. Occasionally a vehicle with Germans would show up, and Jews would disappear from the streets again. The Germans would spend a couple of hours in town, and then leave, and the Jews would surface again. February 1, 1940 the Polish police arrived in Tishevits, the same police as before the war, but with a Volksdeutsche commander. As it turned out, they also expected to be bribed, and the Jews gave them more than they asked for. They created a Christian community with Zarembski as "voit" (city chairman).

We were soon shocked by the terrible news that the Germans were driving the Jews from Chelm and Hrubieszow to the Russian border, and that the entire route was covered with Jewish corpses. From three to four thousand Jews fell on the road from Chelm to Sokol. The remainder, in similar numbers, were driven by armed Germans across the Bug to the Russian side. Many drowned in the Bug, and those who managed to get to the other side, half frozen, were met with gunfire from the Russians. When the Russians became aware of what was happening, they sent an inquiry to the Kremlin. The reply came that they were to be sent back to the German side, and that's what happened. Seven to eight thousand Jews were expelled from Chelm and Hrubieszow, and between 1500 to 2000 returned.

After this saga, my brother-in-law, Avrem'chl Eitl, determined to run away to wherever he could. This plan did not succeed. Only Avrem'chl and his family, and my daughter, Manye, managed to escape to Rawa-Ruska. The rest of my family and I stayed in my brother-in-law's-house. He had a house in the suburbs opposite the orchard. The house belonged to Mattes Weintraub. I brought along a homeless family from Warsaw. We tried to normalize things. The voit, Zarembski, quickly reestablished normal life and took good care of the Jewish population so that no injustice would occur. Together with

[Page 194]

Moishe Ginsberg, Chaim Boxenboim, and Zarembski, we created a business that went quite well. At that time, we undertook to create a philanthropic committee with the participation of the following people: Yehuda Leib Feller, Moishe Lerner, Abraham Laks, Moishe Motl Shalier, Moishe Shmuel Shtengl, Bentche Adler, Ephraim Zuker, and I. Because I had a good residence, all the work was done at my place.

At one meeting Zarembski gave us an allotment of twenty wagonloads of wood to be distributed to poor Jewish families. The wood was a thousand times more important than bread. We received the 20 wagonloads on more than one occasion. That's how we managed to solve the wood problem for the poor population. At the same time, I proposed taking the bread ration cards from the better off, and giving each of the poor a double portion. We also took care of finding some fatty spreads with the bread. Every well off person contributed weekly to this endeavor. This carried on until Purim, 1940. Around this time, Zarembski came running hurriedly by my house, and yelled through the window that he had something of importance to share with the Jewish population, and that I should meet him at 6:00 PM with some 20 friends. The whole shtetl soon heard of this, and various rumors began to circulate. Some good and some contrary. Punctually at 6:00 he arrived, and with a glass of alcohol for him, and butterflies in the stomach for us, he informed us that we had to establish a Judenrat of 12 people with me as chairman. He had to telephone the *landrat* in Zamosc the following morning, and inform them that the Judenrat had been set up in Tishevits. Instinctively, and perhaps against my will, I stated that I did not accept the position. No matter how much the voit and the others tried to persuade me, I refused to accept. The voit turned to Ephraim Zuker, and Leibish Gelber, previously kehila members. They replied that if Finger would not accept, neither would they. The shtetl immediately went into an uproar. The wives of the assembled arrived to take them home. It was known that the voit was a partner of my brother-in-law in the brickyard, and now my partner, so that I had to meet with him several times a day. The shtetl figured that if I didn't want to undertake this, Zarembski must have told me it was a bad thing. The matter became quite serious. I ignored the fact that some of the participants approached me with a finished list, almost entirely of Zionists, if I would only take it on. But after a discussion with my wife

[Page 195]

I gave a categorical no. So Zarembski sat down and made up his own list nominating 12 people. Since I was not on the list, everyone was certain that it was not a good thing. Finally, at 3:00 AM, we reached an agreement that every shtibl or association should delegate 6 people, and throw the names in a ballot box, and draw lots. At this point, a boy arrived from Zileh Zuker with a message for Zarembski that he voluntarily accepts the post of chairman of the Judenrat. Understandably, we straightaway accepted it. There were over 100 men in my house, and we immediately took to the work. The result was the following: from the Husiatyn shtibl, Issachar Helrubin, and Abraham Yakov Kornblum; From the Radziner shtibl, Zileh Zuker and Aharon Med; from the Trisker shtibl, Matisyahu Blachman; from the handworkers, Yosef Vinder, Emmanuel Blecher, Nuteh Schneider–Mendl Tuvieh's son-in-law, and a German Jew, Fishleber, and from the Zionists, Shloime Kreiner as secretary with no duties. Altogether 10 people. First thing in the morning, the Judenrat held a meeting, and they rented a place from Reuven Issac Kopel.

Some weeks passed quietly. Finally the Polish police with a German commandant arrived. Obviously Kotlitzki was also present among the police, and he quickly taught them how to extort money from the Jews. Shushan Purim 1940, he disguised himself with a mask, and with an accomplice, he entered Israel Aharon Eitel's with the intent of robbery. At the time he was living at a certain Wengzenovitch's near the [Catholic] church. Yosef Eilboim happened to be there with a sum of money he was going to sell to Eitel. He tried to prevent them from searching him, and they shot him straightaway. He was the first martyr in Tishevits.

Then several more quiet weeks passed, until one Sunday, around May 5th, three Gestapo came from Zamosc, along with a Jew, a certain Goldman. He also worked for the Gestapo. They drove straight to the Judenrat, and demanded English textiles for three suits, and three pairs of boots. In about three hours it was done, and when they were given the goods, they said that Tuesday they would have to provide 150 Jews for labor in Zamosc. They tried to negotiate with the Jew to provide only 100. They finally settled on 120, and they drove off. The Judenrat immediately called on 50 of the better off Jews. The Judenrat was in a Christian house on Ostrow. I was also present, and they decided to hire volunteers to work. They would pay whatever they asked for. The 120 Jews showed up by 12 at night. The 50 well-off Jews who were there,

[Page 196]

gave increasingly large sums of money, so that every worker received a month's worth in advance. There was about 7500 Zl in the kitty. That was a colossal sum of money. This dragged on until 4:00 AM. As we were going home, after just a few meters, we saw trucks and taxis with Germans. In the blink of an eye, the whole shtetl was surrounded by Germans shouting, "*Juden heraus!*" Within 20 minutes, the whole shtetl of men and women were standing at the plaza by the school in their underwear. There are no words to describe what I saw then, even if no one died. They chose 150 Jews including me. The rest had to sing and dance for over an hour in their underwear in the street in the view of thousands of Poles who came running. They did not touch the Judenrat, and they had the right to exclude their children and near ones.

In my car were Gershon Shtuden with his 18 year old Leibl, Leib (Ronieh's) Eilboim, Moishe Shmuel Shtengl, Moishe Frieder, Israel Kalechstein, Ephraim Zuker with his son Yerachmiel, Dovid'che Garber and his two sons, Moishe Motl Shalier, and others. The people really hurt me with their words. Why had I spoiled such a good plan like being in the Judenrat? Moishe Motl was on my side, and said that we are better off here than in the Judenrat. We have not yet seen the end. They drove us to Zamosc to the *prochownia* and they told us to recite *vidui*, because we were soon going to be shot. We also encountered Jews from Shebreshin, Zamosc, Tomaszow, Komarow, and Bilgoraj totaling about 800 men. The crying was huge. The abovementioned Goldman played the greatest role in the beatings and haranguing. The highest Gestapo officer did not permit himself to do what Goldman did. He beat the women severely. It turned out that my decision not to be in the Judenrat was correct. On the 15th of July, this Goldman was shot like a dog by his best friend, and we could relax a little. The story that we were going to be shot, turned out to be a lie. We were divided into two camps. Half went to the barracks in Zamosc opposite the cinema; the other half was sent to Bialobrzeszin, 12 km from Zamosc. The work consisted of renovations. We were transported every day through Volksdeutsche with song. The work was not hard. Then the good times began

[Page 197]

from the Judenrat in Tishevits. First of all, our wives demanded from the Judenrat the return of the money that was given to hire workers that evening. They did not return the money and gave no explanation. After that, our wives demanded that, after one month, the Judenrat send other workers. At first they agreed and prepared a list of people, but later it turned out to be a ruse by the Judenrat, because why send people to Zamosc and receive nothing in return, when they could raise as much money as they wanted from those not willing to go. We became aware that every day there were scandalous things happening to our wives and parents on the part of the Judenrat who couldn't have cared less. The greater the scandal, the more money they extorted from those staying behind. Finally, around Tisha B'Av, there was a partial end to this also. Jews were being forced into labor all over Poland. Tishevits Jews were also captured and sent to Belzec on the Polish-Russian border to dig 10-meter ditches under the direction of the German Jew-murderer, Rolf. They also brought Jews from Otwock, Lublin, and other places, altogether about 500 Jews. They created a camp in Tishevits. The camp was located in Moishe Dovid'ch's mill. They worked at regulating the flow of the river Huczwa. At that time, my wife, and Bentche Adler learned from the Zamosc Judenrat that one could negotiate our being transferred to the camp at Tishevits. In brief, the matter cost 15,000 Zl and on October 15th we were in Tishevits, almost at home, because every day we had to go to work, but we could eat and sleep at home. We breathed a little more freely. The Judenrat was not happy. Some of us were determined to get revenge, and demanded the return of the money, but we decided to wait. We worked like that by the water until January 15, 1941. Then we were sent to help build a road from Tishevits to Laszczow along with Austrian and German soldiers. We worked day and night, 12-hour shifts. Pesach, the road was finished and the German army began moving towards the Russian border. There were so many soldiers passing through day and night, we were certain the Germans were out to conquer the whole world. People were beginning to fall. Two Jews from Otwock were shot for supposedly trying to escape, Isaac Kopel for hiding a Jew from the camp, Yakov Misheh Geber for being out 10 minutes after curfew, a Jew from Laszczow-met coming early from Laszczow. We began to feel

[Page 198]

the end was approaching. When the war with Russia began on June 22, 1941, everyone was convinced that our days were numbered, disregarding the fact that during the "good" days of their marching on Russia, they had forgotten a little about the Jews. Our fate was sealed. The situation of the poorer population was unbearable. Cases of death by starvation were seen. The previous philanthropic organisations appealed to the Judenrat to restart our work without requiring anything of the Judenrat, and received a negative reply. It is worth mentioning here that 10 days after we were taken to the camp in Zamosc, a German police detachment and murderers arrived in Tishevits. My home appealed to them. So they threw out my wife and children. It was not even possible to get the hidden merchandise out which is still probably lying there and rotting to this day. Notwithstanding the fact that they moved to Mendeleh Finger's gated house a year later, I was still forbidden to return to my residence.

The German police required 30 people a day for labor. A lot of people went to farms to work. A work permit like that cost 3,000 Zl. I also had one of those permits. All the money went to the Judenrat. At the same time, the Jewish police was established: Meyer Shek, commandant, and policemen Dovid Leib Oifir–Betsalel Rimers's son, Melech Shteper, and Heni Lozer, Wishniver's son. Their job was to ensure that the Jews obeyed the Judenrat and the Germans' orders. If not, there was trouble. They did not stop at any punishment, including beatings and arrests. The jail for Jews was in a cellar. The gendarmerie was very brutal. Killings at every turn. People were shot for trivialities. Moishe Bashister and his daughter were shot for being found with a little bit of merchandise. Mendl Tsvilich for nothing, just because. Feivel Stein's boy for telling someone the Germans were coming. Leib Shmeis because he did not chop wood properly at the gendarmerie, or for stealing eight empty beer bottles. Berish Gelbert, and Moishe Stickendreier's sons, both eighteen-year-old boys, for not cleaning the horse stalls well enough. A certain brutal Schultz distinguished himself in his shootings, killing thousands of Jews, Jews from our neighborhood. While we were sweeping the roadway, a girl near me with the name of Shalut, Ephraim Shalut's sister, was shot because he didn't like the way she was sweeping.

[Page 199]

The days dragged on in this manner until about February 1942 when an order was proclaimed that Jews must surrender all their furs. If even the smallest piece of fur was found after this order, the penalty would be death. Within eight hours, every piece of fur was in German hands. There were two martyrs here as well. Yakov Dovid Reichenberg (Shimon Reichenberg's father) for selling his fur to a Christian who turned it over to the Germans, and a woman, Leizer Tillis's wife, Aharon Tillis's sister for being found with a fur collar.

In March 1942, we were shocked to hear the news that they were building a crematorium in Majdanek and in other places. No one could imagine that people were capable of such a thing. We found out that the Lublin Jews were the first sacrifices. Lublin had about 70,000 Jews at the time. The Lublin Judenrat was required to supply 4000 Jews every night. This lasted for three weeks. At first, it was thought that they were being taken to work. We later learned that they had been taken to Belzec, to the crematoriums. We also learned that Jews from France, Belgium, Holland, with their rich baggage, and others were being transported to Belzec. They were well treated until Belzec, but when they arrived at Belzec they saw their true fate. After Lublin, the entire area around suffered the same fate. Pesach, Zamosc joined the others. There were 16,000 Jews in Zamosc then. Every day, they took 1000 Jews. We in Tishevits tried to delude ourselves that they were only concerned with the big cities, but after Zamosc, we felt sure that we would be next. We expected it to happen daily. We began to prepare hiding places. Unmarried people ran off to the forests. Three days before Shavuot, news reached us that, for example, the "voit," Michalkovitch, (Zarembski was in Dachau already) had arranged for 200 horse-drawn wagons for Shavuot. That made us certain that we were next. Shavuot night, the gendarmerie and two vehicles with Gestapo arrived. They sent for the oldest in the Judenrat, and the commandant of the police, and people like Zileh Zuker, Yosl Weiner, and Meier Shek and they were told, "Listen elders, we have come to "resettle" the Tishevits Jews. If it goes well, you will stay, otherwise, *'fast mal auf.'*" The elders immediately understood the significance. Soon about 100 SS arrived, and set to work. Some of the

[Page 200]

Judenrat, one Polish policeman, and 4-5 Germans set out in various sectors where the Jews lived. It was around 2:00 AM. With the knowledge of my boss, a Christian, I made a hiding place under the floor. In that hole were: me, my wife, my Moisheleh, a boy of seven, Moteleh and Nathan Shlafrik's wife and a girl, altogether 6 souls. After an hour of lying there we heard shouting in Polish, "Send out the Jews, or we will kill you and incinerate you." The voice was getting closer all the time. We began to hear shots. We also heard weeping. Not far from us, we heard a familiar voice, and then footsteps and knocking on my boss's door, and the call, "Yasha, otworz!" ("Yasha, open the door"). He opened the door. We recognized Meier Shek's voice saying to the boss, "Give up the Jews immediately, if you want to stay alive. Berish Finger and his family." The Germans said the same in German. The boss replied that he did not know where we had gotten to. As soon as it became dark, they disappeared. They opened the house, and looked in all the hidden places. After 15 minutes of searching they left. Then Yasha closed the gate and opened our hiding place, and asked us if we had heard what Meier Shek had said. If Shek knew that he had to give us up, then we had to leave here; if not, he was going to call the Germans. We all began to cry then. Yasha too broke into tears. This all took an hour in which he kept telling us to leave. This aktion ended with the shipment of 800 Jews to Belzec. My wife and Moteleh went into the fields and hid among the farm equipment, and my child and I hid in an empty stable. Moisheleh dressed like a goy, and went to the village, Mietkie, to a Christian we knew. At night I went to the village, Tyczow, where I found about 200 Jews from Tishevits. Abraham Laks had hidden them all there. (It must be mentioned here that because of this fact, about 6 weeks later, Abraham Laks and his 6 year old son were shot in Tyczow). Among those taken to Belzec were Moishe Yitzchak Dornfeld, Shoshanna Moteh Zilberman with Yenteleh, Gershon Shtuden and his daughter, the rav and his whole family. The following day, he and Moisheleh Lerner returned to Tishevits, but without their families. Almost all the families of the Judenrat had stayed in Tishevits because they had been in the Judenrat during the aktion. Hershel Braun and his family also remained behind. He managed to

[Page 201]

hide in the court of the nobleman from Mietkie, along with Shloime Kreiner and his family. It is worth pointing out that 90% of the detainees were tradesmen and of the poorer class, not having had the ability where and how to hide in the early minutes. Among the dead were Zileh Zuker, the chairman of the Judenrat, and his assistant, Yosl Weiner (for not having provided 30 liters of alcohol during the aktion). Actually, they had provided the alcohol distributing the bottles to each German that entered the Judenrat, but ran out when the officer arrived, and they were immediately shot. Henoch Zeigermacher, Moishe and Shmuel Malier, Azriel Hochgelernter and his family, Malkeh Bergman, Pinchas Zweig, Mendeleh and Abraham Finger, Dovid Zweig and his wife, Fradl Mendl Katsev and family, Isaak Eng and family, Moishe Janower and wife, Yankel Tzvilich and his wife, Liebeleh, and another Yankel Tzvilich. A butcher and his family, Dovid Waxenfeld and family, Shloime Shlegl, Malkeh Zweig, Eliyahu Zweig's mother–shot while lying in bed, Tevl Shteng and family, Yosef Hammer and family, and others. As the Jews were standing in the street prior to being taken away, the Dobuzek nobleman, Kaleczkawski, asked the Gestapo for 100 Jews to work in the fields in order to supply the Germans with wheat. After long negotiations, the Gestapo ordered him to pick 20 men. First he chose those he knew personally: Bentche Adler's two sons, Yehuda Leib Feller's son, Kohat Friedlander and a son, Feivel Stein's son, and others. The German police committed to supplying him with 20 women in the following two days, so that there were 20 Tishevits men and 20 women working for him, as well as some Jews from Laszczow. Two months later, some unknown people came and shot him. Who shot him was the topic of various theories, but the Jews working there felt more insecure. Two days later, twelve SS men came from Tomaszow and shot them on the spot. On that day, I, along with Yehuda Leib Feller, Yosef Zweig, Meir'tche Naster, Dutcheh Helfman, and a son, Gershon Shtuden and his Leibeleh, two Warsaw Jews, Yehoshua Sand and his family, were in Tyczow working at the kolejka[2]. When we returned we ran into the 12 SS who stopped us, but they didn't bother us. It seems that they had planned to shoot us, but they postponed it for a while, because staying overnight in Tishevits, they, along with the gendarmerie, surrounded the courtyard at dawn with the cry: "*Juden, heraus*!" and shot 49 Jews. Among those, Yudl Shtraser and his wife, Meir'tche Naster, wife and

[Page 202]

daughters, Dodl Helfman's wife and sister, Leibeleh Frost and family, Feivl Zeifenmacher and wife, Mendl Shohet's family, and others. They were ordered to be buried right by the city toilets, and that's where they were buried.

Wandering around the fields along with Moteh Fecher, Fishl Shpiz and their families, with nothing to eat or drink, no farmer allowing us to approach, we decided to surrender ourselves to the Germans. Because in the end we still believed they would take us to work. But a neighbor of mine, Panashkova, showed up on a bicycle and said she had been looking for me for several hours, and that it was quiet in town already. They had re-formed the Judenrat with the German Jew at the head, and the Germans were handing out ID cards for those still alive. We returned to the city. Coming to the new cemetery on Ostrow road, we came on the martyrs being carried to their burial. How did this transport look? On one wagon there were about 15 bodies, a head hanging out here, hands and feet from another there. You can't imagine how frightening this was. Seeing this picture, Itelleh Fecher fainted and was unconscious for a long time in spite of our attempts to revive her. Following the wagon were the Jewish police. We, the men, were immediately called on to help bury the martyrs. At the gravesite, the police ordered us to search all the belongings of the dead. Obviously they meant just the money, and we found not a small amount, and the police took it all. Simultaneously, the police went up to all the Jews coming from the villages, and told them that they must bring a certain amount of money within the next two hours, to pay for their ID cards. From me, they asked 4,000 Zl, which was a lot of money at the time. And I had to pay. About 600 Jews were still alive. We thought that those taken away were taken away to work, but our hearts told us that our near and dear ones were no longer among the living.

We collected 10,000 Zl to be paid to Christians to find out what had happened to our people. The Christians brought us some Jewish letters, signed with several Jewish names. This was forced out of those Jews still alive by the Germans. The Christians, the Polish murderers, did not tell us the truth. After two weeks of this near-death life, we were ordered to construct a ghetto in the courtyard near the bridge. This was impossible, because 4-5

[Page 203]

houses stood there. So the Germans allowed us to live with the Christians on Ostrow Street, and also in the few still standing houses like Reuben Kopel's, Leibish Shpiz, Dovid Waxenfeld and others. So half the Jews lived in one part, and half in the courtyard. Thus, the real end began because no Jew was allowed to leave the ghetto. People died of starvation. At the arrival of the Germans, the Judenrat had established a public kitchen, and the Judenrat from Zamosc supplied 4 sacks of rye flour, and a sac of beans every week. All we could cook was water and cabbage leaves. We tried with despair and heartache to do something for the poor but we encountered an opponent in the German Jew, Fishleber. He even threatened to turn us over to the Germans, so we were witnesses to the deaths of the hungry, and were prevented from helping. Some of the poor went to the forest to look for mushrooms and to beg for help from the farmers. But they would not help under any circumstances. Perl Krant gave her two children some mushrooms to eat. They died two hours later.

In the meantime, the Days of Awe for 1942 approached. No author can adequately describe that Rosh Hashanah. Rivers of tears, in the full sense of that word, were spilled by the few hundred Jews in Tishevits. Our hearts told us that the last days, or even hours, were upon us. And actually, a day after Rosh Hashanah, the tragedy of the above mentioned 49 people occurred, and they were all shot in a matter of 10 minutes at 5:00 am. Some of them were only wounded. Among them, Yonathan Hodes' sister, Chentche Leib Frost's wife. Yochanan lived on the Ostrow road. At 6:00 one evening, he was returning from visiting his sister, and he encountered a German, and was shot. At the same time, we received news from Lublin, Radom and other larger cities that there were no more Jews remaining there. We also received news that dozens of train cars were arriving at Belzec every day with Jews from the surrounding areas. On October 2nd, Fishleber came from Zamosc with the news that everything we were speculating about was a lie, because today the Judenrat in Zamosc had received provisions for several months. He had seen it himself. That was on a Thursday. The following morning, the ghetto in Zamosc was surrounded, and in the span of 5 hours, not one Jew was left in Zamosc. We learned this on Friday at noon. Consequently, we also prepared ourselves to leave. We began to consider going to the forest. But how do you go without weapons?

[Page 204]

These were not available for any sum of money. And what do you do with the small children and women? Winter was coming. Several days after the Zamosc liquidation, Sonja Shek suggested to me that we should go hide ourselves at a Christian she knew, a certain Kupitko, but I had to give away all that I possessed. The Christian would hide us in a cellar. Obviously I agreed, and we slowly moved over to the cellar, and the second day after walling us into the cellar, the predictable happened. About 500 Jews from Tishevits fled to the forest, and 70 Jews in all were transported to Belzec. Twenty-two Jews were killed on the spot, and some fled to Christians. After 3 days in the cellar, in a veritable living grave, the Christian threw a letter down telling us that the Polish police knew where we were, and after tonight we had to leave. Nine o'clock at night, he took apart the wall, and ordered us to go. The women and children broke out in tears. The Christian felt bad, asked us to wait, and left. He returned at 2:00 AM, and told us he had a place for 8 people, but we were 10. Two of us had to immediately leave the house. I sent word to Meyer Shek telling him that, from my family, I would leave, and he should choose someone from his family. His answer came that this was his goy, and that no one from his family would be leaving. I answered that I was going, and that anyone was welcome to voluntarily join me. My son, Moisheleh, immediately volunteered, and we both left the house without so much as a goodbye, so angry were we at Meyer Shek.

We cut across the highway and went into a narrow avenue. There we were stopped by a watchman who wanted to report us to the gendarmes, but after a lot of pleading, he let us go. As we were fleeing, we ran into deep mud on the Gwozak. I picked up Moisheleh, and we got out of the mud, and crossed the river Huczwa carrying him on my shoulders. We entered the Turkowice forest, and our running carried us to a Christian, Dirde Nos, in the village of Mietkie. Five in the morning, I let him know that I was in his *plevnik*. He immediately brought us warm clothing and hot food. After being there for three days, I proposed to him that he should make us a hiding place. Maybe we could survive the war here. The women in the family opposed this in no uncertain terms. I also had a lot of merchandise hidden with him. He proposed that I should spend the day in the forest and come to the stable at night

[Page 205]

where I would find food ready, and go back to the forest at dawn. Not having another choice, I agreed. After seven days, the Christian demanded that I leave. So one Sunday before dawn, Moisheleh and I left for the Mietkie forest. When we got there, it had already begun to be day. Suddenly we heard footsteps and voices. We quickly hid in the bushes. To our amazement we heard Yiddish being spoken, and we recognized Surehleh, Moishe Motl's, voice. We went straight over to her. She and Beile Spodek were searching for potatoes in the field. I informed them that it was too late for potatoes, so they went back taking us along. The condition of the Jews I found there was indescribable. Among them were Moishe Motl Shalier and his family, Beile Spodek and her two children, without a husband, Leib Eilboim and his wife Hadass, Cheivl Zeifenmacher's two little girls, Shloime Hirsh Spodek, a girl, Alter Kleiner's wife and a child. All of them in rags and barefoot, and without a groschen, without a piece of bread. I had with me several days supply of food. I immediately distributed it among them and stilled their hunger for a little while. They told me that on leaving the town, the Podbor Christians confiscated everything they had. From Moishe Motl, they took a fortune in money. Also from Leib Eilboim. Unable to witness their misfortune, Moisheleh and I went back to the Christian at night. I told him the whole story, and he took all the clothes he didn't need, filled two sacs with them, and we dragged it to the forest with the last of our strength. The joy was huge. Everyone got warmly dressed, including the little children, and everyone ate well. Then the question became, what next? After many suggestions, it was decided to build a bunker deep in the forest.

I promised to supply merchandise, ie, leather, to make food from as long as we were able to survive. At night, I went to the Christian again. We all had to worry about the provisions for the earlier bunker. Everyone agreed, and the next day we set out to make a bunker in a farther away, deeper in the forest. Everyone who was supposed to be in the new bunker came, 4 of the Zuker brothers, 2 young men from Turobin, exceptionally decent young men. They could do anything, and with luck, we moved into the new bunker.

Every day, at 7:00 am, Liebe Zweig and I gathered together the day's provisions and brought them to the old bunker. One day, while walking along with Shaul Zweig, we came across fresh footprints from Tishevits boots. We followed the footprints for about 3 km,

[Page 206]

and came across a small bunker, and found Abraham Pelz and his wife and 2 sons. They were very happy to see us. We got together often afterwards. When he learned that I was supporting 13 people for 10 weeks, he offered us 500 Zl. I did not want to take his money. I advised them not to stir from the bunker except in exceptional circumstances. One Thursday, Abraham Pelz comes to our bunker and tells us that he has a yohrzeit this coming Shabbes, and that he wanted to come to us on Shabbes to daven and say kaddish. We decided to also invite all the people from the earlier bunker and take the opportunity to have a drink together. We baked some fresh rolls at night. As day broke, while all the others were asleep, I was the only one up, and I heard shooting nearby. Everyone woke up grabbed something to eat with them, and we began to run. The result was the following: Abraham Pelz and his family were the first killed. A few people from our bunker remained. The tragedy was extraordinary. The bunker was burned and destroyed by hand grenades. We spent the whole day warming ourselves by the fire. It was freezing. At two am we separated. Moishele, two young men from Modryn, and I went to the Zukers. We stayed there until Purim. After Purim, we went to Hrubieszow. There, Moishele and I moved into an attic, and spent the summer there. We were captured before Rosh Hashanah and taken to Budzyn, and from there, to camps such as Majdanek, Auschwitz, and others, and we survived. That was just chance. Once in the camp, they took out 800 Jews for the 'selection', and they picked my Moisheleh out of the ranks. I took him back in, held him up so he would look taller, and that's how I saved him.

Tel Aviv, August, 1965

Note from the transcriber: I copied this from the pages of Berish Fingers notes. He became sick and was unable to write or describe further. Shmuel Hochtman of kibbutz Saad knows.

[Page 207]

Some answers from Berish Finger
(He is not able to write himself)

(He gave further clarifications to a few of my questions regarding some issues in his recollections which were written down by P. Landau–Y.Z.)

    1.   Why did I not agree to be a part of the Judenrat? Because I didn't want to work with the Germans. The members of the Judenrat did not want to create any aid funding for the poor needy except for two: they were Issachar Helrubin and Abraham Yakov Korinstein. They were the representatives of the Husiatyn shtibl. The Judenrat had a kitchen, but all they gave out was a little hot water. You can't live on just hot water. So we organized a committee of the following people: Yidl Leib Feller, Moishe Motl Shalier, Moishe Frieder, Moishe Lerner, and I. We raised money and bought products, and helped the needy with them. When the Judenrat found out about this, they threatened to shoot us like they shot Leib (Shamele's) Englstein at that time. As a result, we were forced to cancel the aid plans.
    2.   We were hidden by a farmer during the last aktion, me and my family, and Meir Shek and his family. One day the farmer arrived and told us that two people have to leave because there are too many people in the bunker. Meir Shek said that he didn't want to leave because the farmer was "his." Having no choice, my son and I left leaving my wife, Esther, with my other son to stay.

I knew a farmer called Jan Durce in the village of Mietkie. I kept my merchandise with him. He would occasionally sell some of it, and buy things he would bring to me in the forest where I was hiding with a lot of other Tishevits Jews who benefited from the food that I received.

From the forest, I went to Hrubieszow. From there everyone was taken to a camp called Budzyn. We were there for a year. After that we were transferred to Majdanek. I was there for 13 months. After that,

[Page 208]

we were sent to Auschwitz. We were there for a few days only. From there we were sent to Gleiwitz–in the Blechhammer camp I worked for 6 months until I was liberated.

Some observations: The Helrubin family was killed in 1942 during the last expulsion. In spite of the fact that Helrubin was in the Judenrat, he still conducted himself honorably. He attended very few of their meetings.

I want to point out that Moishe Motl Shalier was not in the Judenrat, and was a scrupulously honest person.

Translator's footnotes:

1.   Moishe Ashpiz states in his memoir that it was Rosh Hashanah Eve. (Ed.)
2.   Narrow gauge railway

Zvi Naor (Finger)
(Son of Sheindel Hodes, grandson of Feivel Finger, the orchardist)

Translated by Sara Mages

Greetings to dear Mr. Zipper,

At the beginning of my answer, I apologize for not replying to your letter in a reasonable time as you requested, because of a complete lack of time.

As you may or may not know, I serve as an officer in permanent service in the Israel Defense Forces with the rank of *Rav Seren* (Major), and I'm sure you'll believe me that I don't have one free minute in a day to devote to matters outside the scope of my duties, and even more so, to sit down and concentrate on something unusual like revisiting a past that brings to mind hair-raising episodes, and very dear people who will never return.

Unfortunately, I will not be able to meet all your requests as detailed in your dear letter for two reasons:

A.   I was only fourteen and a half years old when the war broke out.
B.   After our town, Tyszowce, burned down, and after a series of wanderings, we moved to live in the nearby town of Komarów. We lived in the apartment of a family who had moved to Russia with the retreat of the Red Army, and we resided in Komarów to the bitter end.

It is clear that all the events in Komarów are identical to Tyszowce in terms of method, scope etc., even though the Komarów murderers were quartered in Tyszowce. However, I wasn't involved in the life of Tyszowce, and most of the details and events requested in your letter are almost unknown to me.

At certain stages we had information about Tyszowce and we also met, but I don't have enough facts to answer about all those. As you know, it was forbidden to leave the residential area, a Jew was forbidden to listen to the radio, read a newspaper, etc. - those who possessed them were subject to the death penalty on the spot.

All the prohibitions and decrees were imposed on us gradually and in exemplary method. So, for example,

[Page 209]

at the beginning of 1940 it was announced that within a week a liquidation sale would be held in stores owned by Jews. A month later it was forbidden to own a radio receiver or to buy a newspaper. Six months later, Jews were forbidden to wear furs, and they had to hand them over to the authorities (a Jew who owned a fur collar was shot immediately). A month later, ration cards were issued and they were gradually reduced to only a few hundred grams of bread per person per day. We were concentrated in limited living areas and we were unable to live freely, our movements were restricted and, apart from going to work under Nazi escort, we were not allowed to leave the residential area at all. In the last year and a half it was forbidden to leave the house between six in the evening and six in the morning. This, of course, applied to Komarów and Tyszowce at the same time. In this manner they controlled us in the tightest way and could easily get us at any time.

I will try to answer within the framework of the sections as you requested and with the limitations I mentioned above:

As for the Judenrat: (Komarów and Tyszowce)

It was established at the beginning of 1940, and maybe even earlier, because the Germans demanded it so that they would have an address to turn to with their demands. So, for example, when they appeared in the city - their first stop was, of course, the Judenrat. They demanded from them quotas of people for work in the airports, paving roads, cleaning horses and their stables, and all kinds of humiliating jobs for the next day. Also amounts of silver or gold by weight for the following day and at a certain time, and fabrics for suits for the Nazi officers. In the last years they even took several members of the Judenrat with them as hostages, and the Judenrat made efforts to fulfill their demands without objection.

At the disposal of the Judenrat were Jewish policemen in special uniforms, and they constituted the executive arm of the Judenrat. As for the appointments, I think they were determined by the municipal government and with the approval of the German rule in charge of the local authorities.

Of course, there were Judenrat members whom we defined as friendly, and there were those whom we were careful not to come into any contact with, and they, of course, were treated well by the Germans. The same applied to the Jewish policemen. There were Judenrat members who "made efforts" with the German authorities to cancel a certain decree and even received insults and beatings in public, and there were those who filled the quota as required with full rigor. There were proactive actions by the Germans, "selections," and then, before the transports, the head of the Judenrat and its members appeared and tried to take out the people close to them. If they had to provide a quota of people, it was clear that they went from house to house and skipped their friends' houses. This is where the hatred for the members of the Judenrat came from, because they egoistically protected their family members, relatives, acquaintances and their friends' acquaintances. Today, it is difficult to judge whether it was justified or not, in case there is even the slightest reason for forgiveness.

There were incidents in which the Judenrat resisted handing over people, and then the Germans themselves were forced to collect people - in these cases there were also victims.

As for educational activities:

Generally - I don't remember any. We maintained a religious family identity, and despite the ban, we gathered in private homes, or in cellars, on the Sabbath and holidays for communal prayer. I remember

[Page 210]

that we often dispersed in the middle of the prayer after the guard outside announced that Germans had arrived, but "heroes" were found, especially among the elders who stayed and prayed with great vigor.

In the course of time, there was a certain cooling regarding the faith, and the young people stopped believing. Even among the elders doubts "crept in" regarding the faith, because, according to their perception, incidents or things happened which cannot be logically imagined, and yet they happened. Nothing happened to the perpetrators while the believers were brutally beaten, murdered and everything sacred to them was desecrated.

Once I even heard such a secret debate between elders known to me as religious who expressed themselves, "I'm afraid that I will stop believing tonight," and wept during their conversation.

Obviously, there was someone among them (in this case my grandfather z"l), who encouraged them with the tone "God is stronger." I remember how they warned my grandfather, and literally forced him into the house, when the Germans walked around the city for fear that they would shave off his reddish beard. My grandfather answered with complete certainty that the Rebbe of Kazimierz kept his beard and no German hand dared to raise a pair of scissors, or a knife, on his beard. He was convinced that hand would be paralyzed there and then. And one clear day, when he left the house he was caught by a German who led him to the barber shop. First he took out a knife and cruelly cut his beard with part of the flesh and left the completion of the job to the barber.

This incident destroyed his world. I remember that my aunt came into the house and saw my grandfather sitting in silence, and when she asked, who is the gentile sitting in our house, my grandfather burst into a bitter cry; it was impossible to recognize him.

Despite my free approach today to religious matters (perhaps for such reasons), I fully understand the meaning of such a conversation that came out of the mouths of elders at that time. We will return to education problems: there was no time to engage in educational activities in particular. Every Jew, from the age of 14- 60, had to carry a work card (Arbeitskarte) that was signed every day at a recognized and authorized workplace by the Germans for six days a week, Monday to Saturday inclusive. The owner of an incomplete card - was shot on the spot. We returned from such jobs beaten and wounded, and the next day we went out again.

In the first year they set quotas for work and then the rich paid the poor to go to work in their place, and in the last year almost everyone went out. There were also "comfortable" places of work, such as cleaning the city streets and more, these jobs were permanently given to those close to the Judenrat.

Nevertheless, we sneaked into friends' houses and read a book, studied Hebrew (my aunt Fradel Finger was a Hebrew teacher in Tyszowce before the outbreak of the war), but that was just a drop in the ocean. I assume that you know that the Jews didn't have a school during all six years of the war.

In this way we began to think about the unknown future, and whenever there were rumors of deportations and murders, we started making plans of organizing, escaping to the forest, joining the partisans and resistance actions.

[Page 211]

It's amazing that we also did this secretly, not only out of fear of the Germans, or informers, but rather out of fear of the town elders who feared reprisals.

I must move to another topic, the contact between the Jews of Komarów, Tyszowce and Zamość. The Germans allowed several young men from Tyszowce, Komarów and also other cities (there were 4-5 of them in Komarów), to move freely in the area (mostly in the villages) for the purpose of collecting scrap iron for the German industry mainly for the production of weapons and tanks. The young men were equipped with green armbands with stamps and special certificates, and they wandered around the villages to collect the monthly quota of scrap metal and deliver it to Zamość. The truth is, the farmers collected the scraps and received a substantial payment for them, but it was worthwhile because of the free movement in the area and especially the contact between the residents of Komarów, Tyszowce and Zamość. Among them was also my uncle, Motl Finger, about whom I wrote in my previous short article. The permit holders in Komarów besides my uncle Motel were: Yaakov Khazanold, Ephraim Goldhaber, and Moshe Trost about whom I will devote a few words later. I think these young men paid a lot of money to the Judenrat fund for these permits, but with these young men were those who were able to contribute something in terms of orientation, communication and courage (two of them didn't have these qualities, but because of their closeness to the Judenrat and their parents' status in the city).

These young men brought us the bad news from conversations with the farmers, who were well aware of the situation, and from other sources, about what was carried out in other places. These were the young men who gathered some of the youth (who were considered trustworthy) and planned the purchase of weapons, escape to the forest, joining the partisans, or establishing an independent underground. Some of the discussions were held at our house.

They were made out of an assessment of a situation that the end was near, according to the news they brought from the other cities and under the pressure of time.

I remember that roles were assigned. Instructions were issued for the purchase of weapons from the farmers (from the weapons caches left in the villages from the time of the Polish army surrender). With the tightening of the noose– excessive reduction of the residential area, night curfew, new and cruel decrees, a ban on going for outside jobs, sending people to work who never returned, the increase in the number of victims, etc–an approximate date was set for leaving the city for the forest. Time began to act against us, the situation worsened and weapons in a reasonable and necessary amount had not yet been obtained, and rumors arrived about the total elimination of various Jewish communities in different locations.

It was decided to make one last effort to obtain weapons, ammunition and medical supplies, and in the meantime to maintain close contact within the group, meaning, to sleep dressed at night in three central locations, and to place sentries to serve as a warning. And so, on the night of 15 Heshvan 5703 (October 26 1942), (the date for both Komarów and Tyszowce), we were woken up from our sleep and told that the entire town of Komarów was surrounded and that Germans were continuing to arrive in vehicles and on foot.

We had no contact with the two other groups, because only one group slept in our house. In one breath we got up, I managed to say goodbye to my mother with a hug and a kiss, but I choked on tears and was unable to say a word to her. I took my sister, who was two years older than me (I was 17 at the time), and we slipped out in the dark following the lead group on winding roads, and we managed to infiltrate among the German sentries who started to organize. Shots and shouts separated us and only half of the group managed

[Page 212]

to arrive at the meeting place. The second half didn't arrive at the place we had prearranged in the Komarów Forest. They were killed on the way, and/or captured by the Poles who led them to the Germans.

At the same time, my uncle Motl was in Tyszowce on a mission to purchase weapons. Later, I met him in Tuczapy Forest together with my mother as I wrote in the "Day of Horror in Tuczapy Forest" [page 238].

I will not relate what happened to us from then on, because it already belongs to the biography. I will only mention a few details:

   A.   Shimon Goldhaber and I remained from a group of about twenty people from Komarów.
   B.   My uncle Motl had a very bitter end. About six months later he was captured alive by the murderers in Tuczapy Forest. He was taken to the Gestapo prison in Hrubieszów and was severely tortured for a month. They burnt parts of his body so that he would reveal the location of the partisans (at the same time I was with the partisans), but he remained silent.
When I later became one of the residents of Hrubieszów Ghetto, my co-workers told me that they had buried my uncle Motel and that his body was charred and dismembered. I learned from the prison guards that he had held out with supreme bravery and hadn't revealed anything. On the contrary, he begged them to kill him because he didn't want to tell them anything.
   C.   I promised earlier that I would mention Moshe Trost who had a permit to collect scrap iron together with my uncle Motel.

This young man remained in Komarów after the final liquidation. He wandered in the area with a group of Polish thugs (who were wanted by the authorities), and took revenge on the Germans as well as the Poles who collaborated with the authorities. Upon liberation by the Red Army, he joined their ranks and made it all the way to Berlin. He found part of his family and moved to the United States. After receiving American citizenship he moved to Habash [Ethiopia] for business and from there to Europe. Today he lives in West Germany as an American citizen.

This young man succeeded, after a long pursuit, to locate the main murderer from Komarów and Tyszowce (his name is Schultz, may his name be blotted out). He managed to organize a public trial against him. He sent his wife to bring documents and photos from the archives in Zamość and Lublin (it was quite dangerous), and in April 1964 the murderer's trial took place. I also testified, and in the end he was sentenced to life imprisonment and hard labor. I saw the devotion of a simple young man, a butcher's son from Komarów, who spent a lot of his money, endangered his wife, and didn't rest until the court declared a maximum verdict for the small number of murder cases that we were able to prove before the court. He actually participated in all the selections, and he was the one who killed them all with his own hands before the selections.

I have just gone over the sections in your letter according to which I tried to answer, and noticed your interest in how and from what we made a living in the forest. Of course, it is possible to write a whole book about everything separately, but I will try to limit myself to the main issues only.

In the forests around us were entire families of Tyszowce Jews (in the continuation of my wanderings from Komarów I arrived in Tuczapy Forests near Tyszowce), who fled to every place possible because of the liquidation. These families sent their children to the villages in the area to buy food, or to exchange jewelry for bread, or even the clothes from their backs in exchange for bread and potatoes. Those

[Page 213]

who had no money left, or something instead of money, stole the property of others because they had no other choice. The Germans made sure to reduce the number of families. Every week they conducted attacks on the forests after which they would announce that today they had murdered such and such "bandits." I described one of these attacks in my previous letter - it was also the first meeting with my mother who didn't know about my existence at all. I found her in the company of the townspeople, sitting, crying and pleading that she only wanted to see her children once, and die. I stood some distance from the campfire they were sitting around and listened to all this. When I heard these words I could not hold back any longer, and in a mad rush I fell into her arms to fulfill my mother's wish. I left that day with a number of young men and my uncle Motl who I also found there, and we arrived in the Komarów forests. We took the survivors of the group and my sister who was with them, and two days later we arrived in Tuczapy. Indeed, my mother 's wish was granted to see her two children as she requested, but only to see, because, as I wrote in my previous letter, the attack began at dawn. (This was only a side note because I didn't mean to tell all that). To the question, where did we purchase weapons–at first for money, and then we attacked Germans and stole their weapons. If you ask how I survived, I will also try to answer that briefly (it is also possible to write a book about this). As mentioned, I was accepted into a group of partisans. I succeeded because of my familiarity with the environment, my courage and my diligence (I had nothing to fear because I was sure that the end was near). In one of the attacks on us (there were almost no families in the forest), my uncle Motl was captured alive, and there was anxiety among the partisans that maybe he would return with the Germans and point to our locations like a Russian, who had been captured before him, had done. I informed my uncle, Izik Finger in Hrubieszów, about the situation, and he begged me to join him in the ghetto. On the other hand, my close friends in the partisans told me that if my uncle Motl should return, the partisans' commander would kill me. Another factor, after my uncle was captured, I had to take care of his fiancée (Sarah Reiss) who was with him, and now the responsibility fell on me (she was the daughter of Chaim Reiss who lived near Luther Foigel). On the way to Klantwice[?] I undertook a mission to the Polish underground in Hrubieszów (the partisans' commander had connections, and also knew what was done inside the Gestapo). I boarded a train with Sarah Reiss and we snuck into Hrubieszów Ghetto. I fulfilled my duty, heard from my uncle about the efforts being made to free my uncle, but in vain, and gave in to his pleas to stay with him. Here I would stay for two years, and I will only mention that I went through six concentration camps starting from Hrubieszów, until I was liberated by the Russians in the city of Theresienstadt in Czechoslovakia. There, they [the Germans] had gathered the survivors from all the concentration camps in Germany, and they had [planned] to burn me in a special crematorium built for that purpose. There was a turning point, the commander of the SS, who was in charge of carrying out the operation, considered it and saw fit to report the plan to the Red Cross.

The Red Cross notified the Russian authorities, who were already advancing on Czechoslovakian soil. They changed the line of their advance, reached us and liberated 30,000 survivors who had held out until the end.

[Page 214]

The Labor Camp in Tishevits

(Taken from the book, "Churban Otwock, Falenits, Korczew," by Dr. Binyamin Orenstein, 1948)

Translated by Moses Milstein

The summer of 1940 saw the beginning of the aktions sending young men to the forced labor camps in Lublin, Tishevits near Hrubieszow, and other places.

Three camp inmates from Tishevits. Kalman Horowitz survived. The other two were killed.

A group of butchers from Otwock in the Tishevits camp. Kalman Horowitz survived. The others were killed.

In August 1940, 50 people from Otwock were sent to Tishevits for water management work.

The work consisted of regulating the water runoff from the fields. Ditches 4 meters deep and 3 meters wide were dug. Afterward, the ditches were finished with peat.

[Page 215]

There were 500 Jews from various cities in the Tishevits camp: Warsaw, Otwock, Tomaszow, Tyszowce, and other areas.

The camp was located in a mill that consisted of a one-story building. The inmates slept on the straw covered floor. The rations consisted of 20 decas of bread a day with black coffee and soup for lunch.

The management and the guarding were done by "The Blacks." These were a special commando group (S.D.) dressed in black uniforms. They were degenerate sadists, Volksdeutsche from various lands, who tortured the inmates by constantly calling for roll calls by day as well as during the night.

The inmates gave the camp directors special names. The camp commandant, a Czech Volksdeutsche, was called "Toz." His deputy was called "Red Toz." One of the most brutal camp supervisors was called "Tsik–Tsak," or "Hop-Hop." This was because while marching, instead of calling out one, two, he shouted, "Tsik, tsak, tsik, tsak." He also used to force people to run, shouting, "Hop, hop."

The camp was fenced with barbed wire, and guarded by the "black" guards.

Roll call started at 5:00 am. The inmates were divided into groups. A group consisted of 60 men, led by a group leader. The group leaders were Jews, and their work entailed assuring everyone was present for the roll calls, distributing the rations, and supervising during the work to make sure everyone was working, and no one was escaping.

Torturing the inmates at work or in the camp manifested itself in various punishments. The "black" supervisors would accuse an inmate of not working well enough, and would beat him bloody. Once a guard decided that someone's shovel was dirty and punished everybody. He drove them into a river 80-90 cm deep, and tortured them there for hours. The guard, Tsik-Tsak used to search for a victim, force him to the ground, his foot on his neck, and beat him with the butt of his rifle, or with a riding crop over his whole body until the victim showed no signs of life anymore. When he had to work in the camp at night, the inmates would not get any sleep. Every couple of hours, he called for a roll call count, and beat anyone who fell into his hands.

At night, it was forbidden to go to the latrine alone. One had to be accompanied by a watchman. There were 2 watchmen who carried big lanterns

[Page 216]

and they led and returned from the latrines. It happened sometimes that, because of the poor food, inmates got diarrhea, and couldn't wait for the watchman to return. If they went to the latrine alone, they were shot by the guards.

The Judenrat in Tishevits made efforts to allow the inmates to be freed for Rosh Hashanah and Yom Kippur, and to go and pray. The result of the intervention was that they were freed for the first day of Rosh Hashanah, but on the second day they were horribly mistreated and forced to do twice the work. Yom Kippur, everyone had to work.

The Tishevits inmates expressed their painful life in the following recitation:

Tyszowce

Tra–ta –ta–ta, tra–ta, ta, ta,
Don't ask, don't speak, keep quiet!
500 Jews gathered together in camp,
selected from various cities.
To work, to work for whom, why?
For tyrants, murderers, torturers, what for?
Roll call, arrange yourselves in rows of three
Commotion and wild shouts are heard
Count in the military way, one, two, three, four
That means you too, your turn is coming
Six, seven, eight, nine

There have to be 60 men in each group
The group leader gives a report
On what has happened with the group
Sixty were recorded in the group
Fifty remained for the roll call
Four were sent to the carpenter, five are sick,
The tenth is passed out on the bench.
The commandant runs in rage
What sick? Get up you faker!

[Page 217]

I know fakers well,
Working with everyone hand in hand.
The patient murmurs, working for whom, why?
For tyrants, for murderers, for torturers, what for?
Ready! Left turn, shovels raised
The exhausted Jews march further.
One, two, one, two and three
Left makes the road free,
Tra–ta–ta–ta, tra–ta–ta–ta
Don't ask, don't speak, keep silent, sha!
The sun is shining, the day is hot, but I am cold,
Famished, exhausted by the work in the forest.
A wild guard runs up, a Volksdeutsche,
It is painful, it hurts and I tremble,
All my limbs are in agony.
------why must you beat me I ask
why must you torment and afflict me.
-----to the devil with you and your weeping and whining
A Jew must be tortured, killed and tormented.
Someone is unconscious from hunger and need,
And maybe he was actually tortured to death?
We work, we work, wheel wheelbarrows row upon row
The overseers shout, in time: one, two and three.
The work is finished again in rows of three
Like soldiers marching, one, two, left free.
Halt. Return the shovels to the storehouse,
Thus the day passes in suffering, without sense.
------Midday. Everyone stands in a row meters long,

[Page 218]

Impatiently waiting with their bowls in their tired hands.
The cook spoons the watery soup with his ladle,
The second one approaches and the first departs.
Tsik-Tsak attacks, hits, and creates a racket
He runs around the camp like a wild man
An order, to the water to wash the bowls
After the poor soup, the meager portion.
Friends, someone shouts in the hall
The victim has a lump on his head
We had forgotten completely about him
Let us bring him some food
Place a little straw under him, ease his suffering

And call the doctor he should heal him.
Tsik–Tsak falls in with wild laughter
The hall falls silent with fear.
He drives everyone out to the yard
A commotion and stampede
Fall down, get up, fall down, get up, Hap, hap
Everyone halt, stop, stop
Back to the dark halls to sleep
It's raining, drops fall from the roof.
In the silence of the black night
Only the footsteps of the soldier guard are heard.
A sick man goes out to the yard to do his business
A bullet hits him and makes a hole in his skull
The "black" satanic Tsik-Tsak
Laughs and is joyous at his murderous work.
The one who was shot lies dead
In a red puddle of blood.
Tra–ta–ta–ta, tra–ta–ta–ta
No one wants to remain silent
No one wants to work any more, for whom, why?
For tyrants, murderers, torturers, what for?
Enough martyrs of murder and fires,
Of dysentery, typhus, and plagues.
It's time the sun rose for us

[Page 219]

And freed us from the camp tortures.
May the day of revenge arrive
A consolation for us.

In December, 1940, the camp was closed and everyone was sent back to the ghettos. The people from Otwock also came back, but later in the deportations, they were killed.

————————

The Labor Camp in 1940[1]

Ringelblum Archive

Translated by Moses Milstein

Ringelblum archive, Art. 373
(Jewish Historical Institute, Warsaw)

The reason I was caught and sent to the work camp in August 1940 (one of the first camps in the General Government) was due to the negligence and irregularity of the registration process. From those trying to avoid it, the gmineh recruited the first cadre of camp inmates.

On the 28th of August 1940, I presented myself to the committee on Kawenczinski Street, where the interim doctor– a Jew–declared me fit, in spite of expecting to be freed because of my weak physique. After this interview, I was issued a departure card, and ordered to show up in two days' time.

On the designated day, I found myself at the assembly place–surrounded by barbed wire, and guarded by Polish police–the place where the building of the camp commission on Kawenczinski Street stood.

From the minute you passed the gate that led to the place, you lost the ability to communicate with the outside world. In truth, there was a way to communicate with parents at a nearby wall, namely the shaliach of the gmineh, but this was possible only for a few, because the liaison officer asked to be highly paid.

The crowd gathered in the yard consisted mostly of the poorer levels of society. They were mostly unmarried people between 20 and 30 years of age. Because we had to wait there all day from 8:00 in the morning until evening, we dispelled the boredom by telling jokes, mostly indecent ones. In general the mood was excellent. The perspective of camp

[Page 220]

filled no one with fear. They all figured that for loyal, and honestly fulfilled tasks, they would receive proper living conditions.

At dusk they put us in groups of three (1500 people had been assembled), and led us in groups to the brick building where they gave everyone a nutritious enough meal consisting of soup and bread. After supper, they arrayed us again in groups of three, and led us out in the direction of the yard. We were accompanied by gendarmes carrying rifles with fixed bayonets. In spite of that, there were plenty of opportunities to run away which several people actually carried out. In general, control was not very strict during the march, because the transport had to have 1500 people, so the gendarmes caught and conscripted a certain number straight off the street in order to fulfill their quota. We were accompanied most of the way by the wailing and lamentations of our mothers and families, until they were finally driven away by the Polish police. As the time of the train departure neared, the gendarmes forced us to march ever faster. As a result, the column broke up, we became completely disoriented, and degenerated into a disorderly mad race. In the process, many lost their provisions and other pieces of baggage. I felt German blows for the first time while getting into the freight cars in the eastern train yard. Getting up into those wagons with our loads required a big effort that some were not capable of. The gendarmes exploited the situation, whipping with their riding crops as hard as they could. Finally, they loaded us in, 88-100 people in a freight car, the cars were locked, and sealed, and the train began to move. The gendarmes travelled in the same train, but in the passenger cars. The matter of locking the cars did not at first seem to interest anyone, or bother anyone. But after a while during the 12-hour journey, we became painfully aware of it. It was a question of our basic, elementary physiological needs. But need is the mother of invention, and we managed in the following way: we broke off the tops of the bottles we all carried, and we used the bottom parts as vessels. During the entire journey, a carefree atmosphere prevailed. Everyone was well supplied with food reserves, and they ate as much as they could. And whoever didn't have enough, others gave him. Full stomachs gave rise to confidence in the future,

[Page 221]

and prevented thoughts about a starker future.

After 12 hours we finally arrived at our destination: the freight yard in Lublin. Here the gendarmes began to drive us out of the freight cars, not sparing any blows. On the platform, we were made to stand in rows of three which turned out to be another source of vexation for the inmates as they did it tentatively which aggravated the gendarmes. In spite of the fact the freight cars had been locked, they made us do a count again. After performing the formality, the gendarmes handed us over to "The Blacks." Leading us through the streets of the city, they immediately made their brutality known. For a crooked step, for walking out of line, for being a half a step behind, for the slightest deviation from military regulations, in which they themselves were not proficient, they beat us mercilessly with whips and rifle butts.

In this way, they drove us through the whole city to the barracks on the outskirts that were the assembly point for being sent to the nearby camps. Independent of this transit camp there was a work camp here for those employed at various jobs in Lublin. The inmates who were just temporarily here, lived here generally for only two to four days. We were the exception. We stayed for six whole days.

Our conditions as far as provisions were concerned were a lot worse than those of the workers employed in Lublin, and they took every opportunity to lord it over us. In actual fact our and their food was the same: It consisted of 1/2 kg of bread, coffee or soup: They however, had the opportunity to buy any kind of food in the city, which for us was a dream: aside from that, getting food was disorganized, and very badly managed. (The cook was a Jewish woman).

"The Blacks" in the camp were generally civil enough and familiar. It wasn't until later that I learned the reason for their civility: the inmates gave them a significant amount of money. In addition, "The Blacks" themselves complained in their sad conversations about their lot, forced away from their families. In general, I have to emphasize that initiating or maintaining friendly relations with "The Blacks" was not difficult, and those who excelled in this field had the opportunity to benefit from easier conditions. Above all we tried to befriend the guards. The benefit was, first of all, to be able to go to the city which was very useful,

[Page 222]

because we could bring food into the camp. The prices in camp were around 15% higher, but they varied a lot, because they depended on the number of people who went to the city that day.

It is characteristic that right from the first day of our arrival theft became shockingly widespread, and continued the entire time.

There was no special work defined for us. Whenever they needed someone, they came to us: mostly it involved unloading coal from the freight cars. The work was not hard, and the inmates did it willingly, especially since they could buy things in the city. Soldiers guarded us while we worked. They treated us quite decently. They only beat us when we tried to get out of work. During breaks, Jewish women, sent by a certain charitable society, brought us pots of hot food, and they were allowed to come to us with no particular hindrances. In general, I have to emphasize that the whole time in Lublin we had enough to eat and we never lacked food.

A few words about the appearance of the camp and the commandant. In the middle of the yard stood a tall post with a machine gun on top. It turned out however that it was a big bluff, because every time they took us to work several people ran away, and there was not one case where it led to any consequences.

Upon arriving at the camp, everyone stopped in the yard, lay their packs down on the wet ground and sat on them. After several hours of waiting, the commandant appeared and asked if there were any sick. The inquiry gave rise to whispering and quiet consultations among the inmates, and after a lot of hesitation the general opinion was that the commandant was a fine man, and that strict medical controls existed, and that the ill would be privileged. They would not be required to work, etc., etc. In this sense, it was worthwhile to confess one's own weaknesses. It turned out, however, that the commandant had rather original ideas about treatment: gathering everyone, the sick and the pretenders, he took them into the workshops that were supplied with electricity which he began to touch them with. Inhuman cries from the tortured clearly reached us. It showed that the torture was really

[Page 223]

excellently thought out, and that the one doing it was well experienced. After a short time, the commandant came out leading the stumbling patients along, and he showed fresh enthusiasm for getting another bunch of sick people–but he couldn't find any now. Characteristically, a couple of healthy people voluntarily presented themselves wishing to satisfy the commandant in order to curry favor. But they were bitterly disappointed receiving no privileges, just more suffering.

In the time we spent in the camp, we rejoiced when there was no work. With complete inactivity and freedom, we hung around the camp and did what we wanted with no controls. The nights were, however, quite restless, because they constantly emphasized that we were to leave Lublin in a short time, so we had to always be ready. Quite often, they had night alarms where we had to array ourselves in rows in the yard, and then they herded us back into the building. Finally, one of the alarms had a different ending: they ordered us to march to a certain spot where there were trucks waiting with, to our astonishment, not Germans, but emissaries from the Tishevits Judenrat who paid for the transport.

Tishevits is a pretty big shtetl with about 10,000 residents, 70% of them Jews, a prosperous shtetl in the Hrubieszow region. In August 1939, a bloody battle was waged between the Bolsheviks and the Poles. As a result the city was demolished by the latter. The three nationalities that lived in Tishevits: Jews, Poles, and Ukrainians were doing well. The Jews were in a good position. Their business was mostly in dealing with the farmers around them. It is interesting to note the good relations between the Jews and the Ukrainians who did not hide their sympathy for the Bolsheviks.[2]

[Page 224]

The camp where the trucks stopped occupied a two-story building beyond the burnt- down mill. Our arrival was connected to the departure home of a group of Lubliners. After us, a party from Tomaszow was supposed to come for 8 weeks. They took up the entire second floor. Our group of 150 people was delegated to the first floor, a spacious hall with wooden walls, whitewashed, and full of holes. Not much less full of holes was the ceiling. The suspicious smell coming from there undoubtedly indicated that there were people living above us. The furniture in our hall was very plain, simply nothing. There was nothing resembling bedding, and for the first few weeks we were forced to sleep on the bare floor. Finally they gave us straw from which we made our bedding like animals. I don't need to add that for the entire time we suffered in the camp, the straw was not changed.

The old inmates received us very amicably, and willingly gave us suggestions and information related to conditions in the camp. What we heard about did not sound very pleasant, and led us completely off track because every one of us left for the camp with the complete conviction that the community would send out a new party after the stated term, in this case, 6 weeks. But whoever hoped for such a possibility, and believed the term limit would be respected was in for an unpleasant disappointment. The Tomaszowers acquainted us with the secretive and convoluted penalties and formalities that involved returning home. In any case, there were varied opinions on certain points, but in general, it was agreed that there was no talk of leaving without negotiations which involved certain costs. In the event that the Warsaw community was not interested in our situation we would have to remain until the end of the work. (And that was how it actually turned out). But even that did not guarantee a return, because there was talk about the possibility of creating a winter camp. It has to be underscored that the German authorities did not interest themselves in the matter of changing workers. As evidence, I can bring up the fact that from the Hrubieszow camp they sent–after

[Page 225]

finishing the work which lasted 6 months–all the inmates to us, and no one took on the injustice. In truth, the Judenrat of a small shtetl near Lublin did make certain efforts in that direction–but they demanded such an immense price for the ransom for these white slaves that they gave up. With such perspectives on the future we approached our work.

The first day, we were free (we arrived at the camp around four in the afternoon), but the following day, they forced us to work.

Seven o'clock in the morning, one of "The Blacks" (there were seven of them in all) gave the signal to get up. We were dressed several minutes later. We went out to the yard and stood in columns to get sour coffee and 1/2 kg of bread. (the "vikt" here was the same as in the Lublin camp–maybe a bit better. The soups were certainly better. On this topic, it is worth mentioning that there were times of hunger. And there were times when the soup was superfluous, so that we even poured it out. What caused such contrasts? The matter of feeding us depended on the ease of getting food. And that depended on the amount of money the inmates could raise–namely, whether they could buy food in the city, or the money we were sent from home via the mail which was doled out to us every 2-3 weeks (because the official from the Tishevits Judenrat who controlled the mail contributions, "used" our money in the interim for himself.). Consequently, there were periods of hunger as well as plenty. After eating, "The Black" guards had us stand in rows of three in the yard which had a capacity of a few hundred people and was unusually small and cramped. After several minutes waiting, the commandant appeared–a Sudeten German–assisted by the sub-commandant–a Volksdeutsche. The commandant halted before us: inspected the column with the eyes of a Napoleon, and with a stern voice asked us if there were any among us who had served in the military. Several stepped forward, but the commandant chose only those who were tall and strongly built and designated them as group leaders. The group leader had the duty of maintaining the integrity of the platoon (which consisted of 50 people), and was personally responsible for the integrity of the platoon, and for carrying out the designated work. Fifteen minutes later, the newly-

[Page 226]

minted dignitaries, always under a "Black" escort, led the group in the direction of the Huczwa river whose flow we had to regulate.

The river was bounded at one point by a dam under which we had to deepen the ground and keep back the slope. The technical side was overseen by Polish technicians. Order was maintained by "The Blacks." We were not given much time to look over the work site. Without determining and giving out any information, they ordered us to get to work, which after 15 minutes turned out to be very hard and exhausting. This is what it looked like: There were poles set up in the river on which, in cross section, we threw boards ½ meter wide (around 100 boards), and upon them wheelbarrows coursed loaded by the workers who were standing below up to their knees in mud and water. (The dam leaked). The trip over the boards with the wheelbarrows required unusual skill that we did not naturally possess, and the first 10-20 days it often happened that, to the great schadenfreude of "The Blacks," people and wheelbarrows fell off, a distance of 3 meters, and often ended with serious injuries. For example, one of the workers suffered broken ribs in such a fall. "The Blacks" enjoyed such incidents and they simply collapsed with laughter when one of the inmates fell and painfully barely climbed out of the mud–from the river bed. With the goal of achieving such an effect more often, our tormentors thought of different methods among which the simplest was to instill panic: the methods to achieve this goal were simple and primitive. When "The Blacks" retreated somewhat, we slacked off. You could see rows of wheelbarrows standing unused on the boards along with the resting workers. When the guards unexpectedly appeared, everyone threw themselves into the work with such momentum that 25% fell off onto the ground. After about 10 days, we got used to the work, and the incidence of falls declined. On the very first day, we learned about the cruelty of "The Blacks" who very often availed themselves of their whips which consisted of springs covered with leather. A welt appeared after a blow with such an instrument that could be seen on the skin for weeks. We worked in such conditions until 4:00 o'clock. At that time they gave the signal for the end of work.

[Page 227]

We were arrayed in columns of three, tools inspected, and led off to the camp. There everyone quickly got their eating utensils and lined up for the soup. (The soup distribution, like all mealtimes, regardless of weather, was conducted outdoors). The soups were generally nourishing, and sometimes you could find 15-20 decagrams of meat in them. Aside from that there were sometimes potatoes or kasha, less often, beans. After eating we were supposed to have free time until dusk (there were no lights in the camp). In reality, we were the victims of the criminal activities of "The Blacks." This will be covered later. When it became dark, we were ordered to retire (the second day in camp they confiscated our personal documents and certificates in order to prevent escape.

The food in the camp was never enough or satisfying for anyone. Luckily, we were able to get bread at market prices from the Polish baker whose windows adjoined our yard. Other than that there were two small stores, a Polish and a Jewish one, whose windows also looked out on our yard. The small stores did outstanding business, even though they charged the same prices as in the city, and therefore they competed greatly between themselves–in the end the Polack won, having bribed the commandant, and thus pushed out the Jew.

Daily, the Jewish camp doctor, with the name, Atlas, examined the self-reporting patients. He had the authority to let people off work, but he seldom exercised the privilege because his deliberations were not objective: Dr. Atlas tried to win the sympathy of "The Blacks." They were present during the examination, and his conclusions were generally not in our favor. In truth, you had to be really suffering to get out of work. In addition, it often happened that "The Blacks" nullified the doctor's decision to be let off work, and they hurled insults and threats at him for letting people off work. In general though, the doctor had good relations with the Germans, because he had the right to free someone from the camp for good, the very sick, and thus he made more than one deal with the administration. The exams took place in the ambulatorium which was in a cramped little room with no facilities.

After several days in the camp, our group leaders began to search

[Page 228]

for opportunities to strengthen their power, and to receive sources of revenue. With this goal in mind, they began to propose various, and mostly unrealistic, projects to lighten and make life in camp more interesting. For example, creating an aid fund, a sports club (!), an artistic group, and similar events. Fortunately, we had little trust in our leaders and did nothing to make their plans a reality. The group leaders did not give up, and brought it to the commandant. At first, he didn't respond, but later he exploited it very well: After that day, a hail of blows descended on our backs mostly delivered by "The Blacks"–a litany of threats and shouts so the Jews should not think that they were here on vacation, that they had it too good here, etc. The result was that everyone without exception was savagely beaten.

But our group leaders turned out to be obstinate people, and disregarding the failure, they plotted so long until they found a source of revenue, and a very significant one. They assured us that with the help of an insignificant amount of money they could soften up "The Blacks," and save us from beatings and brutal treatment. From that time forward, we had to pay weekly from the held-back money from Warsaw. The amount of money given was determined by the group leaders, because the money passed trough their hands. Without a doubt, a significant portion of this got lost in their pockets. The bribes turned out quickly to be impractical, (even though it persisted for the entire life of the camp) because "The Blacks" were responsible for getting the work done, and they had to hassle us. Aside from that, their demands grew as fast as they were placated, and every time they demanded more which, in spite of the raises, lasted for less time. (This meant that if the previous payment was good for 5-6 days, then it was shortened to 2-3 days.)

If the "vikt" was not filling enough for someone, he could buy food from Jewish women at the fence, even a kosher meal, or Shabbes cholent, or other tasty meals. The women subjected themselves to the danger of a beating by approaching the fence, because "The Blacks" vigorously guarded against anyone getting near us. Whoever had the opportunity to go to the city came back sated and loaded with gifts of food from the rich Jews. But not everybody had the opportunity

[Page 229]

to steal out of camp, and the opportunities to visit the city occurred very seldom. But in the early days of our being in camp, the group leaders had the privilege of leaving the camp, and they used it to the fullest. This gave them an excuse for self-aggrandizing. In spite of that, their status was not enviable, because they were often beaten when their underlings did not do their work.

The Edenic conditions which had permitted us to buy food at the fence ended quickly with the arrival of a new "Black" with the name of "Tsag-Tsag." Rumors about his cruelty reached the camp much before his arrival. Naturally, the new representative took strict measures to establish order in the camp. His first activity was to forbid loitering around the fence which went on at night on a big scale, for the reason that it was at the end of the yard quite far from the mill–no one paid this order any attention, and it became the cause of some drama. One night, when Tsag-Tsag was on duty, we heard several shots fired, and his voice shouting threats and curses at the Jews–this didn't scare anyone. In the morning, we found a dead Jew who had been shot in the head. The dead inmate was from Otwock, a 22 year old whose name I can't remember. His body was removed, and he was buried in the city cemetery. The effect this had on the camp and the whole shtetl is hard to describe. The Tishevits Judenrat actually intervened with the goal of punishing the murderer, and preventing future such cases. But all the efforts were in vain. Our commandant–who came across as an honest and humane person, deflected every complaint with one laconic expression, "Everything's alright." Tsag-Tsag, possibly feeling a certain remorse, claimed in his talks with the inmates as a mitigating excuse (in spite of the fact no one had asked him to explain) the fact that a day before, a man from Warsaw had escaped from the camp (which had really happened) and he accused the Otwocker of approaching the fence for the same reason. The two new innovations from Tsag-Tsag were the early morning gymnastics which took place before going to work, and consisted of our running around the yard to the calls of "Tsag-Tsag." (From this the name Tsag-Tsag was derived). This innovation was

[Page 230]

Tsag-Tsag's glory, and he considered it a very worthwhile game for us, especially because the mornings were cold. In general, we convinced ourselves that Tsag-Tsag had chosen this as a point of honor to renew and morally rejuvenate the degenerate "Jewish race" and he tried to realize this goal at every opportunity. The morning gymnastics was one such method among others.

In spite of the brutality of Tsag-Tsag, there were opportunities for many inmates to interact with him as well as with "The Blacks." The method was–the ability to sing which, as it turned out, many of "The Blacks" enjoyed. That's how our free hours in the afternoon, for many of us, served as an excellent platform to display our musical knowledge based on ribald songs and jokes, usually Jewish, in the presence of the highest authorities like the camp doctor, members of the Judenrat, and Herr Fishleber (for this creature I reserve a special section). After a while, the camp singers got tired of their being singled out for the small group of spectators, and actually the German audience showed itself to be a lot more grateful because the performance of the talented soloists brought no small benefits, like going to the city, exemption from punishments, picking what to eat, and better food. (In general, "The Blacks" used the technique of privileging one group and abusing another, in order to create divisions among the inmates). In time, "The Blacks" worked the song hours into the schedule, and if we didn't have the inclination to attend, they would drive us into the biggest hall, and with blows, forced us to emit shouts and cries that resembled the bellowing of wild animals for hours on end.

Sunday was different because we didn't have to work. We were, however, not free from all the drudgery that "The Blacks" did not spare us. In the morning, after the exercises, came the report for the commandant which was connected to the attendance list. After that came a drill where we had to perform various military exercises. This lasted until the next meal–this meant until 2:00 o'clock. The first Sundays, after the report, when it was still warm, we were taken to the little river and allowed to bathe until the meal. The afternoons were mainly concerned with the performances. You had to be pretty fleet Sunday to avoid being caught for work that consisted of sweeping the yard and the halls,

[Page 231]

taking out the garbage from the kitchen, etc. Those who distinguished themselves could spend a few hours playing cards, or hunting for insect parasites (a few words regarding them: as long as it was warm, they took us to bathe, so infestations of lice were minimal. But later, it became a massive problem. Because of lack of time, we went weeks without washing. At the very end, we didn't wash at all–because the well froze).

The closer it got to the end of our term, the clearer it became that our return would not occur before the end of the job which had, at the least, weeks to go. We sent frightened letters to our parents, and beseeched the community to intervene and send replacement workers. The letters exposed and illuminated with the darkest blackest hues the descriptions of camp life, in order to upset and motivate our parents to make the greatest efforts to get us out of there.

The time of the Jewish holidays approached. Those who had benefited from the privileges bestowed by "The Blacks," were able to get out into the city and availed themselves of the hospitality of the local Jews. But the majority had to remain in the camp. We were freed from work on Rosh Hashanah, but Yom Kippur compensated for that, because were forced to work a lot longer. Inevitably, this created a somber mood of discontent expressed with anger and curses at the Warsaw community which, as it turned out, took the money from our parents for transport out, and was in no hurry to transfer it. We lived for a certain time in camp with the deadlines for leaving–and when one deadline passed, another was established–in order to mislead us further.

Our work was not anywhere near ending, because after deepening the riverbed, we had to excavate the slope which, according to our reckoning based on our experience, would take at the minimum, two months (and in actuality, that's what it took). In the meantime, the weather was becoming cloudier, but this had a good side, because the supervision was less strict. "The Blacks" stayed away for hours at a time, and seldom stayed at the river, but their every visit made itself felt. Exploiting this, everyone

[Page 232]

who had a few cents in his pocket, stole away to the house of a nearby farmer. This was with the agreement of the technician (a Polack who then got paid by the farmers who took us in), in order to sit for a little in a warm house, and buy something warm to eat. This lasted until "The Blacks" found out about it. The day they discovered our hiding away was terrible. They beat everyone bloody, and did not allow us to rest for a second that day, and forced us to work to exhaustion. This further tried the patience of the inmates. Not a day went by when there wasn't a meeting to send off an urgent telegram to Warsaw, especially when we learned that the delegation that was supposed to come to negotiate our freedom with the Germans was not coming, because the Warsaw community was in no hurry to come up with ransom money for us. This was partly the fault of Herr Fishleber (see the comments below) who had a finger in various dealings with the Lubliner Judenrat upon whom in large measure, the ransom of the workers depended. With a large measure of certainty, I can say that the Warsaw community sent out a new group of people to replace us, but they didn't reach Tishevits, but remained in Lublin, and freed Lublin workers, and Fishleber, who arranged all this, was well satisfied.

As regards the ducking out to the farmers' houses during work that I mentioned earlier, something happened that resulted in the murder of one of the workers. The only volunteer in our camp, under the pretext of going to see a farmer–ran away. (Such volunteers who did so of their own free will were scarce, driven to it by need: there was famine at home. The attitude of the inmates to a volunteer was very unfriendly. Because they considered him a German bootlicker, he was harassed and forced to do all the accumulated jobs like taking out the garbage, gathering up garbage, etc. It's no wonder that the volunteers sought to get out of this environment and get out of the camp) This reached the ears of "The Blacks." Because the group leader was responsible for the integrity of his group, he went off to look for the runaway, and because he was afraid to return to the camp, he also decided to run away. In the meantime, the work ended. We returned to the camp and "The Blacks"

[Page 233]

noted in their report the missing two inmates, and promised to respond appropriately. An unusually strained atmosphere reigned among the inmates. At night, they drove everyone–except the sick, the group leaders, and the excellent singers–to the yard, and brutal exercises began consisting of throwing yourself in the mud, and carrying out other, the most difficult exercises, practiced perhaps only in Dachau. When we were already exhausted, they forced us, under pain of being shot, to reveal possible places of assistance to the group leader (He was quartered with a Tishevits family). "The Blacks" immediately went to the address given, but they did not find him there. They did, however, get information on where he had gone. They immediately organized the pursuit.

The group leader (he was called Stern, 21 years old, from Warsaw) was found wandering on foot in the direction of Warsaw. We learned of his fate the next morning. When "The Blacks" caught him, they tied his legs to the wagon they had chased him with, and dragged him for a distance of 15 km. Stopping in front of the camp, they untied him, and set him free. The second he stepped into the yard, a well-aimed shot killed him on the spot. That was the last deed done by "The Blacks," because on November 10th their service in the camp came to an end.

On the day of their leaving, we chose among us–on the orders of the commandant–guards and other functionaries that replaced "The Blacks." The choosing was conducted in the midst of unheard of enthusiasm and holy pronouncements from the new authorities. We have to admit that our new bosses did not misuse their power, and although they sometimes beat us (naturally less than "The Blacks") they never did so without an important reason. At the same time, we received a whole batch of privileges, like the right to leave the camp by buying a ticket for 1 Zl (the income from this went into the commandant's pocket), as well as the right to buy food from the Jews who were now allowed to come into the yard, and approach us during work times.

In spite of all the improvements, the atmosphere was not much different than before. Life and conditions without any hope of a quick return became completely unbearable. In the letters

[Page 234]

sent through the mediation of the farmers who travelled to Warsaw, we wrote to our parents fantastical, totally fictitious things about our condition, in order to stimulate them to real activity. We had nothing to expect from the German authorities, because they didn't even cover the expenses of transporting the workers. With increasing frequency, we saw people from neighboring camps wandering around alone with no means of survival, dying of hunger, because the Judenrats of their hometowns were not interested in them, and they had no means to pay for the trip on their own. We imagined that the same fate awaited us. One day, a delegation from Warsaw showed up in the person of a plenipotentiary of the Judenrat, Dr. Levin, a Norwegian surgeon–as well as a representative of the elder committee. The delegation however proved to be completely unable to accomplish anything, in spite of the fact that they brought the Germans a mass of gifts (furs, expensive things) and they spent entire days with the local authorities. The reason was the unchanging decision of the Germans, that the time of leaving was when the work was completed which we had already made peace with. In spite of that, the effect of the delegation was useless, because they could have got assurance that there would be no winter camp. In this depressed mood, we rued the fact that "The Blacks" were no longer here, because their presence sped up the completion of the work…

The advantages of freer movement allowed two inmates from Siedlce to escape. This time we were not held collectively responsible because we were allowed to go into the city by the commandant. He did however alert the local gendarmerie. They organized a pursuit, caught the runaways, and shot them on the spot. The commandant later justified himself by saying he had no other option than calling on the gendarmes, because otherwise he would have been accused of working with the Jews.

In the second half of November, as promised, the inspector showed up. Inspecting the work, he indicated that the end would be December 1st. The end was however delayed because we simply did not get the job done. We were at the time so resigned and in such a mood that the news of a quick release brought out no emotion in anyone.

The commandant controlled us less and less and showed up less often at the work site.

[Page 235]

He spent entire days in Zamosc where he completed the job of liquidating the camp.

While he was away, his functions were carried out by a Polish engineer who took part in an incident that almost ended fatally. One night, the engineer was in a "cheerful" mood and wanted to get into the camp with his dog. The Jewish guard did not however want to let him in which he had the complete right to decide. The denial put the drunken engineer in such a rage that he drew his revolver and wanted to shoot the Jew. He avoided death thanks to quick thinking: not reckoning with the consequences, he grabbed the revolver from his assailant's hands. The news of this spread through the city, and the guard, in the space if a few days, became the hero not only of the camp, but of all Tishevits.

Finally, the deadline for finishing the work arrived. The dam on the river was opened, and the inmates began preparing for their return. Almost everyone sold his things in order to buy food. Finally, they gave us the date of departure, December 10th. We did not work on that day. Everyone got a 2 kg loaf of bread for the road, and we went off on foot in the direction of Zamosc (around 4-5 km away), because the vehicles that were supposed to take us back never arrived. Tired and worn out, we dragged ourselves to this destination, and arrived the following day at 3:00 in the afternoon (we had left Tishevits at 8:00 pm). Waiting for us at the train station were freight cars that, after a journey of 24 hours with no food or water, delivered us directly to Warsaw. The Judenrat delegation that had traveled with us, but in the passenger cars, took us to the ghetto. The German guards searched us again and took away all the bread. The rest of the stuff and provisions we were allowed to take with.

Addendum A: Fishleber was a person of ambiguous standing. He most likely determined the question of provisions for the camp, and represented the interests of the Germans. In spite of the fact that in the first weeks he regulated many difficulties in the camp (for example, introducing cards for mealtimes, avoiding chaos) he failed to gain any sympathy, especially among the older inmates, the Tomaszowers. Afterwards, I

[Page 236]

learned that he practiced a trade in "living merchandise" on a big scale, providing whole parties of workers for a fee to Judenrats and labor authorities. The end of Herr Fishleber was a miserable one. The Germans discovered his machinations, arrested him, and in the end, shot him.

Translated from the Polish by Henneh Stern Marder–Montreal

Observations from the translator above: "The Blacks"–these were the first Waffen SS with black uniforms, red swastikas on the left arm, and a death's head on their caps (silver death's head). A black flag with a red swastika, the initials SS, and a silver death's head. "The Blacks" were called "mechablim," demons, by the Jews. They were the first civil administration following behind the first frontlines. Their arrival instilled fear in the civilian population.

The statements about "The Blacks" I received from Moishe Kirschenblat of Radom, who survived WWII in various camps (Dachau, Auschwitz, and others) and lives now in Montreal, Canada.

Henneh Stern-Marder

———

Footnotes:

1. Name of author not given. (Ed.)
2. The author, it seems, got his information from inaccurate sources. The fact is, Tishevits never had 10,000 inhabitants, Relations between the Jewish population, Ruthenians, and the Poles were still very strained from WWI. The shtetl was not bombed out in the "battles" which never took place. The Poles and Ruthenians from the suburbs set fire to the Jewish part when the Jews fled to the forest out of fear of a German bombardment. See the articles by Moishe Ashpiz and Berish Finger who were there at the time. (Editor)

Minutes of Eye Witness Testimony
June 11, 1947 2535/9

Yakov Zuker

Translated by Moses Milstein

Citizen Yakov Zuker, living in Wroclaw on Gnieznienski Street, number 4/5, appears before the Szczecin division of the Central Historical Committee of Lodz. The son of Hershl and Feige (maiden name, Allerhand), born in 1922 in Tishevits, and presents the following testimony after being warned of criminal responsibility for false declarations according to the meaning of art. 140 k.k.

"At the time of the outbreak of the war, I was living in Tishevits. Up to the war, 800 Jewish families lived there. At the beginning of the war, Tishevits was burned down, and the greater part of the residents left for Russia. There remained about 300 Jewish families. During the occupation, the behavior of the Germans to the Jewish population was frightful. In 1941 I believe, there was already a labor camp there. I don't remember the exact date.

[Page 237]

The Jews worked at regulating the flow of the Huczwa River. The workers were not only Tishevits residents, but also Jews brought in from other cities. The working conditions were horrible. They were forced to stand in water all day, the commandant of the camp persecuted them, and every day several victims fell. He was called "Vasser-shed."[1] What his real name was, I can't remember. There were a lot of gendarmes in Tishevits. One of them, Schultz, shot a large number of Jews. There was a labor camp in Tishevits, and besides that, there was the gendarme police station that harassed Jews as well. From 1939 there was a Judenrat, and in 1941 the members of the Judenrat were executed during the first aktion. The behavior of the local population[2] was horrifying; I can give no names, because I didn't know these people well. Before the war, I was studying in Lublin, and during the occupation, I was in Modryn, but I often travelled to Tishevits, so I knew what the local population was going through.

In one of the aktions that took place in Hrubieszow, I lost my family. Then in August 1942, I decided, along with my brothers, my sister, and friends who were working for the bosses, to get to the forest. We made bunkers in the forest and hid there for three months. We had weapons that we bought with our own money. Every one of us had a rifle and grenades. After three months in the forest, where we managed to hide out without losing any people, we were surrounded again, and then I lost my sister and three friends.

In 1942 Jews were obligated to wear a white patch with a Star of David. Being seen without the patch was punishable by death.

In 1942, in the Mietkie-Kolonia (Hrubieszow powiat[3]) the following incident occurred: On the property owned by citizen Raimak there were Jews working. One night, as the Jewish workers were asleep in the barn, they were attacked by Lithuanians led by a German oberleutnant. They were from the Sacharin police station, there for several weeks. I was also with the workers in Mietkie. I slept in the barn, and avoided death through a miracle. All the sleeping Jews were killed with grenades, and with revolver shots. A 10 year old boy was wounded. A few hours later, I went to citizen Raimak with a plea to help the wounded boy. Citizen Raimak, who up to then had behaved well toward Jews, could not do this without informing the militia station. After informing them of the case, and expressing his willingness to take the child to the Hrubieszow hospital, the militia declared that they had their own doctor, and they would quickly render aid. After about a half hour, that very same militia who committed the killings, did show up at the scene of the incident, naturally unrepentant, and instead of helping the child, they shot him. Citizen Raimak had to bury the child himself.

I certify the truth of my testimony with my signature: Yakov Zuker

Eng Gildenman
Representative of the Szczecin division

The minutes were received and written by (Mgr. Froi Eichenbaum)
Translated from the Polish by Henneh Stern-Marder

———

Footnotes:

1.   Water-demon
2.   The non-Jewish population
3.   Equivalent to a county

[Page 238]

A day of horror in Tuczapy Forest
that would never be forgotten from my heart…

To my dear mother
Sheindel Hodes z"l, may HaShem avenge her blood,
and to the family of my grandfather Feivel Finger, may he rest in peace.

Tzvi Naor, of the Feivel Finger family

Translated by Sara Mages

I will admit it, and I'm not ashamed: the writing is difficult for me, my hand is shaking and my heart is constricted. Images pass before my eyes that language has difficulty bringing from consciousness to writing. And yet: sometimes it seems to me that these things never happened. Sometimes it seems to me that only an endless nightmare haunts me, and will haunt me as long as I breathe… However, a dim echo from the depths of those days… whispers to me, "Write, even a little"… Tell, so that those who will come after us know what happened to our people, our brothers and sisters, in moments that were unprecedented in human history on earth. And a supreme order, a sort of internal order tells me, "do"!!!

Therefore, I will try, in my poor language, to give a few impressions, and really only a few - of one day, just one day of those fateful days…

…We are inside Tuczapy Forest. Silence and stillness, it seems that even the trees and the birds

[Page 239]

participate in the sorrow of the person hiding in their shade. The rustling of the trees sounds as if they are whispering to each other. The chirping of the birds sounds like a quiet howl.

The sun is shining and its rays reach the trees and warm the figures running here and there. In every corner of the dense forest a campfire is burning, and despite the sun's rays people are sitting and warming themselves after a gloomy night spent without sleep due to the frost, or the fear that has become the routine of every "resident" of Tuczapy. They look at the flame similar to that of yesterday, and shed a tear for those who have just been torn apart and are no more.

Many have run out of tears and only a heavy sigh chokes the throat and breaks the silence. Who knows what awaits us in a day, in an hour, and maybe in a moment…Who knows if we shouldn't be jealous of those who are done with all the suffering and their souls are hovering in the world to come. But the will to live overcomes all the agony and torture.

The figures warming themselves around the campfires are the survivors of our small town, Tyszowce, which was turned into a pile of ruins and its inhabitants scattered like ashes. These figures, who only a while ago were people who lived in the bosom of their family, taught their children brotherhood and friendship, to love others and to do good deeds, have now become broken shadows who are even willing to steal property that is not theirs just to bring their children a slice of bread and a potato to sustain the shriveled body so that they can continue the struggle for life.

Here and there they bring up memories of the not-so-distant past, of the beautiful days that have passed over the residents of Tyszowce, and are no more. From the beautiful Sabbaths and holidays, from the trips to the Krynitzi Spring in the spring, and the forest in the hot summer days. The participants listen to stories of memories and only sighs break the silence. A boy arrives from the village of Tuczapy with a booty of potatoes and beets that he bartered for a garment or silverware, and with increasing tension they listen to the boy's stories that the village is infested with Germans, and it is clear to all that the next day, in the early hours, a"hunt" will begin for those who are still alive.

Silence, everyone is looking around, looking at each other and a question creeps into their broken hearts- will I be among the living tomorrow?…

Suddenly a noise!!! Tumult!!! Bullets pierce the silence, grenades explode in every direction, battle cries are heard from the mouths of the German murderers - the"hunt" has started ahead of time. Everyone gets up and starts running - but where to?!

The murderers' shouts of rage are heard from all sides. They are accompanied by bursts of bullets that blend in with the cries of mothers who have just given birth, of fathers trying to break through the encirclement ring with a mad run in front of the machine gun muzzles, and in their mouths *Kriyat Shema* to the only God who has been so cruel…

A handful of people remained in the place. They are hiding between the bushes and waiting anxiously for what is to come. This handful included: Moshe Motel Schler, my mother Sheindel Hodes, my sister Golda, Itzik Reiss, Feige Shelprok, my uncle Motl Finger and me.

[Page 240]

We hear the approaching steps of the murderers, see the soldiers' boots, and see the muzzles of the weapons… the heart freezes… the breathing stopped…

My uncle Motl Finger takes a small pistol from his pocket, and points it forward between the branches with bated breath, and everyone is patiently waiting for the next seconds.

The murderers are getting closer and the distance between us is getting smaller and smaller: 30 meters, 20 meters, 15 meters… Tarrach! Motl fired, a German dropped and fell, a hail of bullets opened towards us. Everyone fled in a different direction, some fell on the spot, and some were hit by bullets, a few keep running.

My mother falls as a last call is heard from her mouth, *oy mayne kinder!* [oy my children]. I held my sister with my hand and we continued to run.

Echoes of gunfire, exploding bunkers and screams of terror were heard from every direction. Our game of"tag" lasted for several hours, and with no other way to wrestle with the brutal lead bullets, we clung to the bodies of the murdered, lay next to them pretending to be dead until nightfall.

At nightfall we got up and went to look for those who were still alive.

Once a week we were"honored" with a"hunt" that thinned out our survivors mercilessly.

This is the description of one day… and there were many like it until at the end only four of us remained…

Only four out of all of Tyszowce whose eyes saw the bitter end of the magnificent community that was completely wiped out…

[Page 241]

From the First Days of the War

Moishe Ashpiz (Moishe Diber)–Argentina

Translated by Moses Milstein

I am one of the few people who found themselves in Tishevits during the fire. I will try my best to describe it a little further on, but first, I want to refresh the memory of my fellow townsmen so they may know who I am. I want, in addition, to mention my entire family who were called "Diber."

My uncle Sender Diber had 2 sons, and one daughter who always lived in Tishevits. Their names are Aaron Berish Diber, Mendl Diber, and Sheindl Diber. Sheindl Diber got married to Leibish Ashpiz who was also my uncle, because his brother was my uncle, z"l, who was called Yankl Diber.

My two sisters, Leah'ke and Feige were called "the Diber girls," and had a dry-goods store. I was the youngest in the family. Before my father opened the store in the city, I studied with melamdim in Tishevits, and lived with my uncle Leibish and cousin Sheindl Diber, until my father bought the house from Zuker's son-in-law, Moishe Brenner, who emigrated to Peru. Our neighbor was Moishe Sumess. The house was on the road coming from Komarow, on the street called Pilsudskego.

Now we come to the year 1939 when the war broke out. Our shtetl had a more elegant appearance than earlier. The market was completely paved–Yankl Panich had built a white little fence that beautified the appearance of the city. There were new sidewalks, and it was a lot cleaner.

But a great tragedy arrived with the outbreak of war. Already in the first days of the war everybody had begun to look for ways to save themselves from the bombardments that had not yet reached Tishevits. But the explosions from afar were terrible.

[Page 242]

With the defeat of the polish army, Germans were beginning to be seen. They had not yet shown the evil they were capable of.

Our shtetl became almost empty. Entire families moved out to the villages, some to the suburbs, some to Mikulin, some to Przewale, others to Perespa. We went to Dib [Dub], to a goy we knew. There we were together: My mother and father and I, my two sisters, Leah'ke and Feige, and my oldest sister, Sheindl's, boy, Yosele. My sister, Sheindl, and her younger son, Mendele, remained in their home in Shebreshin [Szczebrzeszyn], and we heard nothing more of them. There were other Jews in Dib, residents of many years. Binyomin Diber and his son, already an adult with grown-up children, Volvish Diber about whom I will write more later, and also Yoski Diber's children, and Zalman Diber who was the son-in-law of Falik Shuster of Tishevits, and also a Jew with the name of Abraham Borg nicknamed, Bidnonye. He used to come to town in a horse and little wagon loaded with flax and other articles that he used to buy in the villages. A long-time resident was also the young tailor, Moishe Goss, now in Israel. There were also Jews who came in from other places and were not originally residents of Dib. These made the local goyim very angry. They told us local Jews that we should expel the newcomers, because the Germans would be more likely to bomb the village because of the foreign Jews.

This lasted several days. Frequent bombardments. Roads filled with people fleeing their homes. Since we were in Dib, father said that it would be more secure if we brought our merchandise over to Dib and hid it in the village. Our store did not have a cellar. But the question arose as to who would drive the carriage. Not one goy we knew was willing. So my father went to see Yankel Moishe Hersh who lived in the forest. He undertook to do the job even though it was dangerous. At night, they did bring a large wagon covered in straw.

Here in Dib, my mother and sisters and I dug a large hole in the stable where we stowed the merchandise, wrapped it well so it would not get ruined, and covered it well with earth on the top because we were afraid of a fire. My mother, a"h, stood over me and wept while I dug the hole. She kept saying," My child, may you at least survive to retrieve the merchandise." She was most afraid for me, because I was then 21 years old, and had been drafted

[Page 243]

into the Polish army, but when the war broke out, I was not mobilized. They had only called up the veterans.

We lived in fear and a lack of food. The starving retreating Polish soldiers took every thing my mother baked or prepared. It was impossible to manage otherwise. We got a little rye, and my mother took it to a neighboring village to be milled. When she returned, she told us how the goyim taunted her, saying that it was certain her men had run away to the Bolsheviks. This was how they made fun of the Jews for the fear that consumed us.

Our house looked very poor. Everything we possessed, even the jewelry, I buried, putting it into the mortar, on the spot where the table stood, burying it deep, and finishing it so no one could tell. But we had a good sign. Rosh Hashanah Eve, around 10:00 o'clock in the morning, we saw heavy smoke in the distance, rising up to the sky, and by our visual calculations we quickly decided Tishevits was on fire. We couldn't tell if it was the suburbs or the city itself. I couldn't help myself, and with the permission of my parents, I ran to the city. Maybe I could save something from our house.

We had only taken away the merchandise. All the household things remained.

A just-married young man, Yoneh Borg, came with me. He was the son of the above-mentioned Abraham, nicknamed, Bidnonye, who was a resident of Dib, and was occupied with buying flax and similar things from the villages. This son married a girl from Tishevits, a seamstress. Her father was Moishe Glazer. I think he was called Moishe Chazer. We agreed to run to Tishevits together. He had new furniture in his newly furnished home. The closer we got to the city, the clearer it became that Tishevits itself was burning. When we got there, we saw the entire side where our house stood, from the Komarow road to the pharmacy, was already incinerated. The pharmacy and the whole row of houses kept burning.

We heard loud explosions, and it was impossible to move about because of the fire. However, seeing that our house was already burned down, I ran over to my cousin, Mendl Diber's house, because the fire had not yet reached there.

[Page 244]

There, I saw goyim from the Ostrow road packing out as much as they could carry.

The fire was burning on all sides. The town hall was already destroyed, as well as the side of Moishele Pshivaler and the Bashisters up to the school, down there where the Mazar family lived. This was all burned down except Srulke Farak's side, Meir Brick's soda water factory was still standing, but the fire grew stronger with the burning of the pharmacy. You could hear loud crackling. I don't know how many people I saw running around, but very few, less than ten. Suddenly there came a loud roaring from bombers overhead. Then I ran back to the bathhouse, and over the bridge that was near the bath, to the toilets. There were several trees there, and I lay down under them.

There were other men and women sheltering there, as well as some children. Lying there too was the young man who had come with me from Dib, and we both came to the conclusion that even though it was too late to save anything, it was perhaps fate that we should be there to witness the destruction of our shtetl Tishevits.

The roaring of the airplanes, and the cracking of the fire were very loud. The women and children who were lying there under the trees were crying and screaming, and the older ones yelled at them to keep quiet so that we would not, God forbid, be noticed.

When the noise settled down, we both began to return to Dib. Remnants of the houses were still smoldering. Nothing was left, not the synagogue, not the besmedresh. If I remember correctly, the bathhouse remained.

These were my last moments in Tishevits as a city. When we got back to the village, I related everything about our house. Understandably, they broke out crying, but we hoped to survive, and afterwards, God would help. Unfortunately, the hope only applied to me–not to my parents or my sisters. In the evening, we went to the minyan to daven. It was after all Rosh Hashanah Eve. We davened together in fear, but we davened. Around us, there was a large movement of Polish military, shooting, bombs exploding, but we Jews did what we had to. The owner of the house we were davening in was Volvish Diber, Binyomin Diber's oldest son. He bought my uncle Sender's house before the war, and since we davened in that comfortable house during the holidays, this year we also

[Page 245]

got together a minyan in the house. It was, of course, dangerous for so many Jews to come together in a village, but the spirit of Rosh Hashanah overcame the fear.

It was a time when there was practically no government, the Polish army completely disorganized.

Gangs were running around, they threw away their uniforms, their weapons, and burned them. We still had not seen any Germans in our neighborhood, because they went to the larger places first, and where there were paved roads. There were in Dib already a lot of refugees, Jews who had fled their homes, and from territories that had already been taken over by the Germans, mostly around Krakow. They fled with whatever means they could, some with horses and large wagons, some in automobiles, some in carts.

My father invited two men for a meal. They were very fine and rich people, but they were already homeless. They told us about the difficulties of finding food along the way, and of travelling. The military filled the roads, and civilians were barred. I did not imagine that I too would soon be homeless. After a few days passed, my father and I went to town.

Coming into the city, we came to our little hill with its destruction, and we looked around and we saw many people doing the same thing. They were looking into cellars, to see if the fire was still smoldering there. In the market, several people were standing around talking about politics just like before. Some had hammered together shelters in order to have a roof over their heads, like Moishe Pshivaler and his son-in-law, Leibish. My father and I started to gather some charred stones, but the work didn't go well, and we abandoned it, and we went back to the village to our family. As I mentioned earlier, there were a lot of Jews in Dib. Among them was Mendl Diber, my cousin, and his wife Esther, and son, Gedalia, and another young boy. He lived in one of the colonies, that is to say, with a goy who lived close to his fields. Berish Diber and his family lived on the Ostrow Road. He had a house there because his previous big house near the river had burned down, and Sheindl Diber with her husband and children went to another village. They had fields there. My uncle, Sender Diber, also came back to Dib, because a little time before the war, he had sold

[Page 246]

his big house in Dib to the previously mentioned Volvish Diber, and moved to Tishevits.

On Yom Kippur, a lot of Polish soldiers assembled in a large field near the yard, gathered their weapons together, and burned them. After that, they went away, some on foot, and some captured horses that were wandering around. One of them was leading a horse and had a hand grenade in his hand saying, "No one is going to take his horse from me." I also managed to get a little revenge on the Polish antisemites. There was a young schoolteacher in Dib. He was a big antisemite. When the Polish army fell apart, he, with the rank of second lieutenant, hid near our house. There he lay, deep in the earth, full of fear like us. Within a few days, we already knew that the Germans had taken the entire neighborhood and that they were the bosses now. It was sad enough for us, but there were very few of them still, and they were staying in the orchard where Hershel Brown lived. It was even said that they were handing out chocolates to the children. We had not yet heard of any terrible things. Then suddenly, they disappeared. For several days it had been rumored that the Red Army was coming to our area. Suddenly we heard a lot of shooting and the entry of so many soldiers the like of which we had not seen to this point. They brought with them lots of heavy artillery. It was fearful to look at. When they entered Dib, there was a lot of heavy shooting. My father and I were not at home. So we began to run, but we had to hide under a pile of straw, because the volleys of bullets were so heavy. When it had quieted down a little, we got back to the house, and we saw a piece of artillery near our house shooting into the forest.

With the first shot, all the windows in the house shattered, and all the lime fell off. We all jumped into a nearby hole, and we all took cover there. My mother cooked a pot of grits, and we ate some, and stayed there until evening.

With the new bosses, the Jews could breathe a little easier. We thought we were saved. Better the Russian than the German. My father went to Komarow. We had a lot of family there on my mother's side. They were my aunts and uncles. We brought them some food because it was easier to get food in the village. When my father returned, he brought the good news with him that the Russians were very good to the Jews. They call everyone "tovaresh," they give rides in their cars on the roads, they give out bread, it was a holiday! On another day, when we went to Tishevits, to see what was going on, I found it quite changed. The market was full of Russians. They were buying everything available from the Jews, like a piece of material to make pants, or material for a woman's dress. They paid very high prices. At the time a Russian Ruble was equal to a Polish Zloty, but you could get any price you asked for. Anyone who had anything dragged it out for sale. What will you do with the money? Nobody knows. Everybody knew there was no merchandise available to buy in return. This was on the day of Sukkot.

These few days with the Russians went by quickly, and suddenly, we heard that the Russians would be retreating from our area. They were going back over the river Bug, and the Germans would reoccupy our area. From that point on, the flights began. Anyone who was able ran away. I talked it over with my cousin, Berish Diber, about whether he would go away. He answered me, "If you want to, run away! I'm not running. How can I? My kids are grown up already. My daughter, Sheindl, has a fiancée from Laszczow. I don't want to separate them," and so on. He was not willing. My father also claimed that he could not, because with the girls, how could he. But among the young men I heard that many were getting ready to go away. So I was tempted as well. I was lucky that my cousin, Elke, actually my uncle Sender's daughter, had gotten married in Zamosc to someone called Moishe Rubinstein. They also had a dry goods store in Zamosc. During the bombardments, they had also buried their merchandise with a goy in Dib. When the Russians were beginning to leave Zamosc, my cousin, Elke, convinced a Russian soldier to drive to Dib to collect the merchandise, because when the Russians were leaving they said to everyone, "Come with us, and if you have anything, we will take it with." And so she came from Zamosc with an automobile. This was exactly on Simchat Torah.

The driver of the truck said he would take as many as could fit.

Then all the young people in the Village began to get ready to leave, because we had a good opportunity.

[Page 248]

I approached my father: What do you think, father? What should I do? Other young men were looking to see what I would do. If my father would give me permission, they could go too. My father answered with these words: "You, my child, are young. Maybe you can save yourself." This was my father's blessing which accompanied me during my worst suffering and the pain to come. The following people came with us: Moishe Goss who is now in Israel with his family, Israel Goldman who is now in Israel, Etl Yoski Diber's daughter, a divorcee and her two daughters. She was married to David Treger of Tishevits. There was also a young boy Abraham Goldman, a grandson of Falik Shuster of Tishevits. A Jew from Komarow who was a son-in-law of Yoski Diber. I don't know if the latter survived.

This Simchat Torah was very sad for us. My mother put two small loaves of bread, a little sugar, and a few other things to eat, in a kerchief, and my father embraced me and kissed me. His long beard pressed against my face, a feeling that will stay with me for the rest of my days. My mother wept bitterly. My sisters hugged me, and my little nephew, Yoseleh, was also weeping. And the Russian driver was shouting, "Faster!" And so in haste we parted. I climbed up on the truck and cast a last look at my father, my mother, and my sisters, Leah'ke and Faige, and my little nephew, Yoseleh.

From that point on, I wandered as a refugee through all kinds of inconceivable hardships until the year 1947, a span of eight years, until I ended up in Argentina where my older brother had already been living. If I would have the opportunity to describe my further experiences, that is, from 1939 to 1947, it would surely be a chapter of Jewish suffering. When I arrived in Argentina, the Tishevitsers already here organized a get-together where I gave them an overview of the devastation I had lived through. There are about 40 families from Tishevits in Argentina. Every year before Rosh Hashanah, we get together to remember our home that was destroyed, and all our dear ones who were so brutally murdered. In ending, I want to describe an episode that I heard about involving 50 young boys and girls from Tishevits and from Komarow who were brought together by the aforementioned Volvish Diber. He was the milkman

[Page 249]

of the Diber court. The landowner at the time was a German officer, but one who wanted to save the lives of some young people by giving them work. He managed to get together 50 children. There, they worked and lived with plenty of hardships, but hope still lived on. Unfortunately however, after the harvest, when the wheat was being threshed, three officers from the SS arrived. They dug a grave in the Diber Woods. The children were stripped naked in the orchard of the court, and from there, they were driven to the grave. All 50 children were shot there. Volvish, who felt he was to blame, asked to be the first, along with his wife and children, to be martyred, so he wouldn't have to see the many children he wanted to save, murdered. Among them was my sister, Feige.

Holy is their memory.

Toba Kornblit, z"l

Mindl Kornblit (Dum)–Israel

Translated by Moses Milstein

I am not in a position to express my sadness on the destruction of our shtetl, Tishevits.

The first victim in the Second World War was my younger sister, Toba, z"l. Instead of being led to the chupah, she was led to the cemetery. May these few words serve as a consolation and everlasting memorial.

[Page 250]

Memories from the Holocaust The Valley of Slaughter
(Eyewitness testimony from Mrs. Esther Katzenhandler
who was miraculously saved from certain death)

Efraim Kuperstein (Haifa) Israel

Translated by Sara Mages

In the village of P'yatydni, a distance of about seven kilometers from Ludmir [Volodymyr], Wolyn Oblast, there is a huge mass grave. More than thirty thousand Jews, men, women, the elderly and children, were shot to death there, and also buried alive. All from the cities: Ustyluh and Ludmir, the survivors from the surrounding area, and also from our city Tyszowce z"l, who fled to the border of the Bug River from the Nazi hell after the Stalin-Hitler pact.

The Kuperstein family

The murder selections began on the 19 of Elul 5702 (September 5, 1942), and lasted for about fifteen days. The German murderers, together with their helpers, the Ukrainian and Polish killers, executed all the Jews in the mass grave that had been prepared beforehand.

[Page 251]

The German murderers gave instructions over the loudspeakers: "The people should take off all their clothes and also remove prostheses and eyeglasses." There were some people who refused to undress, so their tore clothes were torn off and they were beaten brutally.

A period of twenty-five years has already passed since the great disaster in the history of our people, the likes of which history has not seen before. Ever since the German Nazis invaded Europe, and annihilated European Jewry, they specifically chose Poland as the place of murder and annihilation of the magnificent Jewry in this country.

It is impossible to believe that someone is able to write, and remember, all the horrors we have gone through.

Therefore, we will vow, and will remember and perpetuate together, in this holy book, everything that happened to our people, and it will serve as a tombstone for those who perished during the Holocaust.

In the aforementioned mass grave is also my family, the Kuperstein family z"l - the grandfather, R' Menachem Mendel, the father, Eliakum Getzel, the mother, Leah, the sisters, Ruchele and Chayale, her son, Shalom and her husband, Yosef of the Appelbaum family of Ludmir, and the brothers Avraham and Moshe.

I write down their names to commemorate them for eternal memory in this holy book.

My mother Leah z"l:

A native of Hrubieszów from a very privileged family, the family of Shalom and Basha Zimmerman (my grandmother was known by the name, Basha *di esik makher* [the vinegar maker]). Who didn't know my mother? A noble mother, educated, dedicated in heart and soul to the Zionist idea and kind-hearted. She did not refrain from giving help and encouragement to the needy, and, above all, was endowed with courage and fortitude.

In 1932, she drove away a masked robber with a gun in his hand who attacked us in our house in the evening. "Silver and gold!" he shouted and demanded. Mother didn't stop to think: she quickly jumped through the window to the balcony, summoned help, called the police, and after a battle with the policemen, he was seriously injured and died. Then we learned that the robber was Franek, the well-known communist from Ostrów. That's how my mother was, and I will never forget her, may her soul be bound up in the bond of eternal life.

My grandfather: R 'Menachem Mendel z"l, was very devout, from the strictest of the strictest. An honest man, rich, and yet he lived modestly. He always lived together with my grandmother Rivka at my parents' house. He engaged in Torah and Talmud study day and night. May his soul be bound up in the bond of eternal life.

My father Eliakum Getzel z"l:

My father was a public activist, cantor, community leader and chairman of Agudat Mizrachi, and was loved and accepted by all the strata of townspeople. A member of the Jewish community committee, philanthropist and hospitable, and was among the major and richest merchants, and always worked not in order to receive a reward. May his soul be bound up in the bond up of eternal life.

My brother, Avraham z"l, was a real genius in the written and oral Torah, observant and devoted to the ideology of the Betar Movement. May his soul be bound up in the bond of eternal life.

My brother Moishele z"l:

According to hearsay, he managed to escape from the ghetto to the forest, to the Jewish partisans, but the Polish partisans frequently attacked the Jewish partisans, and after a battle with the Poles many Jews fell, among them Moishele. May his soul be bound up in the bond of eternal life.

Honor to the memory of my family, my sisters and brothers, they will remain engraved in my heart, and in my memory, for eternity.

————

[Page 252]

Memories of our Experiences
in the Time of the Second World War

Told by Shosheh and Hersh Englstein

Written by Moishe Sachar

Translated by Moses Milstein

It is not possible to remember every moment of the tragic war era. It is hard to believe that a person can undergo such frightening experiences. And in truth, still today–so many years later–I can see before me the sorrowful moments and shadows of that tragic experience. I was born in Tishevits, and lived there until 1928. My wife was from Hrubieszow which is why we lived there until 1939.

With the outbreak of the Second World War, fate landed us, after fleeing and wandering around, in a shtetl, Tyczyn, near Rowne.

With the entry of the Germans, the Jews of the shtetl, along with the refugees who had fled from various places, were imprisoned in a ghetto. Their number was from two to three thousand Jews. The Jews lived there for about a year. The leader of the Judenrat, a certain Getzl Shwartz, had good relations with the residents. He was not one of those who collaborated with the Nazis. He was among the first to call for resistance.

When by chance it was discovered that the Germans were preparing to liquidate the ghetto, and they had prepared graves in the forest not far from the shtetl, we decided not to allow ourselves to be led to our graves, and every family got some naphtha or benzene ready with the goal of setting the houses on fire, and even to be burned alive, so as not to allow ourselves to be murdered by the Germans.

In 1942, two days after Yom Kippur, the Gestapo came with trucks to take the Jews to their graves. When the Gestapo informed the leader of the Judenrat, H' Getzl Shwartz, that they wanted to take the Jews out of the ghetto, H' Shwartz expressed his opposition,

[Page 253]

and was shot on the spot. The shot was a signal for the ghetto residents, and the ghetto went up in flames immediately. Very many were burned alive. Among them, my wife's mother, Beile Fink, z"l, with one of our children who was with her.

The Gestapo surrounded the burning ghetto and shot anyone who tried to escape. Only a small number succeeded in getting to the forest. We split into groups in the forest, so we would not be concentrated. Naturally, the groups consisted of city families and acquaintances. Every group was a family of its own.

Once, I left the village to look for food for my wife and children, but I could not, under any circumstances, find my way back to them. I wandered around day and night searching with no luck. My wife, seeing that the children would starve to death, went off to look for me in the forest leaving the children alone. She met people from other groups along the way, but no one knew where I was. At one point she came across a young man, and asked him if he had heard of a Hersh Englstein. So he told her in secret that there was a Hersh in a certain group, but not Englstein. She had heard about this Hersh, because we knew him. She figured that she might learn something from him, so she went along with the group in order to find that Hersh. But the group was against her joining them, because it would make their lives more difficult–yet another person in the group, a woman to boot, weak and exhausted. But my wife told them categorically that she would under no circumstance leave the group without finding her husband. Seeing her determination, and having no other option, they agreed to let her go along. Going with them, she did in fact find the other Hersh's group. He really did know in which group and where I was, and he brought her to me. As soon as we were reunited, we went off to return to our children. We found them half unconscious from hunger. I gave them something to eat and they revived.

We decided to build bunkers, and to find ways to get some weapons for self-defense.

We suffered like this for two years from 1942-1944. A life of pain, suffering and hunger. We used to work for the farmers in the villages, and

[Page 254]

get some food that way. We also scoured the fields for anything to still the hunger. The situation at the fronts worsened. The Germans began to retreat from their positions. As a result of the complicated situation, the Germans, with the help of the Banderites[1], began to rampage through the area. First they killed the Poles in the area, and then they turned their attention to the Jews.

Some farmers from the village let us know that the Germans, with the help of Ukrainians, were planning attacks on the bunkers in the forest. What could we then do? The situation was hopeless.

One day, in 1944, the Germans, and the Banderists, entered the forest, and wherever they ferreted out a bunker, they threw in hand grenades. We could hear all that, and we were in fear of death knowing that our turn would come soon. We really expected to die, because what sense does such a life have? But, it was either fated, or simply a miracle, that night had fallen before our turn came. The attacking units, it seems, received the order to stop the attacks via a trumpet signal. That night, we resolved to go to the river Sluch that was in that area.

We moved like shadows at the edge of the forest in the direction of the river. The farmers from that neighborhood told us that the river was not frozen in spite of the cold weather. Not having any option we went all the way to the river. But how to get to the other side? The river was pretty wide and deep. There was once a farm near the river with a large horse barn. We noticed a deep, large trough the horses used to drink out of. We wanted to turn the big wooden trough into a boat. We tied ropes around it, and lowered it into the water. But when the first two people got into it, and pushed off from the shore, it was caught by a strong current, and the two people barely managed to make it back to shore. We saw that our "boat" was unfortunately not feasible. Not having any other options, we decided to go back to the forest. We did not, however, know which direction to take. After a short discussion, we gave a young boy who was with us, Moishe Weisbrod, the job of pulling out a handkerchief with a knot in it, to determine which of us would go left and which right. Our group was to go right. We divided ourselves into two groups: one to go left and one to go right. In the middle, we sent out

[Page 255]

scouts. While walking along, we saw two human forms in the distance. They looked very fat. The closer they got, the fatter they looked. Fear in those days was a natural phenomenon for us. We ordered the two forms to halt! If not, we would open fire! They stopped, and we got closer to them. They were carrying sheaves of straw on their heads. We saw that they were farmers who lived in the area.

They exchanged hellos with us, and with enthusiasm, they told us that there was a village not far from there where there were more of "your own." By this, they meant the Russian partisans who had come to scout out the area before the Red Army arrived.

We felt some relief at that, of course. As we continued along the road toward the village, we noticed smoke and light issuing from the huts. When we entered the homes, the farmers told us that they were baking bread for the partisans who were in a nearby village, and that the partisans were going to come and pick up the bread. We waited impatiently for the partisans, but they did not show up so quickly. We couldn't wait much longer knowing that day was coming, and the light would put us in an uncomfortable position. So some of us went off to the village where the partisans were, in order to find out the truth. When the delegation returned, we found out that the partisans had left for another destination. We determined to follow them. We got to that village and met the Russian partisans. They greeted us amiably, and actually helped us get over the river Sluch, where we came to a village called Stara-Huta.We came across Soviet army units stationed there, as well as partisans. We breathed a little easier then.

Our only desire was to rest and to get something to eat. But typhus was raging through the whole village. We entered a house where everyone was laid up sick. Near them was some food. I took some of it and gave it to my children.

The memory of these frightening experiences makes me shudder, thinking about how people could have survived this.

One of the Soviet officers told me then, "I know you Jews don't like to fight, and you will certainly now go to Palestine." They younger ones among us were immediately drafted into the army. The rest went to Poland hoping to find family members. From our group, only 60 people remained. Among the 60, only two intact families. We went to Lodz, where the returnees were concentrating.

After a certain amount of time in Lodz, Poland, we saw that we could not continue to live there, and to tie our children's future there. So we decided to go to Israel somehow. Our children left with the children's aliyah before us. We came via the DP camps of Germany, after the founding of Israel. We live here now, and are happy. From our children, we have *nachess*. We have eight grandchildren, and beg God for health and peace in the land. The specter of war makes us tremble, remembering the tragic times we lived through.

Footnote:

    1.   Stepan Bandera, Ukrainian antisemitic, far-right nationalist.

[Page 256]

Episode Engraved in my Memory

Esther Bluzer-Kizel (America)

Translated by Moses Milstein

At the beginning of the war, when they had begun bombing our shtetl, Tishevits, all the Jewish residents fled to the closest wooded areas outside the city, hoping to survive the first horrible days of the war. A few days later, the whole shtetl was engulfed in flames.

The panic was unbearable, and cries echoed through the whole forest.

Everyone was faced with the same question: where will we go now? And what awaits us in the future? Like other young people then, I gathered my courage, and went back to the city to see if our house had also burned down.

On the way out of the forest stood our rabbi, R' Artshele, with his whole family, huddled against the wall of a farmer's house. His gentle face was white as chalk. His blue eyes were full of fear. His whole body trembled. In his face, you could read the entire Jewish experience of grief.

[Page 257]

His eyes were pleading for help, and at the same time, expressed all the pain of the Jewish population of the shtetl, Tishevits.

But I was shattered even more by the distress of his wife, the Tishevits rebbetsin, and their helpless children.

Although I was not especially religious, I had always had special feelings for our religious, spiritual leaders, and my heart was truly breaking. But unfortunately, I could not help them in any way. That was the last time I saw our rebbe. But this scene has remained forever in my memory.

In the first row, standing, from right to left: Yechezkl Singer, Sholem Rov (Spodik), Chaimtche Zwillich (chazzan), Moishe Dovid Samit, Yankl Adler (Dutche's), Leibish Gelber, Berish Gelber
Second row: Moishe Singer, Dovid Adler (Ozer's), Artshe (the rabbi), Moishe Zalman Lifsh (Kvetcher), Nataniel Gelber (Sani), Yasheh Shammes, Moishe Adler (Pshivoler)

[Page 258]

Chaya Halfman z"l:

Translated by Sara Mages

Chaya Halfman z"l was born in 1922, was a member of the partisan organization in the Tyszowce forests (Lublin Province).

In the summer of 1942, she was killed in the forest by a soldier of the Polish Home Army.

[Page 259]

Shaya (Yeshiyahu) Shtengel of Tishevits, Active Participant in the Warsaw Ghetto Uprising

Sholem Krishtalke (Montreal, Canada)

Translated by Moses Milstein

Tishevits is considered one of the smaller shtetls in Poland. Nevertheless, it possessed a goal-oriented youth, an active youth, in almost all political movements and hues of Jewish life.

Shaya Shtengel, z"l

The youth of Tishevits could not stand by and remain indifferent to the events occurring in the world, and to be satisfied only by reading reports in the press.

No, they wanted to take part in all the historical struggles occurring at the time, whether in Poland, or in Russia.

[Page 260]

This active contingent of young people went out into the world to fight, each according to his intellect and moral convictions.

Moishe Krempel volunteered to fight in Spain in 1936, in the Botvin Brigade[1] against Franco and his fascist regime. Other young people left for the larger cities to fight and to be more effective in their national and social aspirations.

One of these idealists was Shaya Shtengel. Shaya began his idealistic social activities in "Yung-Bar," continued in "Yugent Komitet" of the leftist Poalei Zion, was a a keen student in the "evening courses for adults." In 1931, he moved to Warsaw and immediately became active in Poalei Zion "Yugent."

By trade a painter, he was very active in the professional association of his trade. He was treated by everyone with great love and respect.

During the war years, Shtengel was the editor of Poalei Zion's monthly journal, "Die Freieh Yugent." On November 11, 1933, my wife, Shifre, and I travelled through Warsaw on our way to Canada. Shaya Shtengel, with a cousin of ours, Yidl Danziger, a student at the religious teachers seminary, came to visit us and to say good-bye.

After receiving greetings from the shtetl, the talk turned to the sad world situation in general, and the Jewish case in particular where we saw a significant win by the Nazi party in the elections to the Reichstag; and the sad situation of the Polish Jews, who were not being allowed to travel to Palestine because of the British quota system. And whoever had the ability to save himself, should do so. It was an aware person and Jew who stood before us, who understood and had correctly evaluated the situation at that time, but who was nevertheless full of faith that our ideals were right and would triumph.

Looking for material on the subject "Tishevits in Holocaust literature," I came on the name, Shaya (Yeshiahu) Shtengel in the large, monumental work of Melech Neustadt–"Destruction and Resistance of the Jews in Warsaw–Testimonies and Memorials–Tel Aviv 1948, 2 volumes. And in the section–the Fallen on Guard–page 693, Melech Danziger writes:

"Shtengel Yeshiahu (Shaya): From the shtetl Tishevits near Chelm. A construction worker, a rare occupation among Polish Jews. Shaya was very respected in his shtetl. A loyal member of the youth movement of the leftist Poalei Zion. Coming to Warsaw before the war, he faithfully continued his work as an active and important

[Page 261]

doer of "Yugent." He was also involved in the youth section of the professional union of construction workers. In a letter from Poalei Zion to their colleagues in Eretz-Israel–of May 21, 1944–he is mentioned as one of those members who remained active at their posts until their final moment. He was 30 years old at the time.

In a second spot in the above-mentioned book, page 232, in a letter from Adolph (Dr. A. Berman) of the central committee of Poale Zion, Warsaw, May 24, 1944, to the comrades in Israel, Dr. Berman gives a report about the progress of the resistance and life in the ghetto, the activities of various comrade-leaders, how they conscientiously performed in all aspects of the work, and helped in the ghetto. Among others, Dr. Berman singles out a number of comrades "who actively worked up to the last minute of their lives, taking part in the organization of the armed resistance, or fighting until they fell in battle."

One of the 35 participants cited was our comrade, Shaya Shtengel.

Yakov Kenner in his book, "Kvershnit," 1897-1947, New York, 1947, in the third part under the name, Yizkor, memorializes with words of gratitude the martyrs, and holy warriors who died in the battle against the Nazis, may their name be erased.

Yakov Kenner dedicates a whole part of his book to Shaya Shtengel, page 271, which we publish here in its entirety.

"Shaya Shtengl, a painter worker from the shtetl, Tishevits, between Chelm and Hrubieszow–came to Warsaw in order to benefit culturally and to take part in a large mass organization.

As a painter, he also made a living in Tishevits. Tishevits possessed a strong Poalei Zion "Yugent," but no party could develop there, because when a young person grew up, he wandered away abroad, or at least to Warsaw, because at home an adult worker had no future. An exception in this regard in Tishevits was Shaya Shtengel. Because of the painter's trade he inherited from his father and brother, he looked for bigger prospects than the shtetl could provide. Every Shabbes, he wanted to hear a new speaker, he wanted to see Yiddish theater, and

[Page 262]

he wanted to rise to greater political activity in the ranks of the party organization not available to him in Tishevits.

So he came to Warsaw full of naïve imaginings, and honest ideals. He quickly got himself set financially in his trade, and quickly became active in the youth section of the Jewish construction union under the leadership of the late comrade, Lazar Stolier. He associated early on with the "Yugent," as a political-cultural organization, and he slaked his thirst somewhat for culture in the widely diverse cultural activities available.

The last few years, he belonged to the party, but he never gave up his ties to "Yugent" where he was politically and spiritually raised. He was strongly motivated to emigrate to Israel in latter years, where he could put his skills as a certified painter in the service of the country. He was just waiting for his newborn son to get a little older. In the meantime, war broke out which put an end to his hopes. Later came the underground activities of the Jewish battle organization, and he became its technician. He built the central bunkers, installed the secret underground command radio station, and when the ghetto uprising broke out, he died a hero's death. "

Shaya Shtengl received a Jewish upbringing in his home, and in his shtetl. In the Poalei Zion party, he learned the spirit of justice, and the synthesis of socialism in the workers' Eretz Israel.

And when the time came to fight against the greatest enemy of the Jewish People, Shaya Shtengel stood in the first ranks to defend Jewish honor in the spirit of our Maccabees. He died a hero's death on the battlefield.

Footnote:

1. In December 1937, a Jewish company, the Botvin Brigade, was formed from mainly Polish Jews and political emigrés from France and Belgium. It was named after Naphtali Botvin who had been executed by the Polish authorities in 1924. (Jewish Chronicle)

[Page 263]

Memories

Tova Mendelowic (Pump) (Israel)

Translated by Sara Mages

Much has been told, and more will be told, by eyewitnesses to what the Nazi soldiers did to their Jewish victims. Many will never see the light of day. The massacred took their secrets to the grave. Only a few of the survivors managed to draw from the depths of their souls the tragic events that befell entire families and individuals who left no sign or trace of their existence on earth. And the oblivion- covers layer upon layer, a whole wide world that has been destroyed. About breastfed babies who were murdered before they tasted the taste of life. The heavens were shut. My cousin, Tovale, brings up one of the unknown tragic events that befell the youth who were plucked before they blossomed, helpless people who expected salvation from the grace of Heaven, and Iszai and her mother Rachel Pump of the Zwilich family (Mendelowic).

When the war broke out in 1939 I was about eight years old. The school year had come to an end, and we had been looking forward to the festive ceremony of handing out the certificates for the end of the school year the following day. But the echoes of gunfire, and the panicked flight in every direction, transported us to a different reality. Tyszowce went up in flames. That night we found ourselves on a wagon loaded with belongings and a little food on the way to the village of Kraczew near Komarów. We were not the only ones who escaped on that sleepless night. Some escaped in wagons and some on foot, not knowing where to go. The sky turned red and lit the way to the entrance to the forest. The mystery of the forest did not frighten me at that time. I was too young to feel the magnitude of the threatening danger, and what we were afraid of. We kept quiet. Here we found shelter for a while with a farmer we knew. A considerable number of Jews stayed with gentiles in the Tyszowce area for another six months. Among them were my uncles Mendl and Melech Zwilich and some of their family members, as well as Iszai Zwilich and his family (my uncle Zachariah and his family had left Tyszowce at the outbreak of the war). From time to time I came to them with the help of a farmer from the village and brought them food. One day, a gendarme took my uncle Mendl outside while he was making soap, and killed him on the spot. The fate of the other families was no different. Some found their death in the Zamość Ghetto, and some saturated the damned Tyszowce soil with their blood with the active assistance of their neighbors. Twelve families from Tyszowce hid for about a year in the village of Kraczew, until a rumor spread that the Germans were conducting searches for Jews in hiding in the villages, and that every farmer who sheltered a Jew would be executed. The twelve families immediately left the village and found refuge with a landowner (pritz) from Chortkov. He badly needed manpower on his farm and probably with the Germans' knowledge. Here, they were forced to do hard physical labor from sunrise to sunset, in exchange of a loaf of bread and a place to live in a shabby storeroom.

[Page 264]

It was also a death trap for the handful of Jews. In the morning of November 12 1942, the illusion reached its tragic end in accordance with the best of Nazi organization and methods. At dawn, several vehicles loaded with Germans surrounded the farm from all sides, and took every Jew who was outside the farm, while shooting in the air in every direction. They gathered together all the inhabitants of the village, young and old, and the farm workers, to watch the horror show. It is hard to describe this horrible sight the way a ten year old girl saw it! I would never forget the screams and cries that reached the heavens.

The Germans, in order to sate their sadism, ordered three Jews to dig a large grave, and when it was completed they aimed their weapon at them and killed them. This is how they abused the last Jew in the place.

I don't know how it happened. When I stood there next to my parents by the open grave, a Christian boy, one of the farm workers, grabbed my hand, pulled me to the side and shouted at me to come home at once. The Germans were too busy and did not notice what was happening, that's how I escaped and saved my life. From a distance of several meters I heard the shots that killed my parents and my brother David. I fled from the place and hid in a pit in the field. At night I came out and returned to the big grave. I cried there all night. I knew that from then on I wouldn't have a living soul to take care of me and protect me. From then on I felt, in a tangible way, the concept of fear of humans. The animals were closer to me. They didn't hurt me. I hid in the forest in a tree, collected scraps of food in the forest and in the fields, and revived my soul. On days when I couldn't get anything to eat, I ate tree bark. I also collected some sacks from the fields which served me as clothes and cover from the cold. I wrapped my legs in rags, and so I wandered from place to place at the mercy of Heaven. Amazingly, I never got sick in the years of hell, not even once. Over time, I lost count of the days; I didn't know when it was a holiday. The ringing of the bells reminded me it was Sunday, and the gentiles' holidays aroused fear in me.

In 1944, when the first signs appeared that the war was about to end, I came out more in the surrounding area in order to hear news from the girls in the village. From them, I learned that a number of Jews who were hiding in the villages and the forests were flocking to Zamość, to a concentration station for Jewish survivors from the entire area.

The son of one of the farmers took me to Zamość. There I met for the first time strangers brought closer to each other by the shared fate of being Jewish. From then on, I was no longer lonesome and haunted by my own shadow. I moved with them from place to place towards the final stop, Eretz Yisrael.

However, all the hardships of the war years did not pass without leaving their mark on me. First, I fell ill with typhus, and all the rest came one after the other. The wounds on my body may have healed, but I will never forget the scars left on my soul and spirit from that day and night of horrors of November 12 1942, and the years of loneliness in the forest.

In 1947, I arrived in Italy together with groups of Jewish youth who had survived the camps. Here, they took good care of us in an Israeli atmosphere, and tried to give us back some of the joy of youth that had passed forever. We studied part of the curriculum of the schools in Israel, geography, singing, dancing and the way of life in Israel, and here I also found my future husband in one of the instructors who, like me, was a Holocaust survivor, and we built a new nest in our country.

[Page 265]

A Visit to Tishevits After the War

Berl Eidelsberg

Translated by Moses Milstein

Related by Berl Eidelsberg, (son of "Der Weisser Yosef," and Fradl Oizer's) and his wife Elke (nee Adler, daughter of Bentche Datcheh Oizer's and Miriam, descended from the "Tsapess") who lived in the suburbs. They left Tishevits with the arrival of the Germans, and survived along with their two children. They now live in Israel.

When the Germans, may their name be erased, left Poland, we began to look for our relatives, but unfortunately we were unable to find any alive. We were in Tishevits twice, once at the beginning of 1945. The goyim, our well-known neighbors like Frenek Dziabinsky, who lived in the same courtyard as my father, and other neighbors, said that they helped the Jews a lot, above all my father and brothers. But when I asked them why they didn't hide any of my brothers or sisters, they had no answer. We looked for traces of anyone at all, but we could not find any information. A year later, when we were living in Lodz, some goyim approached us to buy our house. We learned from them that my brothers Voveh and Laizer, and other young boys and young women from Tishevits were provided with work by the nobleman from Dobuzek, Kalaczkowski, My uncle, *a"h*, appealed to him that he should ask the Germans to give him ten young men, and several women for work. They worked there until, one day, some Germans arrived, demanded that the Jews be taken from their work, and shot everyone. They told me this took place in the summer of 1942. Then we traveled to Tishevits for the second time. We wanted to gather the bones together of all the martyrs in one grave. They told us however

[Page 266]

that no one knew exactly where the Jews were buried, because the majority of the Jews were sent to Belzec. There were gas chambers there, but they shot our brothers and sisters in the city and the suburbs. Obviously, we were unable to accomplish anything by ourselves. Where the city of Tishevits once stood is now an empty place. Where the market once was, only a few booths and stalls remained. It was a Wednesday, a market day, farmers brought everything like they had done before the war, only a little less, but the Jewish stores, the Jewish taverns, the Jewish mills, the Jewish granaries, the Jewish streets, were no longer there. We visited the place where the old cemetery was, now a field of rye. The rye was growing tall and beautiful, nicer and higher than in our rye fields. We also went to visit our mothers who are buried in the new cemetery. On the way there, we found ourselves walking on tombstones, torn away from the graves it seems, or maybe not yet inscribed, because we could see no letters on the stone. It was Wednesday, and the farmers were traveling to the market from the villages. They recognized us, and even greeted us. How are you? Where are you? Where are you living? They were "happy" to see us, showed us "love," and spoke with hatred of the Germans. Every one of them assured us that we could come live in Tishevits together in peace.

Then we asked them about our brothers and sisters and why none of them were capable of hiding a Jew. They had no answer. We then traveled back to Tishevits with the thought that we would organize all the Tishevitsers found in Poland, and we would all make an effort to gather the bones of our martyrs. We soon joined with the Tishevitsers from Wroclaw. We decided on a date to meet in Wroclaw. I was then in Wroclaw. I myself contributed 25,000 zlotys to encourage others to contribute. We decided to establish a committee with Moishe Krempl as chairman, and approach the Tishevitsers from America, Argentina, Peru, and other countries to raise an amount of money in order to travel to Tishevits, and arrange for the burial of the scattered victims. But unfortunately, not everyone was so enthusiastic and dedicated to the task. The initiative went over to Wroclaw where the majority of the Tishevitsers lived. But they dragged it out so long that the Tishevitsers left Poland. Once in Israel, we heard that something was done in that respect.

[Page 267]

The following letter was written by a Christian from Tishevits in 1950 to Dov Shpiz in Israel. In the letter, she mentions his parents, Leibish Dovid Garbert and wife Ruchel Tzalkess, and their four children, and also Bentzieh Shpiz and his family. The Milstein family is also mentioned here. They were called Rozers.

(The letter is translated from Polish)

2.1.1950

Dear Berko,

The letter we received from you brought us a lot of joy, because we learned that you were among the survivors. None of your parents survived. They were killed by the Germans. After you left, Lubeh married a Jew from Warsaw. The Jews from Warsaw were brought to Tishevits to control the river flow. He got to know Lubeh, and they got married. He stayed on in the shtetl, because in Warsaw there was no food. People were dying of hunger there. Within the year, she gave birth to a boy who later died. The Germans continued to persecute the Jews, and in 1943, Shavuot, they attacked the Jewish homes at night, drove all the Jews out to a square, loaded them onto trucks and the remainder onto wagons, and took them to Zamosc, and murdered them there. Among those who traveled in the wagons was Lube, and with a few others, she managed to escape. The driver was an acquaintance, and the German had fallen asleep. Returning to the shtetl, she was unable to find her husband, and she went to her parents. Your father, mother, Etl Chava and Moishe were hiding in the house, Lube with them.

The Germans persecuted the remaining Jews even more. Your mother and children crossed the river and hid in the meadows, and your father fled to the forest. While Chavah was off looking for your father, your mother and the children were burnt in the Meadows. Chavah stayed with us because she had nowhere else to go, and was waiting for her father to come back from the forest, and take her with him. Your father used to come to us every second night to get some food, and he took her with him. There were four of them, your father, Chavah, Mendl Ruben's, and Somer's boy. They were in the forest until February. When they were captured, they refused to reveal who was providing them with food, so they were burned. There is no one left from your family.

[Page 268]

About your house: the Germans sold it for demolition, and it was demolished. The place was taken over by the "Tibulchikin." We wanted to build a house on the place, but she wouldn't allow us. On your grandfather, Dovid's, place, where Bentche had built a brick house, Faral Leon lives there now. His wife and daughters were hidden at Maliss's in the stable. They were discovered and burnt in the "valley." The sons, Yekl, Chaim and Motl worked in the village for a nobleman, and they were murdered there. The rest of the places are free. You should know that Ludwig Stelmalczik died, and his sons, Kazik, Vladek, and Franek, and Stelmalczik Ignaz, and Walaszen's wife and son, Stach, two Tibulik brothers from Komarow, and others, altogether 9 people were murdered in the Zamosc prochawnia. Now it's called the "rotunda."

We are all in good health, but my brother, Tomek, died in 1944. My older son, Czecho, got married, and is attending a trade school. He lives in Szczeczyn. My mother is still alive. She is 80 years old. I write to you about certain neighbors. Masheh Chazer's had a bunker in her house where 10 people stayed. They were able to hide for a few days. After that they were discovered, and in the courtyard near the bridge at Hodes's place, they were killed. A lot of people were murdered there. Today the place is called "ghetto." Itche Chazer, who went with you to Russia, stayed there a short time, then returned to the shtetl. He hid for a year in the village with his brother, Hersh. Later, they were murdered near Koles's house, and buried in the valley on the other side of the river.

I will end here. Next time, I will write you everything about who was killed and where they are buried.

Awaiting your reply, your neighbors,

Manke and Ignasz.

Greetings to your brother, Yakov, and greetings from all.

[Page 269]

Where is the City?

Sholom Stern (Montreal, Canada)

Translated by Moses Milstein

(A chapter from "Pages From a Trip to Poland"–also printed in "Pinkas Zamosc"–written in 1948)

The bus grinds over the sandy dirt road between Zamosc and my home town, Tishevits, I am sunk in my own difficult experiences of the day. Y. L. Peretz, the great Jew and poet no longer reposes in Warsaw. How can he lie quietly in his resting place, between his best friends Dinezon, and Ansky, while his fellow Jews were being exterminated? Y.L. Peretz was tortured with every Jew individually on the road to Belzec. With every Jewish congregation, he was there.

It is the evening of Tisha B'Av. The bus speeds to the suburb, over the long bridge, passing through the courtyard, bumping over the other little bridge at the beginning of the shtetl. But where is the city? We stop at the police station on the other side of town. Where did the shtetl disappear to? Where have we strayed to? My throat constricts with a burning thirst as if I were wandering around in a desert. There is no shtetl.

It was burned down by the retreating Poles in September 1939.[1] There was a labor camp in Tishevits. No trace of a house. I can't find the place where our house stood. No memory of a city, no wall, chimney, no foundation, just holes and overgrown graves from which black, angry crows scream. Who has so devastated the shtetl? The Poles, our neighbors for hundreds of years, lay in wait for the Jewish poor to rob them. They, who shot at the retreating Red Army, they who wanted to undermine the new peoples' government with savage impassioned shouts in Lublin: " Daj nam boga, give us God!" These were the very ones who helped murder the Jews. They searched and rummaged for gold

[Page 270]

and money in the walls, in the cellars. They looted everything; stole, and left blind graves overgrown with spiky grass.

The sky is burning. The sun is a bloody revolving circle, and blood pours from brick stairs into the desolation. The crows fly off with frightened crowing; they play in the burning rays of the sun.

What day is it today? Tisha B'Av. But I am hearing the Sabbath Eve song of Shir Hashirim. Here, it seems, the Husiatyn shtibl stood, the besmedresh, the shul with its paintings of trumpets, the tribes with flags, the ark of the covenant, the Jews wandering in the desert, the Leviathan eating its tail, because if he takes it out of his mouth, the world comes to an end and returns to emptiness and desolation. The sky at twilight flickers above us. Here it descends and flames encircle us. We stride through a world that shouts in flames but is not consumed. A wasteland! Hot dust whirls. Black rooks crow, jump over the ditches. An old Polish woman who speaks Yiddish wrings her hands, "I don't remember you, but I knew your parents, mamelach! God in heaven, do you remember my husband, my Benedict? The bandits killed him too."

The Polish lawyer in town, Jeremczik, and his wife (who lived in Detroit as a girl) take us around. He himself was in Auschwitz for five years. She tells me in English certain facts about the slaughter. A lot of Jews are buried in the meadows, in the fields. We come to the river that led to the pasture. The bathhouse was once here, the poorhouse. A broad, swift, current circled around the gardens and willows. Now the river is dry, a swampy-green sheet spread over the pools of water. We jump over. You see, in these very pools, blood flowed for hours from the Jews shot and stabbed. Twice, the great slaughters of annihilation took place: the first, Shavuot 1942, and the second and last, two weeks after the Days of Awe. Here behind the cabbage and beet gardens lie the majority of Tishevits's murdered Jews, as well as Jews from Czechoslovakia. Here in the lavatory ditch, they slaughtered and threw the still breathing Jews, and boarded it up with wood.

I tear open a board: skinned bodies, broken skulls. I fall on the prickly thorns. Only my lips are burning with thirst. The sun bloodies the Lipowiec forest. To me, it looks like the smashed wheel of the incinerated mill. The wheel is in flames. Blood murmurs and swims over its blades. I do not cry, but the pain is like someone holding glowing iron against my darkening eyes. I am blinded.

[Page 271]

The wife weeps and says, "I myself was sick. There was a Jewish girl living with me. Beautiful and good as an angel. She came to beg me to hide her. But how could you hide anyone in a shtetl that had burned down? And the non-Jewish residents–the Poles, and Ukrainians actively helped the Nazis. That was the most horrifying. Polish neighbors leading their Jewish neighbors to death. I parted from the girl, and as soon as she left my house, she was dragged by her golden braids, and stabbed to death by the haystack, her and her parents, and her little brothers and sisters. Do you see this little room? Here they used to lock up the sinners."

I went out to the meadow. The moon rose, and glistened among the shattered skulls. Flocks of crows were shouting from the poplars. I thought I was going to go mad. I hear all this, and I am mute.

I want to weep, but the well of tears has dried up. I want to scream, but the shout will not tear itself out. It is quiet; night is falling in the meadow. A shepherd boy behind the haystack in the pasture whistles a sad melody. The wooden church is old and sunken. The smell of cut hay spreads over the meadow. We jump back over the river. It's beginning to get dark. We head for the orchard in the courtyard, to the old cemetery. But we are walking on tombstones, letters worn out. But here and there, something remains: "*Ma'aseh b'shnei achim*," "*Haniftar bakash shelo yichtivo acheirav shum shebach*." The cemetery is ploughed up. A garden of all kinds of weeds. A high school has been constructed where the gate was. My grandfather's grave, my older brother's tombstone leaning on a hollowed out tree–no trace remaining of the big holy place where, according to legend, Meshiach Ben Yosef rested. Jews had worn grooves on his grave, in their stockinged feet, and left notes to God. The Nazis ploughed up the field, desecrating life and death.

Darkness descends on us. I remember in deep sorrow that it is Tisha B'Av tonight. I cannot, under any circumstances, remember the sad melody of "Eykhe," even as I picture the Jews in their socks, on the overturned benches. I do not walk among ruins. Everything has been destroyed. Why am I not shouting? It is as if we were paralyzed. It becomes dark. Dense darkness covers the desolation.

Burning thirst. I go to the well. But as I am about to raise the bucket, a broad shouldered farmer appears behind me. He grabs the scoop and pours the water back. "Before you can drink the water, you have to boil it. The water is not clean. Once, when the Jews were here, there was a pump. Today, there are no Jews, no

[Page 272]

shtetl, no pump. Dead. My name is Kalmik. The police station on the second floor is mine. You are, it seems, the son of the zhezhnik?" (The shochet's son). Yes, I reply.

"Do you know, perhaps, where and when my relatives were killed?" No, he scratches himself and groans. "Where, you know yourself already. But how, this I can't tell you. Better you don't know. See, there behind the stable, Jews are also buried. Their heads were split with iron bars as they tried to escape to the Lipowiec forest. Who did this? And if you did know, how would it make things easier for you?"

I can't fall asleep.It seems to me, that the darkness froths and pours, like waves of water, over me. I am covered with hot cold sweat, and tears are running from my eyes. Grief tears open the well of tears. I bury my head in the straw sack, and sob. My friends dream and groan. They sob in their dreams. Suddenly, I think it's Shabbes. Shabbes candles are blinking in the shtetl, but they do not flame for long. They go out. I try, my eyes closed in the darkness, to relight them, to get them to shine and tremble again through the windowpanes. But I can't, under any circumstances, see the same picture of a Friday evening with lit, winking Shabbes candles. They have gone out.

The following day, the desolate view of my home town disappears with the bus. Silver dew trembles on the thorny mass grave. Again tears gush from my eyes. We know that they will lie there like that, in the middle of a pasture, without a gravestone. No Jew will come here anymore to grieve over them. We are the last ones to walk over their graves in sorrow. We also know that what happened to my birthplace Tishevits, Komarow, and Zamosc, also happened to all the Jewish cities and shtetlach in Poland.

My entire body is pierced by woe. In sorrow and rage, I clench my fists, "*Zacharta et asa l'cha Nazi-Amalek!*" Arise, take revenge on the annihilators of our people, and the fascist beasts everywhere!

————————

Footnote:

1.   The author was incorrectly informed. The shtetl was set on fire by the local villagers. See the pinkas regarding these events. Ed.

————————

[Page 273]

Extracts from the poem

I Returned to My Destroyed Home

Yakov Zipper (Montreal Canada)

Translated by Moses Milstein

And suddenly, I am here again
The old cemetery
Is now a wheat field
The door squeaks no more
In the wind.
The red stone
Of the holy R' Aharon Kozak[1]
No longer towers with courage
Over the fence
And the hunched little tree
Over the *latutnik's*[2] grave
No longer shades
With secrets and obscurity.

Everything is open now
And so true,
As is written in the verse:
Tzion sadeh techaresh[3]

[Page 274]

O how grandmother and mother
Bewailed this verse
Every *Tishebov*.

I stand here now
In the open field.
Somewhere here
Your grave is hidden.
Your memory–
Arisen in green.
A muted cry
Hovers in the air,
A hidden shudder
In the grass.
It's quieter than quiet.
Destruction passes
In silence.

The whole shtetl–a desolate
field.
Stone upon stone

And catastrophe upon catastrophe
Among grass and moss.

When you, my brother, were
pierced
By the bomb,
The first disaster in our house–
Everyone wept.
Even the gentile street,
With sorrow crossed themselves
And the white church
Let the bells ring
A whole night.
Father became grey overnight.
Lost himself in study
And sang of the tragedy.
Suppressed the groans
Like his face with the dense
beard.
Only his eyes gently caressed

[Page 275]

our little heads,
bent over the Gemara.
Enlightened us with simplicity
And simple understanding.

Mother shriveled up
And became thinner.
Trembles over us and flutters;
Fills her days and nights
Urgently bustling around
Over poverty's houses
On our street.
Touches fevered heads and
examines
Swollen tongues
Places *bankes*[4] and cleans
Vermin with ointment
And above all–
Takes on so much
Of someone's problems,
Her own to conceal.
"What do you know, dear father-
in-law,
How many calamities, God
forbid,
Are dug into the rags
Of our street."–
She consoled grandmother Sarah
Who at the hollow chimney
By the guttering night lightv
Lamented in her prayers

Along with her horror
That hovers over the house
Since uncle Yoineh
Stopped sending from the front
The short interrupted postcards.
Like an open wound the tragedy hangs
Over the house,
And grandmother Sarah laments it
Every morning with the *korbn minche*[5] siddur
And groans through the night

[Page 276]

leaning her head
on the pillow with the red stone.
And when the heart overflows,
They both cover themselves
In black scarves,
And hurry through the back alleys
To you and fall upon
Your stone.
"Run to the divine throne,
Issachar my crown,
Move heaven and earth
With our weeping;
Do not let grandfather rest
In his Garden of Eden,
And all the good pious people, rise up
With a warning call,
ki ba'u mayim ad nafesh."[6]
Now there is no more weeping–
There is no one running to move
heaven and earth
No one to run to in the desolate field.
There remains at least a
tombstone for you;
From uncle Yoineh a memory arrived,
A brown envelope with a black border.
So they wept over this,
And nevertheless accepted the decree.

But from them, from the whole family
And all the neighbors–
Nothing remains–

Empty nothingness.
Aunt Chayeh with all her loved
ones,
Aunt Nechameh and her
household,
Eighteen in number I think,
And uncle Sholem, aunt Beileh
And the entire "vull."

Maybe I actually came

[Page 277]

To raise the interrupted melody
Of the whole family
Laid out on the meadow
Over the bridge
And near the water mill;
And all our neighbors
The people Flekl, Hammer and
Shtift,
With hands like briquettes
And shoulders like walls.
The whole neighborhood they
Renewed and coated;
Taken to markets
And out into the world;
Filled all the taverns
With open speech and noise
And the anterooms of "good
Jews"
Like quiet lambs.
Their daughters mouths were full
of
Folk songs,
And their boys
In the trade unions
Fought with their own father.

It's quiet in the "vole,"
No one's about,
No one is coming.
Just a page, half-burned
From some library book
Lies in the dirt.
You know
The pharmacist with the pointy
moustache
Who once showed the Cossacks
Where a Jew was hiding in the
"voul,"
He is here.
He is still buddy-buddy
With the rascal from the other

side of the bridge.
They both live

[Page 278]

In the big wall
Not far from here.
All day long they rummage in
the ruins,
Practically explode
From joyous laughter
With every find.
Like their great grandfather
Liach the greedy, king of the
swamps–
Half man half devil–
They reign here with
schadenfreud
In their idleness.

Also Yanina, the crazy whore
Is with them.
Drink away the Sundays
together
With full kiddush cups.

They are here,
"Protected and shielded
To the glory of the lord
From all eternity
And his redeemer."
So all the bells ring out
From the white little church on
the hill.

But from our family
With all the neighbors–
No one.
Only in me,
Are they present,–
Just like you with the mute
tombstones
With which the muddy roads
Were paved.

I wander about here aimlessly
For the last time.
My feet stagger on the "*Po
nitmanas.*"
The fields around shudder

[Page 279]

And the earth is silent
Under the hot sun.
My senses are alert
I start at every rustle
Of a leaf in the wind.
"Maybe a sliver of a word
An echo of a *nigun*[7]
That accompanied our
grandfathers
For a full 7 hundred years.

I have come to bid farewell
And take what I can,–
You and all of them,
And anything I can find.
Even a sign carved long ago
In a crumbling tree;
An unfinished song,
That wanders around here
At loose ends.
I'll gather everything up:
The memory of the chests
Where "Chmiel" the oppressor
In his day,
Slaughtered little children
Glatt kosher;
And the echo of our mustering
On the clay mountain,–
Readying themselves for the new
murderer
Lying in wait

In the cool sand here around,
Mutely congealed
The frozen tear
Of generations that go
To the graves of their ancestors.
The happy chatter
Still hovers around
From the just newly hatched
'*Hador Hatsa'ir*.[8]'
Our green dream
Still hangs on every tree

[Page 280]

And our defiant call;
Chazak ve'ematz, shalom!"[9]

I want to see it just one more
time
And hurry away from here,

Because bread herev Now rises
In mute lament;
The dew falls
On a bitter community.
The corn sways
In horror
From the interrupted nigun.
And the grass shimmers
In the shadows,
That wander orphaned
Without a *tikkun*[10].

A great demand arises
From our streets that once were,
A demand and a warning:
"The ripe apples in the
nobleman's orchard
blaze again
over the fence
with red lit skin."
But see and apprehend:
"On the fence of the nobleman's
orchard
A dessicated fleck–
The blood of *chaver* Yochentche
And his household.
Their blood spurted
On the blooming trees."
Succulent red death
Flooded the green grass
And silenced his yearning
Beloved little nigun with his last
note;
To the fence he was dragged

[Page 281]

By death,
And the blue eyes
With a velvet glance,
Saw the sun
And the green sacrificial altar
For the last time.

Who then can consume
An apple that fell from the altar?
Who can breath the aroma
Of green and ripe fruit,
That tastes of the last breath
And red death?

So I will take you and his last
look
Away from here

And take it with me over oceans.
Somewhere there is still land
Where grass is just grass
And bread–
Doesn't rhyme with death.[11]
And here–
May desolate solitude
Join with the ruins;
Sate itself and give birth to oaths
That will curse
And never reward
The earth,
That makes things grow drunk
On blood and murder.
Even a migrating bird
Must avoid this place.
No free lusty twitter
In the land that blooms with
death.
Only mournful fear
And terror
Shall nest in field and forest,
In the garden and the house

[Page 282]

Of our "beloved" neighbors,
Who if they alone did not
Wield the axe–
Always had ready prepared
The open sac.
And their bed–our goods,
And their house–our bounty:
Our closet
And table and chair,
And also the shirt off our back
And the shoes off our feet.
May they tremble
At the horrible roars
Of our bloodied dove:
"Rob all the houses!"
Even the road with its silent dust
Gives testimony:
"Rob all the houses!"
Thus our dove grumbles.

And if there were one
Of their whole race,
To whom no part
Of this obtains,
He was also singed by the
flames,
And he becomes one of us.–

So our dove squirms.
With anxious silence of the dead
She shudders alone,
Black and naked
On every ruined stone.

Footnotes:

1.   Author's footnote: According to shtetl legend, R' Aharon Kozak, a horse trader, defended the shtetl against Chmielnicki's hordes and fell on the spot.
2.   Author's footnote: According to another legend, around the 1600s, a latutnik (cobbler) who lived in the shtetl was Moshiach Ben Yosef. When the holy men from Tsfat and Lublin found out about it, and asked him to reveal himself, he suddenly died one Friday morning. Every Tishebov they placed written requests for the well-being of Jews on his tombstone.
3.   Micah 3:12 Zion shall be plowed as a field
4.   moxibustion
5.   women's prayer book in Yiddish
6.   Psalm 69: For the waters have reached my neck
7.   A melody, often accompanying scripture, or wordless
8.   The Young Generation. Zionist youth group
9.   Be strong and of good courage, peace!
10.   Perhaps a kabbalistic reference to salvation of a soul in torment by the prayers of the living, or the concept of redress.
11.   In Yiddish, "broit" and "toit."

[Page 283]

The Last Markets
"Remember what was done to you...–Poland

Henne Stern-Marder (Montreal Canada)

Translated by Moses Milstein

With empty wagons–they came
Polish farmers–to the last market…

On empty wagons–Polish farmers
Loading the Jews–in last dawns.

Murderous louts–Polish farmers
Driving the Jews–to the crematorium.

They were our neighbors–
Used to bring vegetables to the market.
Saturated with thousand-year hatred–
Full of jealousy and killing–the huts and
the courtyards.

Readied graves–gas ovens–
Boiling waves–bloody lakes.
The fields and the forests and Poland's
witches
Silenced witnesses–in windblown fires.

Embers and fires–lighting the nights
Smoke swirls–choking the air–
Curling the clouds–covering the
whispers
Glowing and burning–souls in ashes–
Skies ashamed–flames wipe away…

Empty wagons–Polish farmers
With hatred annihilated–the Jewish
neighbors.

[Page 284]

An eternal curse–in Polish profanity–
Hurl–"*karban tamim*"[1] –at Poland's dishonor!!!
Roar–"*kharomes*"[2] –and flames for Liech– *Shfoykh khamoskho*[3] --lament–*Ein sof*!!![4]

————

Footnotes:

1. Innocent victim
2. Vehement curses
3. Invoking divine anger against the enemies of the Jews. Recited on Passover night
4. Forever

————

[Page 284]

Brother

Ish Ya'ir (Montreal, Canada)

Translated by Jerrold Landau

It's already fifty, plus one,
Since the desolation of late Av
When choking in your blood
on the lap of your father
you gasped out the last: Until when?

The Kaiser, the Kaiser,
Already bored by the hunt
for petty prey in the wild;
They're enticed by the game
Of a giant combat
So fate decreed
World War!

I hear all the laments
Of your orphaned mother
Though she's been concealed so long
In the abyss.

Your gravestone – a footbridge
For the protected German.
On your grave
grass is growing
Pan Stach.

Yes, they complain in Galicia;
Indeed, they are weeping in Odessa...
But the Jew remains shamed
With his disaster...

———————

[Page 285]

The Bearer of News

Ish Ya'ir (Montreal, Canada)

Translated by Jerrold Landau

And pathways,
        And overflowing water.
When indeed
        Are you coming
                The bearer of news [often the term *Mevaser* refers to the harbinger of the Messiah]
To sprinkle
        Flowing water
Over the ashes
        Of Treblinka?

    Tread in mud,
        Weary,
On weeping dirt paths.
Limbless, the trees
Hear the dead laugh:
Travelling here, with a horse and wagon,
Is a great Tzadik;
Hassidim, enveloped in devotion,
Joining with the Divine Presence.
To the huts,
        Bringing redemption,
A Jew slinks,
        A rebel.
Where then does the red *lane* burn?
Who indeed is the murderer?

   Plush grass,
Hidden pathways.
Chopin notes complain.

[Page 286]

   On piano keys
            The dead cry,
Until day breaks
Shrouds are woven
Deaf murderers
On Poland's desolate roads.
For whom does the red *lane* burn,
If not for me?

   Forest,
      And path,
               And flowing water.
It is already time
Hurry,
      Get going already, messenger,
                  Do not be late for the *Ge'uleh*

————————

We are Asking

Ish Ya'ir (Montreal, Canada)

Translated by Moses Milstein

Lush is the grass in the meadow;
A little lamb prances in the valley.
Compassionate, gracious Creator,
You once held me close…

Through storms, in innocence, you led me.
A *taliss* of *tkheyles*[1] –my shawl.
A sled, a bell, an echo;
An infant's smile–amazed.
Early spring. a snowman, melting;
The mild winds defile his end.
The heart tormented with doubts.
The throat of the infinite opens wide.
Where then to flee from sorrow,
Does father's bosom protect you?
Or is it so to speak in your mind?
In Auschwitz the babies are burning,

[Page 287]

We wonder bewildered,
On crooked paths.
You yourself make our lips stutter.
You choke our insolence.
The gases asphyxiate;
You hurl into the abyss
Our refuse…
The grass in the meadow is burned.
The little lamb–bones in the valley.
Conceal, don't be jealous, Creator,
You once held me close?

Footnote:

1.   Sky blue, the blue wool thread woven into a taliss in biblical days.

Remember What Amalek Did to You…Do not Forget!

by Dr. Israel Stern (Montreal, Canada)

Translated by Moses Milstein

Can someone forget, even if he wants to? Whether it be those of us who come from there but were not present then, or the few survivors, like smoking embers; they do not need to be reminded; the nightmare is remembered in sleep, and the heart aches while awake. "*Ki kol levav davi, v'kol rosh lacholi.*"[1]

Only the doubt niggles: Do we have to do so publicly?…Sometimes, remembering may, God forbid, produce the opposite…And if we do remember publicly, then the question becomes: what, why, and how?

Our remembrance should be conducted according to the tradition of "*Achrei mot kdoshim emor*"[2] Or should we sin on the other side, by learning a lesson from the holy tragedy?

Even though it is written: "*Katuv zot zikaron bsefer,*"[3] I have doubts about whether the widespread custom of memorializing a destroyed community through a yizkor pinkas is a positive phenomenon or not. Previous generations have found effective methods to anchor the pain of Jewish misfortune in their descendants. Through *Kines, Sliches, Taanitim,* and messiah-belief they hammered out a survival mechanism that served us until now. And us? We sit shivah for a third of a people on a page of paper in a pinkas, or in a stale mass gathering. Maybe preparing a pinkas heritage for the archives is actually a sign of the estrangement of our own heirs…

[Page 288]

It's also possible that we have already wasted the pain and the glory of the last sacrifice.

Is it not more fitting to be silent? Thinking logically, it can be seen as a desecration. Nevertheless, I want to share these very unconsoling meditations of a mourner, even though I feel therein a trace of minimalization and desecration.

Which world?

Is it the world that did, or helped, or in the best case, helplessly looked on, to the murders in Biafra? Is it the world that sees thousands of bodies floating in the waters of Cambodia, and goes on with its crazy ways? Is it the world that chooses when to be outraged at the mutual atrocities in Vietnam following the baton of a master conductor, and political sympathies? Is it the world of the new Left which uses the word Auschwitz fairly often, but really only to create sympathy in everyone who is kosher in their eyes, but not for the Jewish people, the original and eternal victims of genocide?

Thereby we have to remember that even to our "friends" we are no longer some kind of pathetic weakling, but like in Hitler's demonic Torah, some sort of superpower, an international conspiracy. Can we expect to soften the hearts of the Arab Muslims and their cynical patrons? Is it the Soviet Union and its satellite robots where it's usually forbidden to mention that Hitler singled out the Jews for special annihilation? But rather they steal our bloody martyrdom, desecrate our victims, and remind us of our plight and their "big favors and compassion" when it suits them to damn Israel and Zionism?

Which world do we want to remind?

The Asia-Africa world is used to such victims, both from natural cataclysms, and man-made ones. Our open wounds make no impression on them. At most, it strengthens their conviction in the downfall of white people. And according to them, and to the Black extremists in America, we are white, economically powerful, culturally and politically powerful white people who have nothing to complain about, but on the contrary, we dare to criticize them. First, the most sensitive of the Asian-Africans , and the Afro-Americans, can't be surprised at our tragedy, can't apprehend it, those who are steeped in the religion and philosophy of India and China. Our view of life and existence is diametrically opposed to theirs. On the contrary, our uncovering of our wounds to the world is repugnant to them.

[Page 289]

(That they complain loudly when something affects them is another matter).

We can divide the European-American world into three categories with individual exceptions:

The vile category of zoological antisemitism: These lent a hand, actively or passively, directly or indirectly, to our annihilation. They saw, and still see in us the source and essence of all that is bad and contemptible. A large part of their hatred for us came from the theology of the majority of Christendom in all its hues. Western literature–even the works of the so-called "European consciousness"–is steeped in the poison of Jew hatred and loaded with arrows of mockery and slander. Whether this particular poison came down from the devilish upper classes to the masses, or the deadly hell gases came from below to the elite, makes no difference.

On a higher level are the Christians who imbibe their religion from a cleaner well. Some of them are even of the "*chasidei omot haolam*": some were refugees and were persecuted by the Hitler animals. Individuals even paid with their lives. But the fact that they accept Jesus as their savior, and the cross as the symbol of their redeemer (oh woe), makes them see our tragedy from a different aspect, and in a manner opposed to ours. For the best of them, it seems, that our tragedy (our carrying the cross in their terminology) is a new confirmation of our free will...the *ata bachartanu*[4] which is so cheap and repulsive among "progressive" Jews, is for them the greatest pedigree, the sun of creation and of history. To this is added their different views on sin, guilt, forgiveness, and atonement.

Even a religious socialist, and refugee from Hitler, like Favel Tillich, comes to the conclusion that the post-Auschwitz Germany can be rehabilitated, because his religious- philosophy investigations lead him to the conclusion that the individual only shares responsibility, but not, God forbid, guilt for the actions of the state. And between responsibility and guilt there must lie the way out for the rehabilitation of the blond beast. The irony is that his chief worry is for the moral fate of the murderous folk, and not for the survivors of the massacre. Even the martyr, Dietrich Bahnhoffer, who was hung by the Nazis in 1945, writes in his "Ethics" that because of the sacrifice of Christianity, nothing is demanded of the guilty for them to pay in full for the evil done: It is acknowledged that what has passed can't be restored, and the wheel of history can't be reversed. Not all wounds can be healed.

[Page 290]

The main thing is that there should be no new wounds. The law, an eye for an eye, a tooth for a tooth, is the prerogative of God, the judge of nations. In the hands of men, this law can lead to tragedy.

This is not a criticism of their religion, or their authenticity, profundity, or the righteousness of their philosophy. It is only meant to remind us that as far as feeling our suffering in our Jewish historical context, they are incapable. Sympathizing with our not wanting to, and not being able to, forgive is taken for granted.

The third category consists of the secular-humanistic-scientific world which also includes the political world, because politics, as is well known, dresses-up in scientific clothing. Modern science and technology that also has a humanitarian tradition of serving the general welfare, has in essence, turned into a religion, idol worship for a large part of its servants and representatives, and even more so, for the common people. Science, secular philosophy, and art, have at the same time shattered the medieval worldview, and also dethroned that kind of person from his royal throne, as the pinnacle of creation, to the level of minor element in the universe. Man is today less significant than he was as matter in the hands of the creator. According to the misguided science of today he is matter in the hands of matter even though the idea of matter, in the classical sense of the word, is not recognized today in modern physics. What demonic discoveries science has led to everyone knows. And yet everyone dances at the devil's wedding. Even organized religion searches, if not for support, for an agreement from it. Obviously, no one wants to be seen as a backward obscurantist.

Even science had a hand, maybe unknowingly a big hand, in our mass annihilation. The belief that the law of the jungle, sly objectivity, all permissiveness, the theory of evolution with its jungle morality, the mechanization of man, the equality of men and beasts, all these theories, and even more evil winds, blow through modern science.

In truth a lot of spiritual people left the world broken seeing the destruction that their hands and brains brought about, and are still liable to bring about. These geniuses began to look for a scientific basis for a new ethics and morality. But these weak efforts are basically condemned to fail, because the underlying philosophy of modern science is false and harmful. We are all entranced by its desirable fruits, but consuming them we obey the suggestion of the biblical serpent…modern mathematical logic has determined–if such

[Page 291]

a determination was generally necessary–that no thought system is self-sufficient. Therefore, it is not conceivable that science can generate for itself ethical principles. Ersatz ethics and made up morality, like a pattern of paper flowers, are actually not hard to produce. But after a life-threatening event one must reach and draw oneself to the transcendental, over and above science, above reason, above the merely human. *Ein chabush et atzmo mebeit ha'asurim.*

Scientists do not accept the charge of guilt. Artists and philosophers do not even try. To art, as is well known, everything is permitted. But as regards shared guilt, or shared responsibility for the victims–and this we are all–it is a paltry distinction.

And science is triumphant…we can fly to space…we can walk on the moon…we will soon, at any moment, create life while at the same time remaining strangers to the notion of dignity. Who's talking about holiness, of life…where do we fit in with our mourning in this Moloch-orgy?

As individuals, some of the latter two categories feel our pain. But this is, basically, in contradiction to their fundamental beliefs.

So we are almost completely alone in our pain. How alone we are, we saw often during and after the Six Day War. I would say that the more one is spiritual–and every one of us is far from there, from the idea of thinking and feeling, believing and reacting, from the naiveté of the innocent martyrs, from the little shtetlach–the more incomplete is his mourning. Our greatest tragedy lies perhaps in this. It turns out that really grieving, lamenting, and causing a great stir, only the martyrs alone do "*bei nacht oifen alten mark.*"[5]

Staying with our own misfortune and orphanhood, we must not fall into a kind of masochistically sweet satisfaction with our woe. Even though *ahoves-Israel* is an important matter, we must guard ourselves from falsifying it. And that is so cheap, and easy. On the contrary, all of us, from religious orthodox to free-thinking atheist, from extreme right bourgeois to extreme left, must examine their ideals, because aside from the fact we are part of humanity, and therefore indirectly also responsible for what happened, we have other, most intimate calculations to make: everyone with himself. Not to look for sins elsewhere, but in one's own self. Even if we let the martyrs, and the period of their sacrifice, out of this national self-criticism, we can't allow ourselves to be exempted. Our handling of the catastrophe during the time of trouble, after the tragedy, and now, must be reexamined. The rationalizations must stop,

[Page 292]

both the scientific, and the religious dogmatics. The way must involve re-establishing moralizing by oneself, and finding the way by oneself. We must look for a spiritual strengthening of our national existence, because without this, our physical existence can't survive. Furthermore, our history, and the history of Western culture, has shown that every Jewish quest is always more than just Jewish. Those, again, who feel that they have already found it, because they have never lost anything, more power to them. But the richest can sometimes turn out to be the poorest.

It is true that searching and researching deeply and freely can lead to the most extreme heresy and disappointment. So shall we feed ourselves with self-delusion? If there really doesn't exist, according to our human understanding, no law and no judge, no spiritual sense for our Jewish existence and continuation, then why should we stand in the way of history? The world, and our own youth, are already sick of "I'm okay, I'm an orphan" psychology. Hitler exterminated us physically. The western world, and the so-called communist world within it give many of us as individuals the opportunity and the possibility of melting as salt in water. And many of our people take advantage of this opportunity. With what kind of power can we hold them back? What right do we have to hold them back? Because of what and for what shall we call them home?

The questions hurt, and cause pain. But we must not silence them just because of our fear of pain. We can't respond to them anymore with worn out phrases. Such answers can only appeal to the dullest of the generation, to those who want to remain among their own because they have nothing to show the outside world, or to those who don't want to mix with the outside world because of base prejudices.

Scientific-rational motivations for Jewish existence, such as historical, material-economical needs, might be enough for certain communities at certain epochs. They can even give support to Jewish charitable activities even today. But for Jewish continuity, it is no longer enough. "We exist because we exist," means thinking in a vicious circle. The truth is that the Jewish people today are vegetating more than existing. Naturally, there are isolated individuals who live with a Jewish sensibility. There are even great Jewish creators. But the people, as a rule, have no shared minimal *ani maamin*. Whether we like it or not, the Jewish people were never just a people in the ethnic sense of the word only. They were formed as a carrier of an idea, and only thus can they have an existence. The people don't have to be exactly homogenous, poured from one source, but

[Page 293]

a spiritual backbone they must have. And this they no longer have. The Jewish people cannot vegetate like the remnants of an American Indian tribe on a reservation. They also can't be a museum exhibit.

It has become the fashion lately to say that the {Israeli}state has become the focal point, the shared longing of all Jews. It means, therefore, that the state is, if not the physical, then the spiritual backbone of the Jewish people. Even if one accepts this premise, one has to state that the state itself is based on "*ein breirah*"[6], and what if there is a "*breirah?*"

They console us: We don't have to use Kabbalah to hasten the end of the exile. "*Mizion teitzei Torah*" will come to be. In the meantime, there are bigger worries. What are we expecting from a young plant?... And so on…Yes, *shearei hatirutzim lo ninalo*. The excuses ring familiarly from other nations who have come to realize another great dream. But if you don't prepare for Erev Shabbes, how do you await Shabbes? Unless it falls from the sky. We have a rule: Trust in miracles, miracles happen, and will happen. But people have to do theirs, and after that there will be a miracle, if something comes of it. In the meantime, the country is still far from becoming the spiritual center. Unfortunately it often happens that the spirit which comes from Israel to the diaspora lacks a Jewish flavor and spirit, and is in fact, the opposite.

It is unfortunate that even among those who remember the Holocaust, there is no shared mourning. And in Israel where it is remembered perhaps more than in the diaspora, people go home and they magically bring out, from time to time, and quite frequently, the specter of Kamtza and Bar Kamtza.[7]

The country of Israel, even though we take its existence for granted, is still a miracle. We cannot, and we must not, throw everything onto the shoulders of the beleaguered Israeli. Nevertheless, Israel is the most natural place where the spiritual, original-Jewish essences can again begin to circulate in the veins of the Jewish people. Connected with that is a changed social atmosphere. And we have to start with ourselves, and not wait for our adversaries to make the first move. I do not believe in a totalitarian, homogenous, *ani-maamin* which obligates every individual. I am against a lazy compromise that satisfies no one. The idyll of *shalom beit Israel* can become a stagnant swamp. There is a difference between spiritual struggle that is rooted in a consciousness of spiritual partnership, and fighting unrelentingly for the sake of a mitzvah. This is, politically, harmful and awful. But spiritual innovation and strengthening are of course not possible in such an atmosphere. Therefore, calls for repentance, which came from deep in the heart, from sincere

[Page 294]

lovers of Israel, fall on deaf ears and hearts. Everyone is convinced that the call is meant for their adversary, because one is personally flawless, really perfection. The truth is that no Jewish movement today has a lot of real opponents that it must fight in a life and death struggle, and where there is nothing in common. Unfortunately, we are all confronted with giant waves that threaten to drown us all with our trivial, often only personal, disagreements. It is therefore past time to learn to debate, and challenge each other with restraint and respect, acknowledging the goodness in the opponent, and instructing him in his mistakes by not copying them. One can lead others by being a good example in daily life, and not with the worn-out bombastic phrases that, delude, falsify and deceive one's self and others, but construct nothing.

It has been 27 years since the uprising in the Warsaw ghetto; 37 years since the unspeakable settled on his demonic throne in Germany; almost 31 years since the outbreak of WWII; 25 years since the liberation of the camps; 22 years since our sole consolation–the country of Israel. And we are still mourners, and the mourners increase, to our great tragedy.

If one takes a good look around, around at the Jewish world, it turns out that exactly now the whole Jewish expansion, wherever it is–and not just in Israel–is surrounded as in a hostile ghetto. Of course there is a difference of where and when: and one may not, under any circumstances, compare it to the most horrid, incomparable. But it nevertheless seems to be that Providence wants to remind the quietest of the quiet, the most sated of the sated, that in every generation man is forced to see himself as if he were in Auschwitz or Treblinka. Every Jew must feel something of the horror.

How much has already been spoken of, and been written about, the heroism, as well as the horror, in the time of the great tragedy. In the last quarter century, a Holocaust literature has accumulated in many languages, but especially in Yiddish–the language of the martyrs. It is written with "blood not with lead[8]," by those who were not in Treblinka, or by those who were persecuted, or by the few survivors. But the physical destruction was so horrible, it can't be weighed or measured in any human language. The spiritual and demographic disturbance in the Jewish organism is so shocking that only a few can begin to comprehend it. The people won't begin to feel it until more time has passed. Remember the *Churban* we must, but we also can't help it. Remembering it in public we are allowed only if it is not in vain. We must sit shivah without cease, as long as we are alive

[Page 295]

if there is, God forbid, nothing Jewish to live for. In order to confirm that there is a sense to Jewish existence and continuation, we must stand up from our shivah, search for and unplug the sand-filled wells that have been dug by Jews from Abraham until today. Hopefully, the refreshing waters of life will well up for us again, and for the kind of person created in God's image.

לאנדם-מאנשאפט קאנפערענץ פון טישעוויצער ין
תולר ורצלאוו דעם מאי .1948

Landsmanschaft conference of Tishevitsers in Poland. Wroclaw May 2ⁿᵈ 1948.

Footnotes:

1. Every heart aches, and every head hurts. Isaiah, 1:5.
2. To speak kindly of the dead
3. Write this memory in a book
4. The Chosen People
5. A play by Y. L. Peretz, *At Night in the Old Marketplace*, 1904
6. No choice
7. Midrash about internal tension among Jews leading to the destruction of the 2ⁿᵈ temple.
8. Line from the anthem of the Warsaw Ghetto

[Page 296]

Open For Me

by Sholom Stern

Translated by Moses Milstein

O, God, open for me
The gate of mercy.
The world in ruins
The murderer lies in wait.

O, open for my people
The gate of mercy.
Let me be the pure sacrifice.
The pages of grandmother's yellow, family siddur
Flutter in silent woe.
Remember, record all the anguish again,
Take revenge for the blood of my murdered
brethren.

O, God, the suffering
Has bored through my body.
Redeem us from misery
Do not leave the world alone.
Everything is but
The work of your hands.
Be merciful to man,
For his blundering understanding.
Let your peace rest
Over the earth, in every land.

Should you need a guardian.
Know, your people have the purest tears.
You alone, be their intercessor, their savior.
And goodness in the world will increase.

O, God, open for me
The gate of mercy.

[Page 298]

In Memory of the Martyrs

לזכרון עולם לקדושי

טישובצה לוב' הי"ד

שהושמדו ע"י המרצחים הנאצים

ביום ו' לכסלו שנת תש"ג

15.11.1942,

ארץ אל תכסי דמם

ת נ צ ב ה

The plaque to the memory of Tishevits among all the destroyed communities in Poland on Mt. Zion in Jerusalem

[Pages 299-304]

List of Martyrs

Transliterated by David Sosnovitch

Edited by Yocheved Klausner

א Alef	ב Bet	ג Gimmel	ד Dalet	ה Hey	ו Vav	ז Zayin	ח Chet	ט Tet	י Yod	כ Kaf
ל Lamed	מ Mem	נ Nun	ס Samech	ע Ayin	פ Peh	צ Tzadik	ק Kof	ר Resh	ש Shin	ת Tav

Family name(s)	First name(s)	Maiden name	Sex	Marital status	Father's name	Mother's name	Name of spouse	Additional family members	Remarks	Page
א Alef										
EIDELSBERG	Yosef		M							299
EIDELSBERG	Peretz		M							299
ADLER	Ben Tzion		M							299
ADLER	Miriam		F							299
ADLER	Dov		M							299
ADLER	Eliezer		M							299
ADLER	Wave		M							299
ADLER	Moshe		M							299
ADLER	Sara		F							299
ADLER	Bentshe		M							299
ADLER	Dvorah		F							299
ADLER	Chava		F							299
ADLER	Avraham		M							299
ADLER	Rivka		F							299
ADLER	Yehoshua		M							299
ADLER	Ozer		M							299
ADLER	Dov		M							299
ADLER	Moshe		M							299
ADLER	Yosef		M							299
EITEL	Arye		M							299
EITEL	Telze		F							299
EITEL	Israel		M							299
EITEL	Beila		F							299
EITEL	Rachel		F							299
UNRUCH	Feiga Rachel		F							299
UNRUCH	Hendel		F							299
EITEL	Avramze		M					and her family		299
ALERHAND	Welvel		M					and his family		299
EILBOIM	Israel		M							299
UNRUCH	Tzvi		M							299

Family name(s)	First name(s)	Maiden name	Sex	Marital status	Father's name	Mother's name	Name of spouse	Additional family members	Remarks	Page
UNRUCH	Chana		F							299
ADLER	Moshe		M							299
ADLER	Beila		F							299
ADLER	Chaia		F							299
ADLER	Lea		F							299
ADLER	Ben Tzion		M							299
EITEL	Israel Aharon		M							299
EITEL	Tzipora		F							299
EITEL	Dvora		F							299
EITEL	Moshe		M							299
EISEN	Moshe		M							299
EISEN	Lea		F							299
ELBOIM	Arye		M							299
ELBOIM	Yehudit		F							299
ELBOIM	Shlomo		M							299

ב Bet

Family name(s)	First name(s)	Maiden name	Sex	Marital status	Father's name	Mother's name	Name of spouse	Additional family members	Remarks	Page
BECHER	Eliezer		M							299
BECHER	Refael		M	Married	Eliezer		Marie			299
BECHER	Mari		F	Married			Refael			299
BECHER	Binyamin		M		Refael	Marie				299
BECHER	Leibel		M		Refael	Maie				299
BECHER	Dvora		F		Refael	Marie				299
BECHER	Feiga		F		Refael	Marie				299
BECHER	Chaia		F		Refael	Marie				299
BECHER	Chana		F		Refael	Marie				299
BICHER	Yehuda		M	Married			Bat Sheva			299
BICHER	Bat Sheva		F	Married			Yehuda			299
BICHER	Sonia		F							299
BICHER	Shimo		M					and 1 child		300
BICHER	Shulka		F							300
BICHER	Esther		F							300
BICHER	Chana		F							300
BICHER	Bezi		F							300
BARG	Yehoshua		M							300
BARG	Bluma		F							300
BARG	Avraham		M							300
BARG	Yitzhak		M							300
BARG	Yehoshua		M							300
BARG	Bluma		F							300
BARG	Avraham		M							300
BARG	Chaia		F							300
BARG	Luba		F							300
BARK	Shlomo		M							300
BARK	Nesha		F							300
BARK	Sonia		F							300
BRAUN	Tzvi		M					and his family		300
BRAUN	Chanitche		F		Tzvi					300

BLECHMAN	Barka		M						300
BLECHMAN	Esther	MARDER	F						300
BLECHMAN	Chaia		F						300
BLECHMAN	Rivka		F						300
BARG	Rachel		F						300
BARG	Raah	MARDER	F						300
BARG	Bat Sheva		F						300
BARG	Moshe Eliezer		M						300
BARG	Chanale?		F						300
BARG	Refael		M	Married			Mina	Synagogue caretaker	300
BARG	Mina		F	Married			Refael		300
BARG	Moshe		M						300
BARG	Minka		F						300
BARG	Yaffa		F						300
BARG	Yoel		M						300
BARG	Malka		F						300
BLANK	Melech		M						300
BLANK	Rivka		F						300
BLANK	Sara		F						300
BLANK	Idel		F						300
BLANK	Reizel		F						300
BLANK	Bela		F						300
BIBEL	Moshe		M						300
BIBEL	Esther		F						300
BIBEL	Chana		F						300
BIBEL	Necha		F						300
BIBEL	Yitzhak		M						300
BIBEL	Yerahmiel		M	Married			Chana		300
BIBEL	Chana		F	Married			Yerahmiel		300
BLECHMAN	Matityahu		M						300
BLENDER	Yeshayahu		M						300
BASCHISTER	Fishe		F						300
BASCHISTER	Yaakov		M						300
BASCHISTER	Fradl		F						300
BASCHISTER	Moshe		M						300
BASCHISTER	Feiga		F						300
BECKER	Zalman		M						300
BECKER	Mordechai		M						300
BECKER	Hinde		F						300
BECKER	Yosef		M						300
BECKER	Fesha		F						300
BINBERG	Bluma		F						300
BERGMAN	Reizel		F						300
BERGMAN	Gitel		F			Reizel			300
BERGMAN	Aharon		M	Married			Lea		300
BERGMAN	Lea		F	Married			Aharon		300
BERGMAN	Avish		M	Married				and children	300
BERGMAN			F	Married			Avish	and children	300
BURG	Aharon		M					and his family	300

Family name(s)	First name(s)	Maiden name	Sex	Marital status	Father's name	Mother's name	Name of spouse	Additional family members	Remarks	Page
BURG	David		M						and his family	300
BIBEL	Gedalia		M						and his family	300
BIDERMAN	Akiva		M						and his family	301
BIDERMAN	Shmuel		M						and his family	301
BLOZER	Rachel		F						and her family	301
BLECHMAN	Chaim		M						and his family	301
BLECHMAN	Berel		M						and his family	301
BIDERMAN	Yitzhak		M							301
BIDERMAN	Reizel		F							301
BIDERMAN	Avraham		M							301
BIDERMAN	Yaakov		M							301
BIDERMAN	Chaim		M		Yaakov					301

ג Gimmel

Family name(s)	First name(s)	Maiden name	Sex	Marital status	Father's name	Mother's name	Name of spouse	Additional family members	Remarks	Page
GLANZ	Itchele Dov		M	Married					Town rabbi	301
GLANZ	Rabbanit		F	Married			Itchele			301
GLANZ			M		Itchele Dov				first son of Town Rabbi Itchele GLANZ	301
GLANZ			M		Itchele Dov				second son of Town Rabbi Itchele GLANZ	301
GLANZ			M		Itchele Dov				third son of Town Rabbi Itchele GLANZ	301
GLANZ			F		Itchele Dov				daughter of Town Rabbi Itchele GLANZ	301
GEIST	Gershon		M							301
GEIST	Ita		F		Gershon					301
GUTHEIT	Rachel		F							301
GELBER	Moshe		M							301
GELBER	Rachel		F							301
GELBER	Miriam		F							301
GLETER	Israel		M	Married			Rivka			301
GLETER	Rivka		F	Married			Israel			301
GLETER	Chana		F			Rivka				301
GLETER	Reizel		F			Rivka				301
GLETER	Zemale		F			Rivka				301
GLETER	Esther		F			Rivka				301
GLETER	Freida		F			Rivka				301
GLETER	Chaia		F			Rivka				301
GLETER	Rachel		F			Rivka				301
GEBEL	Chaim		M	Married						301
GEBEL			F	Married			Chaim			301
GEBEL	Binyamin		M	Married						301

Family name(s)	First name(s)	Maiden name	Sex	Marital status	Father's name	Mother's name	Name of spouse	Additional family members	Remarks	Page
GEBEL			F	Married			Binyamin			301
GLICK	Moshe		M							301
GLICK	Meitche		M					and his family		301
GLICK	Shmuel		M							301
GLICK	David		M							301
GAM	Yerahmiel		M							301
GAM	Reizel		F							301
GAM	Meir		M							301
GAM	Lea		F							301
GRINBERG	Tzvi		M	Married			Grina			301
GRINBERG	Grina		F	Married			Tzvi			301
GRINBERG	Meir		M			Grine				301
GRINBERG	Chaim		M			Grine				301
GRINBERG	Chaia		F			Grine				301
GINZBERG	Pinhas		M							301
GINZBURG	Shabtai		M	Married	Pinhas					301
GINZBURG			F	Married			Shabtai			301
GINZBURG	Yerahmiel		M	Married	Pinhas					301
GINZBURG			F	Married			Yerahmiel			301
GINZBURG	Yaakov		M	Married	Pinhas			and 2 children		301
GINZBURG			F	Married			Yaakov	and 2 children		301
	Freidel		F	Married	Pinhas			and husband		301
			M			Freidel			Mother's maiden name was GINSBURG	301
			F			Freidel			Mother's maiden name was GINSBURG	301
			F			Freidel			Mother's maiden name was GINSBURG	301
			F			Freidel			Mother's maiden name was GINSBURG	301
GUTHEIT	Rachel		F							301
GOLDMAN	Mendel Wolf		M	Married			Esther			301
GOLDMAN	Esther		F	Married			Mendel Wolf			301

ד **Dalet**

Family name(s)	First names(s)	Maiden name	Sex	Marital status	Father's name	Mother's name	Name of spouse	Additional family members	Remarks	Page
DORNFELD	Moshe Yitzhak		M							301
DORNFELD	Soshana		F							301
DROCH	Tzivya		F							301
DROCH	Liba		F							301
DROCH	Hirsch		M							301
DROCH	Moshe		M							301

Family name(s)	First name(s)	Maiden name	Sex	Marital status	Father's name	Mother's name	Name of spouse	Additional family members	Remarks	Page
DICKER	Fishel		M					and his family		301
DERSCHITZ	Abish Meir		M	Married			Beila	and children		301
DERSCHITZ	Beila		F	Married			Avish Meir	and children		301
DANZIGER	Yehuda Leib		M							301
DANZIGER	Nahum		M							301

הﬧ **Hey**

Family name(s)	First name(s)	Maiden name	Sex	Marital status	Father's name	Mother's name	Name of spouse	Additional family members	Remarks	Page
HALROBIN	Issachar		M	Married			Nchama			301
HALROBIN	Nechama		F	Married			Issachar			301
HALROBIN	Zeev		M		Issachar	Nechama				301
HALROBIN	Yoheved		F		Issachar	Nechama				301
HALROBIN	Malia		F		Issachar	Nechama				301
HALROBIN	Henia		F							301
HALROBIN	Yehuda		M							301
HALROBIN	Nahum		M							301
HALROBIN	Feivel		F							301
MARDER	Etel Lea	Hertzberg	F							301
HELFMAN	David		M							302
HELFMAN	Tova		F							302
HELFMAN	Binyamin		M							302
HELFMAN	Yehuda		M							302
HELFMAN	Chaike		F							302
HODES	Yehoshua		M							302
HODES	Batya		F							302
HODES	Reizel		F							302
HODES	Rivka		F							302
HODES	Avraham		M							302
HODES	Yitzhak		M							302
HASER	Moshe		M							302
HASER	Beila		F							302
HASER	Yehiel		M							302
HASER	Shimshon		M							302
HASER	Leib		M							302
HASER	Refael		M							302
HAMMER	Mordechai		M							302
HAMMER	Mala		F							302
HAMMER	Rechel		F							302
HAMMER	Moshe Shlomo		M					and his family		302
HAMMER	Israel Meir		M					and his family		302
HAMMER	Sigar		M					and his family		302
HAMMER	Azriel		M							302
HAMMER	Hinde		F							302
HAMMER	Sheindel		F							302
HECHT	Avish		M							302

Family name(s)	First name(s)	Maiden name	Sex	Marital status	Father's name	Mother's name	Name of spouse	Additional family members	Remarks	Page
HECHT	Basha		F							302
HECHT	Chaim		M							302
HECHT	Mordechai		M							302
HECHT	Yekutiel		M						first name appears in list as Yektiel	302
HECHT	Moshe Zalman		M							302
HORN	Leib		M					and his family		302
HODES	Avraham		M							302
HODES	Yochanan		M					and his family		302
HOCHGELERNTER	Welvel		M					and his family	family name appears in list as HOCHGELERNTER	302
HOCHGELERNTER	Azriel		M					and his family	family name appears in list as HOCHGELERINTER	302
HOCHGELERNTER	Pini		M					and his family	family name appears in list as HOCHGELERINTER	302
HOCHGELERNTER	Yaakov		M					and his family	family name appears in list as HOCHGALERINTER	302
HECHT	Shmuel		M					and his family		302
HASER	Moshe Eliyahu		M							302
HASER	Moshe Eliezer		M							302

ר Vav

Family name(s)	First name(s)	Maiden name	Sex	Marital status	Father's name	Mother's name	Name of spouse	Additional family members	Remarks	Page
WACHSENFELD	David		M							302
WACHSENFELD	Gitel		F							302
WACHSENFELD	Michael		M							302
WACHSENFELD	Hodes		F							302
WACHSENFELD	Anshel		M						first name is possibly Antchel	302
WACHSENFELD	Yosef		M							302
WACHSENFELD	Esther		F							302
WACHSENFELD	Mordechai		M							302
WACHSENFELD	Chana		F							302
WACHSENFELD	Moshe		M							302
WACHSENFELD	Shmuel		M							302
WACHSENFELD	Yitzhak		M							302
WACHSENFELD	Yaffa		F							302
WACHSENFELD	Gitel		F							302
WACHSENFELD	Tzvi		M							302
WACHSENFELD	Serki		F							302
WACHSENFELD	Eliahu		M							302
WACHSENFELD	Hirshel		M							302
WACHSBAUM	Moshe Volf		M					and his family		302

Family name(s)	First name(s)		Sex					Additional family members		Page
WACHSBAUM	Heshel		M					and his family		302

ז Zayin

Family name(s)	First name(s)	Maiden name	Sex	Marital status	Father's name	Mother's name	Name of spouse	Additional family members	Remarks	Page
SINGER	Efraim		M					and his family		302
SINGER	Baruch		M					and his family		302
SINGER	Yechezkel		M					and his family		302
SINGER	Mendel		M					and his family		302
SINGER	Moshe		M					and his family		302
SOBERMAN	Moshe Mendel		M					and his family		302
SILBERSTROM	Yaakov		M					and his family		302
SIGMAN	Naftali		M							303
SIGMAN	Peretz		M							303
SIGMAN	Shmuel		M							303
SIGMAN	Israel		M							303
SIGMAN	Yocheved		F							303
SIGMAN	Rachel		F							303
SIGMAN	Zela		F							303
SIGMAN	Mala		F							303
SIGMAN	Freida		F							303
SIGMAN	Barka		F							303
SIGMAN	Moshe		M							303
SIGMAN	Chaia		F							303
SILBERMAN	Mordechai		M							303
SILBERMAN	Yaakov		M							303
SILBERMAN	Malka		F							303
SILBERMAN	Yente		F							303
SILBERMAN	Avraham		M							303

ט Tet

Family name(s)	First name(s)	Maiden name	Sex	Marital status	Father's name	Mother's name	Name of spouse	Additional family members	Remarks	Page
TUCH	Eliezer		M					and his family		303
TUCH	Yitzhak		M					and his family		303
TURIM	Tzvi Yosef		M							303
TURIM	Chaia Sara		F							303
TURIM	Lea Yehudit		F							303
TEITEL	Yaakov		M					and his family		303
TENNENBAUM	Moshe Baruch		M					and his family		303

ל Lamed

Family name(s)	First name(s)	Maiden name	Sex	Marital status	Father's name	Mother's name	Name of spouse	Additional family members	Remarks	Page
LEIBEL	Avraham		M							303
LEIBEL	Rivka		F							303
LEV	Henya		F					and 5 children		303
LEV	Gitel		F							303
LEV	Israel		M							303
LEFLER	Leibish		M							303
LEFLER	Rachel		F							303
LEFLER	Meir		M							303
LEFLER	Malka		F							303
LERNER	Moshe		M					and his family		303
LERNER	Chaike		F							303
LERNER	Eliezer		M							303
LERNER	Eliezer		M							303
LERNER	Tova		F							303
LERNER	Professor Mordechai Yosef		M							303
LAFISH	Getzel		M					and his faily		303
LAFISH	Chana		F					and children		303
LAFISH	Dina		F	Married				and husband and children		303
LAFISH	Mendele		M							303
LAFISH	Chavale		F					and her family		303
LACHS	Aharon Berish		M	Married						303
LACHS			F	Married			Avraham Berish			303
LACHS	Avraham		M		Avraham Berish			and his family		303
LACHS	Dina		F							303
REICHENBERG	Esther	LANDAU	F	Married	Shlomo		Yaakov David			303
REICHENBERG	Yaakov David		M	Married			Esther			303
REICHENBERG			M		Yaakov David	Esther				303
REICHENBERG			F		Yaakov David	Esther				303
REICHENBERG			F		Yaakov David	Esther				303
REICHENBERG			F		Yaakov David	Esther				303
LERNER	Sara		F	Married			Moshe			303
LERNER	Moshe		M	Married			Sara			303
LERNER			M		Moshe	Sara				303

LERNER			M		Moshe	Sara				303
LERNER			F		Moshe	Sara				303
LERNER			F		Moshe	Sara				303
LIFSH	Berel		M					and his family		303
LIFSH	Reuven		M					and his family		303
LIFSH	David		M							303
LIFSH	Shmuele		M					and his family		303
LANDAU	Yitzhak		M	Married	Shlomo				family relationship was based on Pages of Testimony	303
LANDAU			F	Married			Yitzhak			303
LANDAU			M							303
LANDAU	Yaakov		M	Married					family relationship was based on Pages of Testimony	303
LANDAU			F	Married			Yaakov			303

מ Mem

Family name(s)	First name(s)	Maiden name	Sex	Marital status	Father's name	Mother's name	Name of spouse	Additional family members	Remarks	Page
MILSTEIN	Moshe		M							303
MILSTEIN	Sara		F							303
MILSTEIN	Shmuel		M							303
MILSTEIN	Chava		F							303
MILSTEIN	Yitzhak		M							303
MILSTEIN	Yaffa		F							303
MILSTEIN	Gitel		F							303
MILSTEIN	Tzvi		M							303
MILSTEIN	Eliyahu		M							303
MED	Avraham		M							303
MARDER	Esther		F							304
MED	Avraham		M					and his family		304
MED	Aharon		M					and his family		304
MARDER	Binyumtzi		M					and his family		304
MINZBERG	Fritz		M					and his family		304

[Pages 303-309]

List of Martyrs from Tyszowce, Poland (cont.)

Family name(s)	First name(s)	Maiden name	Sex	Marital status	Father's name	Mother's name	Name of spouse	Additional family members	Remarks	Page
נ Nun										
NUSTER	Eliahu		M					and his family		304
NUSTER	Yenkel		M					and his family		304
NUSTER	Meir		M					and his family		304
NEIMARK	Hershel		M					and his family		304
NEIMARK	Gershon		M					and his family		304

Family name(s)	First name(s)	Maiden name	Sex	Marital status	Father's name	Mother's name	Name of spouse	Additional family members	Remarks	Page
ס Samech										
SACHER	Moshe		M	Married	Aharon Issachar		Chana Sheindel			304
SACHER	Chana Sheindel		F	Married			Moshe			304
SACHER	Nahum		M					and his family		304
SACHER	Yaakov		M					and his family		304
SOBOL	Mendele		M	Married						304
SOBOL			F	Married			Mendele			304
SOBOL	Gila		F		Mendele					304
SOBOL	Hershele		M		Mendele					304
SMIT	Moshe David		M					and his family		304

Family name(s)	First name(s)	Maiden name	Sex	Marital status	Father's name	Mother's name	Name of spouse	Additional family members	Remarks	Page
ע Ayin										
ENG	Shmuel		M							304
ENG	Aharon		M							304
ENG	Henya		F							304
ENK	Izaak		M					and his family		304
ENK	Moshe		M					and his family		304

Family name(s)	First name(s)	Maiden name	Sex	Marital status	Father's name	Mother's name	Name of spouse	Additional family members	Remarks	Page
פ Peh										
PETER	Lemel		M					and his family		304
FUCHS	Eli Reuven		M	Married			Bluma			304

FUCHS	Bluma		F	Married		Eli Reuven				304
FUCHS	Shimon		M	Married		Fruma				304
FUCHS	Fruma		F	Married		Shimon				304
FUCHS	Moshe		M						possibly Zisel's husband	304
FUCHS	Zisel		F					and children	possibly Moshe's wife	304
FEINER	Shimon		M	Married		Frimza				304
FEINER	Frimtze		F	Married		Shimon				304
FEINER	Sara		F							304
FEINER	Moshe		M							304
FIGLER	Leibush		M							304
FIGLER	Sara		F							304
FIGLER	Yetta		F							304
FIGLER	Mindetz									304
FIGLER	Tova		F							304
FIGLER	Shprinza		F							304
FIGLER	Tuvia		M							304
FIGLER	Shlomo Meir		M							304
FIGLER	Serl		F							304
FIGLER	Bracha		F							304
FIGLER	Esther		F							304
FIGLER	Sara Freida		F							304
FIGLER	Pinhas		M							304
FUTER	Sonia		F							304
FUTER			F			Sonia				304
FUTER			F			Sonia				304
PECHER	Mordechai		M							304
PECHER	Frumtche		F							304
PECHER	Yetale		F							304
PECHER	Fishel Shpiz		M							304
FINGER	Avraha		M							304
FINGER	Esther		F							304
FINGER	Shindel Hodes		F							304
FINGER	Feivel		M							304
FINGER	Golda		F							304
FINGER	Cheile		F							304
FINGER	Mordechai		M							304
FINGER	Fradl		F							304
PAUL	David		M							304
PAUL	Frieda		F							304
PAUL	Ettel		F							304
PAUL	Yosef		M							304
PAUL	Feivel		M							304
PAUL	Reizel		F							305
PAUL	Frieda		F							305
PAUL	Moshe		M							305
PAUL	Dvora		F							305
PAUL	David		M							305

PELTZ	Mordechai		M	Married				305
PELTZ			F	Married		Mordechai		305
PELTZ	Moshe		M					305
PELTZ	Necha		F					305
PELTZ	Feiga		F					305
PELTZ	Esther Malka		F					305
PELTZ	Moshe		F					305
PELTZ	Pinhas		M				and his family	305
PELTZ	Avraham		M				and his family	305
PELTZ	Yaakov		M				and his family	305
PELTZ	Michael		M				and his family	305
FIRSHT	Shmuel		M					305
FIRSHT	Necha		F					305
FIRSHT	Chana		F					305
FIRSHT	Avish		M	Married				305
FIRSHT			F	Married		Avish		305
FIRSHT	Feiga Etel		F				and her family	305
FRIEDLAND	Kehat		M					305
FRIEDLAND	Simtche		F				mother of Shlomo, Reizel, Sara, Esther and Rachel	305
FRIEDLAND	Shlomo		M		Simtche			305
FRIEDLAND	Reizel		F		Simtche			305
FRIEDLAND	Sara		F		Simtche			305
FRIEDLAND	Esther		F		Simtche			305
FRIEDLAND	Rachel		F		Simtche			305
FRIEDLANDER	Beila		F				mother of Chaim, Dora & Mania	305
FRIEDLANDER	Chaim		M		Beila			305
FRIEDLANDER	Dora		F		Beila			305
FRIEDLANDER	Menya		F		Beila			305
FREIDEN	Freida		F				relationship in accordance with Pages of Testimony	305
FREIDEN	Bluma		F		Freida		relationship in accordance with Pages of Testimony	305
VOGEL	Eliezer		M				and his family	305
VOGEL	Yitzhak Itche		M				and his family	305
	Yekutiel		M	Married		Chantche	and his family	305
	Chantche		F	Married		Yekutiel	and children	305
VOGEL	Yosef		M					305
VOGEL	Shlomo		M					305
FUCHS	Mordechai		M					305
POMP	Yosef		M				and his family	305

Family name(s)	First name(s)	Maiden name	Sex	Marital status	Father's name	Mother's name	Name of spouse	Additional family members	Remarks	Page
FINGER	Eliezer		M					and his family		305
PAPIER	Natan		M							305
PAPIER	Beila Gitel		F							305
PAPIER	Nahma		M							305
PAPIER	Chaia Hinde		F							305
PAPIER	Chava		F							305
FINGER	Mendel		M					and his family		305
FINGER	Esther		F					and her family		305
FINGER	Mania		F							305
FINGER	Shalom		M					and his family		305
PETRUSHKA	Leibel		M					and his family		305
PETRUSHKA	Moshe		M					and his family		305
FRIEDLANDER	Simtche		F						mother of Shlomo, Reizel and Sara	305
FRIEDLANDER	Shlomo		M			Simtche				305
FRIEDLANDER	Reizel		F			Simtche				305
FRIEDLANDER	Sara		F			Simtche				305
FRIEDLANDER	Beila		F						mother of Esther and Rachel	305
FRIEDLANDER	Esther		F			Beila				305
FRIEDLANDER	Rachel		F			Beila				305

צ Tzadik

Family name(s)	First names(s)	Maiden name	Sex	Marital status	Father's name	Mother's name	Name of spouse	Additional family members	Remarks	Page
ZUKER	Efraim		M					and his family		305
ZUKER	Uziel		M					and his family		305
ZUKER	Feiga		F					and her family		305
ZWEIG	Bezalel		M							305
ZWEIG	Malka		F							305
ZWEIG	David		M					and his family		305
ZWEIG	Yosef		M					and his family		306
ZWEIG	Pinhas		M					and his family		306
ZWEIG	Leiba		F							306
ZWEIG	Hinde		F							306
ZWEIG	Shaul		M							306
ZWILICH	Yaakov		M					and his family		306
ZWILICH	Ishai		M					and his family		306
ZWILICH	Yenkel		M					and his family		306
ZWILICH	David		M					and his family		306
ZWILICH	Mendel		M							306

ק Kof

Family name(s)	First name(s)	Maiden name	Sex	Marital status	Father's name	Mother's name	Name of spouse	Additional family members	Remarks	Page
KNOBEL	Yitzhak		M							306
KNOBEL	Freida Bluma		F							306
KNOBEL	Aharon		M							306
KNOBEL	Mali		F							306
KNOBEL	Malka		F							306
KNOBEL	Liba		F							306
KUPERSTEIN	Menahem Mendel		M	Married			Rivka			306
KUPERSTEIN	Rivka		F	Married			Menahem Mendel			306
KUPERSTEIN	Elyakim Getzel		M	Married	Menahem Mendel	Rivka				306
KUPERSTEIN	Lea		F	Married			Elyakim Getzel			306
KUPERSTEIN	Avraham		M		Elyakim Getzel	Lea				306
APPELBAUM	Chaiale	KUPERSTEIN	F	Married	Elyakim Getzel	Lea	Yosef			306
APPELBAUM	Yosef		M	Married			Chaiale			306
APPELBAUM	Shalom		M		Yosef	Chaiale				306
KUPERSTEIN	Rachele		F		Elyakim Getzel	Lea				306
KUPERSTEIN	Moshe		M		Elyakim Getzel	Lea				306
KLEKS	Yaakov		M					and his family		306
KOPEL	Yechezkel		M							306
KOPEL	Sara		F							306
KOPEL	Avraham		M							306
KOPEL	Necha		F							306
KOPEL	Efraim		M							306
KLEINER	Arish		M							306
KLEINER	Nesha		F							306
KLEINER	Feiga		F							306
KLEINER	Tevel		M							306
KLEINER	Chana		F							306
KLEINER	Yosef		M							306
KLEINER	Chaia		F							306
KREINER	Shlomo		M							306
KREINER	Rivka		F							306
KREINER	Pesah		M							306
KREINER	Yaakov		M							306
KALMANOVITZ	Henia		F							306
KALMANOVITZ	Rivka		F							306
KALMANOVITZ	Aharon		M							306
KALMANOVITZ	Tzila		F							306
KOPEL	Tzvi		M							306
KOPEL	Malka		F							306
KOPEL			F			Malka			Malka's first daughter	306
KOPEL			F			Malka			Malka's second daughter	306

Family name(s)	First name(s)	Maiden name	Sex	Marital status	Father's name	Mother's name	Name of spouse	Additional family members	Remarks	Page
KOPEL			F			Malka			Malka's third daughter	306
KOPEL			F			Malka			Malka's fourth daughter	306
KOPEL			F			Malka			Malka's fifth daughter	306
KAUFMAN	Rachel		F							306
KOPEL	Eliezer		M							306
KLENBERG	Kopel		M					and his family		306
KRISTAL	Moshe Chaim		M							306
KRISTAL	Eliezer		M		Moshe Chaim			and his family		306
KRISTAL	Aharon		M		Moshe Chaim					306
KRISTAL	Akiva		M		Moshe Chaim					306
KRISTAL			F		Moshe Chaim					306
KRISTAL			F		Moshe Chaim					306
KOPEL	Eliezer		M					and his family		306
KOPIL	Reuven		M					and his family		306
KREMPEL	Chanan		M					and his family		306
KRENT	Peretz		M					and his family		306
KORNBLIT	Avraham Yakov		M					and his family		306
KOPEL	Yechezkel		M					and his family		306
KLENBERG	Kopel		M					and his family		306

ר   Resh

Family name(s)	First name(s)	Maiden name	Sex	Marital status	Father's name	Mother's name	Name of spouse	Additional family members	Remarks	Page
RUB	Moshe		M	Married			Chana			306
RUB	Chana	MARDIR	F	Married			Moshe			306
RUB	Sara Yehudit		F		Moshe	Chana				306
RUB	Tzvi		M		Moshe	Chana				306
RUB	Rivka		F		Moshe	Chana				306
RUB	Michlola		F		Moshe	Chana				306
REIS	Chaia Rivka		F							306
REIS	Hene		F							306
REIS	Rachel		F							306
REIS	Niunia Sarale		F							306
REIS	Hodel		F						listed as Yissocher'l	306
REIS	Frimtche		F							306
RUB	Yehuda		M	Married			Feiga Etel	and family		307
RUB	Feiga Etel		F	Married			Yehuda	and family		307
RUB	Chantche		F							307
RUB	Moshele		M							307

RUB	Sarale Yehudit		F							307
RUB	Hershele Leib		M							307
RUB	Rivkale		F							307
RUB	Mechliele		F							307
RUB	Yitzhak		M							307
RUB	Yehoshua		M	Yitzhak						307
RUB	Israel		M	Yitzhak						307
RUB	Yosef		M	Yitzhak						307
REIS	Mordechai		M							307
REIS	Fradel		F							307
REIS	Avraham		M							307
REIS	Moshe		M							307
REIS	Rachel		F							307
REIS	Chana		F							307
REIS	Avraham		M						possibly was Moshe's father-in-law	307
	Moshe		M						"son in law" appears in the list and possibly son-in-law of Avraham REISS	307
RUB	Moshe		M							307
RUB	Breina Rachel		F							307
RUB	Aharon		M							307
RUB	Glikel		F							307
RUB	Teme		F							307
RUB	Mordechai		M							307
RUB	Bluma		F							307
RUB	Sonia		F							307
RUB	Esther		F							307
RUB	Perel		F							307
ROSENMAN	Shlomo		M							307
ROSENMAN	Chana Bracha		F					and her family		307
REICHENBERG	Hanoch		M					and his family		307
RUB	Meir		M					and his family		307
RUB	Avraham		M					and his family		307
RUB	Shalom		M					and his family		307
RUB	Itzi		M					and his family		307
RUB	Yitzhak		M					and his family		307
RUB	Eidel		M					and his family		307
REIFER	Yosel		M					and his family		307
REICHER	Shiye		M							307
REICHER	Etel		F							307
REIS	Moshe Baruch		M							307
REIS	Chana		F							307
REIS	Lea		F							307

Family name(s)	First name(s)	Maiden name	Sex	Marital status	Father's name	Mother's name	Name of spouse	Additional family members	Remarks	Page
RUB	Moshe		M	Married			Chana			307
RUB	Chana	MARDER	F	Married			Moshe			307
RUB	Yissocherl		M		Moshe	Chana				307
RUB	Frimtche		F		Moshe	Chana			listed as Yissocher'l	307

ש Shin

Family name(s)	First name(s)	Maiden name	Sex	Marital status	Father's name	Mother's name	Name of spouse	Additional family members	Remarks	Page
STENGEL	Yosef		M	Married				and children		307
STENGEL			F	Married			Yosef	and children		307
STENGEL	Meir		M							307
STENGEL	Rachel		F							307
SCHALT	Hentche		F							307
SCHALAT	Shlomo		M							307
SCHLEGEL	Shlomo		M	Married			Dvora			307
SCHLEGEL	Dvora		F	Married			Shlomo			307
SCHAFIR	Shlomo		M							307
SCHAFIR	Peshe		F							307
STRIGLER	Yechezkel		M							307
STRIGLER	Chana Sheindel		F					and children		307
SCHERER	Zalman		M		Pesah					307
SCHERER	Avraham		M		Pesah					307
SCHLEGEL	Yocheved		F							307
SCHLEGEL	Bintche		M							307
SCHLEGLE	Pesah		M							307
SCHLEGEL	Sara		F							307
POMF	Sara		F							307
SCHAFIR	Hanina		M							307
SCHAFIR	Dvora		F							307
SCHAFIR	Yaakov		M							307
SCHAFIR	Yetman		M							307
SCHPIZ	David		M							307
SCHPIZ	Herzke		M							307
SCHPIZ	Ben Tzion		M							307
SCHPIZ	Fishel		M							307
STURMAN	Naftali		M							307
STURMAN	Yetta		F							307
STURMAN	Moshe		M							307
STURMAN	Hirsh		M							307
SCHECHTMAN	Irish		F							307
SCHECHTMAN	Sara		F							308
SCHECHTMAN	Avraham		M							308
SCHECHTMAN	Chaia		F							308
STICH	Yitzhak Meir		M							308
STICH	Hinde		F							308
STICH	Chaike		F							308
STICH	Avraham		M							308
STICH	Reizke		F							308
SCHERER	Zalman		M							308

SCHERER	Avraham		M						308
SPRITZ	Yeshaiahu Eliezer		M						308
SPRITZ	Esther Yehudit		F						308
SPRITZ	Ben Tzion		M						308
SPRITZ	Tzirl		F						308
SPRITZ	Lea		F						308
SPRITZ	Nahum		M						308
SPRITZ	Kalman		M						308
STENGEL	Simcha		M	Married			Chava		308
STENGEL	Chava		F	Married			Simcha		308
STENGEL	Shlomo		M		Simcha	Chava			308
STENGEL	Rachel		F		Simcha	Chava			308
STENGEL	Yaakov		M		Simcha	Chava			308
STENGEL	Hanoch		M		Simcha	Chava			308
STENGEL	Gedalia		M						308
STENGEL	Tevel		F						308
STENGEL	Eidel		F						308
STENGEL	Shlomo		M						308
STENGEL	Sara		F						308
STENGEL	Mina		F						308
STENGEL	Ben Tzion		M						308
STENGEL	Yitzhak		M	Married			Malka		308
STENGEL	Malka		F	Married			Yitzhak		308
STENGEL	Rachel		F						308
SPRITZ	Hirsh		M				and his family		308
SCHAFIR	Reizel		F					family name listed as SHAFER	308
SCHAFIR	Dvora		F						308
SCHAFIR	Grina		F						308
SCHAFIR	Yosef		M						308
SCHAFIR	Sara		F						308
SCHAFIR	Gitel		F						308
SCHAFIR	Bashe		F						308
SCHLAFROK	Feishe		M				and his family		308
SCHLAFROK	Zeev		M				and his family		308
SCHMUTZ	Zelig		M				and his family		308
STENGEL	Shlomo		M				and children	listing unclear	308
STENGEL	Avraham Shlomo		M				and his family	first name listed as Shlodmo apparently an error, probably Shlomo	308
STENGEL	Godel		M				and his family		308
STENGEL	Liebel		M				and his family		308
STENGEL	Ozer		M				and his family		308
STENGEL	Naftali		M				and his family		308
STENGEL	Moshe Shmuel		M				and his family		308
STENGEL	Yehoshua		M						308
SCHPIZ	Arye		M						308

SCHPIZ	Rachel		F							308
SCHPIZ	Luba		F							308
SCHPIZ	Yaakov		M							308
SCHPIZ	Lea		F							308
SCHPIZ	Itel		F							308
SCHPIZ	Chava		F							308
SCHPIZ	Moshe		M							308
STUDIN	Simcha		M					and his family		308
STUDIN	Leibush		M					and his family		308
STUDIN	Gershon		M					and his family		308
STUDIN	Fishel		M					and his family		308
STENGEL	Simcha		M							308
STENGEL	Chava		F							308
STENGEL	Gedalia		M							308
STENGEL	Tevel		M							308
STENGEL	Eidel		F							308
STENGEL	Shlomo		M							308
STENGEL	Sara		F							308
STENGEL	Mina		F							308
STENGEL	Ben Tzion		M							308
STENGEL	Yitzhak		M	Married			Malka			308
STENGEL	Malka		F	Married			Yitzhak			308
STENGEL	Rachel		F							308

[Page 309]

Supplement to the List of Martyrs

Family name(s)	First name(s)	Maiden name	Sex	Marital status	Father's name	Mother's name	Name of spouse	Additiona family members	Remarks	Page
PAUL	Fania		F						listed as - granddaughter of his sister - whose sister apart from Mindel, Leizer and Tcharne?	309
PAUL	Yosele		M						listed as - grandson of his sister - whose sister apart from Mindel, Leizer and Tcharne?	309
PAUL	Moshe Leib		M						Mother's maiden name was BERG. Listed as the son of his sister - whose sister apart from Mindel, Leizer and Tcharne?	309
PAUL	Chana		F	Married				and children	listed as wife of his sister - whose sister apart from Mindel, Leizer and Tcharne?	309
PAUL	Feiga		F						Mother's maiden name was BERG. Listed as the daughter of his sister - whose sister apart from Mindel, Leizer and Tcharne?	309
FINGER	Mindel	BORG	F	Married			Zelig		listed as his sister - whose sister apart from Leizer and Tcharne?	309
FINGER	Zelig		M	Married			Mindel		listed as his brother-in-law - whose sister apart from Leizer and Tcharne?	309
FINGER	Bracha		F		Zelig	Mindel			listed as his sister's daughter - whose sister apart from Leizer and Tcharne?	309

FINGER	Zanvel		M		Zelig	Mindel			listed as his sister's son - whose sister apart from Leizer and Tcharne?	309
FINGER	Tile		F		Zelig	Mindel			listed as his sister's daughter - whose sister apart from Leizer and Tcharne?	309
FINGER	David		M		Zelig	Mindel			listed as his sister's son - whose sister apart from Leizer and Tcharne?	309
BORG [BARG?}	Leizer		M	Married			Malka		listed as his brother - whose brother apart from Mindel and Tcharne?	309
BORG [BARG?}	Malka		F	Married			Leizer		listed as his brother-in-law - whose brother-in-law apart from Mindel and Tcharne?	309
BORG [BARG?}	Tila		F			Malka			listed as his brother's daughter - whose brother apart from Mindel and Tcharne?	309
BORG [BARG?}	David		M			Malka			listed as his brother's son - whose brother apart from Mindel and Tcharne?	309
BORG [BARG?}	Feiga		F			Malka			listed as his brother's daughter - whose brother apart from Mindel and Tcharne?	309
UNRUCH	Tcharne	BORG	F	Married			Leizer		listed as his sister - whose sister apart from Mindel and Leizer?	309
UNRUCH	Leizer		M	Married			Tcharne		listed as brother-in-law of his unknown wife - whose apart from Mindel and Leizer?	309
UNRUCH	Tila		F			Tcharne			listed as sister's daughter - whose sister	309

									apart from Mindel and Leizer?	
UNRUCH	Chaia		F			charne			listed as sister's daughter - whose sister apart from Mindel and Leizer?	309
UNRUCH	Yerahmiel		M			Tcharne			listed as sister's son - whose sister apart from Mindel and Leizer?	309
SINGER	Yechezkel		M	Married			Malka			309
SINGER	Malka		F	Married			Yihezkel			309
SINGER	Peretz		M					and his family		309
BOIM	Yaakov		M	Married			Chaia			309
BOIM	Chaia	SINGER	F	Married			Yaakov			309
HELBROBIN	Issachar		M	Married			Sara			309
HELBROBIN	Sara	SINGER	F	Married			Issahar			309
HELBROBIN	Hersh		M			Sara				309
HELBROBIN	Avraham		M			Sara				309
HELBROBIN	Shechna		M			Sara				309
STENGEL	Leib		M				Feigele			309
STENGEL	Feigele		F				Leib			309
STENGEL	Feigele		M			Feigele				309
STENGEL	Esther		F			Feigele				309
STENGEL	Chanale		F			Feigele				309

[Page 310]

Pictures from Memorial Services
in Honor of the Tishevits Martyrs

Translated by Moses Milstein

Some of the participants in a haskore in honor of the Tishevits martyrs that took place in Germany,
in the Neu-Ulm camp in 1947

[Page 311]

The cantor recites the el maleh rachamim for the martyrs

Some of those gathered in the hall

222   Pinkas Tishevits

[Page 312]

The Tishevits landsleit in America at a haskore in 1965

[Page 313]

On Har Zion in Jerusalem, 1963

[Page 314]

The haskore in the basement of the Shoah at the monuments to the destroyed communities in 1963

[Page 315]

Minutes from the Founding Meeting of the
"Association of Former Residents of Tyszowce in Israel"

On 15 August 1950, the former residents of Tyszowce: 1. Yitzchak Kolenberg, 2.Yehoshua Weinberg, 3. Hanoch Chavkin, 4. Yehoshua Hertzberg, 5. Moshe Sachar, 6. Pinchas Landau, gathered for the purpose of founding the "Association of Former Residents of Tyszowce in Israel." With the consent of all present it was decided as follows: -

1. To found the aforementioned association.
2. To call all former residents of our city who are in Israel to a "memorial" meeting.
3. According to the testimonies of former residents of Tyszowce who had fled the city before the extermination, the Nazis liquidated Tyszowce Ghetto the day before Rosh Hashanah 1943, and annihilated all the Jews who were then in the ghetto. Therefore, it was decided to hold a "memorial" meeting every year on the aforementioned day for the martyrs of our city, and this year we will hold the "memorial" on September 10 1950, 29 Elul 5710.
4. To inform all the former residents of our city about the "memorial" meeting. Since we do not know all the addresses of former residents of Tyszowce, it was decided to publish a notice in the newspapers and to ask everyone who will read the notice - to inform all the former residents of Tyszowce with whom they meet about the aforementioned "memorial."
5. On the night of the "memorial" to inform those gathered about the establishment of the association and its purpose, which is: A. to maintain a constant contact between all former residents of our city, and

mutual aid. B. in order to maintain the mutual aid, it is desirable that the organization will have at its disposal *Kupat Gemilut Hasadim* [charity fund] and with it to help those in need of financial help.

Tel Aviv, August 15 1950

Minutes from the first memorial held by the
"Former Residents of Tyszowce in Israel"
in memory of the martyrs of Tyszowce who were destroyed by the Nazis

About one hundred and twenty people from Tel-Aviv and Haifa, all natives of Tyszowce, gathered at "Beit Hachalutzot" hall in Tel Aviv. After the introductory meeting of the former residents of our city, who had not seen each other for a long time, even before the World War, the elders of our city who survived the annihilation by fleeing to Russia, from there to Germany and from there after the war to Israel, got on the stage. And they are: Pinchas Wachsbaum, Yakov Becher, Pesach Sherer (three in total), and Lemel Weinberg an Israeli resident since before the war. The gathered elected the member Yitzchak Kolenberg to conduct the

[Page 316]

memorial meeting. When he got on the stage, he eulogized the martyrs of our city with a few words. After the recitation of *El Malei Rachamim* by Yitzchak Gelber, and the recitation of the *Kaddish* by our city's elders, the first part of this meeting was ended. The second part of this meeting was opened by the member Pinchas Landau who explained to those gathered the necessity for an association of former residents of our city, and the need to create means for mutual help. A. to elect a committee that will handle the affairs of the association. B. to establish *Kupat Gemilut Hasadim* [charity fund] of former residents of Tyszowce, and each of those gathered would contribute a sum of money for this purpose according to his/her ability. The member Hanoch Chavkin spoke about the purpose of the association and the fund. The members, Yehuda Ginzburg, David Chavkin, Shlomo Roth, Moshe Sachar and Shmuel Knobel, also spoke about the nature of the donation and its size. After a short debate between several speakers, it was agreed that each person would contribute according to his ability and generosity.

With the consent of all those gathered, the members of the committee for Tel Aviv and Haifa were chosen under the name, "The Committee for the former residents of Tyszowce." The five committee members for Tel Aviv - Hanoch Chavkin, Yehoshua Weinberg, Mordechai Miller, Moshe Sachar and Pinchas Landau. And the five members of the committee for Haifa: Yitzchak Kolenberg, Yehoshua Herzberg, Tzvi Kiesel, Pesach Sherer, and Moshe Burg.

The meeting closed with the singing of "Hatikvah."

Tel Aviv, September 10 1950

[Page 317]

Activities of the Tishevits Committee in Israel

Moshe Sachar (Israel)

Translated by Moses Milstein

After the end of the Second World War, as soon as the first rescued Jews began to appear bringing the terrible news of the destruction of Tishevits, the survivors who came back from the Soviet Union and other places met up in Poland, later in the DP camps in Germany, and finally in the land of Israel.

Wherever they were, they organized memorial gatherings dedicated to the memory of the martyrs. It is worth noting that in all the gatherings everyone had the same desire–not to rest until the memory of our fathers, mothers, sisters, brothers, sons, and daughters who died *al kiddush-hashem* was immortalized.

* * *

The 1949-1950 wave of aliyah brought with it a larger number of Tishevitsers, at which point the work of the committee really began. This was actually the organizing committee, at the head *chaverim*: Pinchas Landau, Itzchak Kolenberg, Yehoshua Weinberg, Moshe Sachar, and Yehoshua Herzberg. The main job of the committee at that time was to help the newcomers in any way possible. Of course we had little financial ability, but the newcomers felt they were with their own, originating from the same shtetl. In the meantime we established bonds with our *landsmanschaften* in America, Canada, Argentina, Peru, and other countries, wherever there were Tishevitsers. And thanks to the help we received at that time, we organized a *Gemiles Chesed* bank, and we were able to help the new *olim* by granting loans, understandably within our small means. And with time a living bridge was created, like brother and sister, between the old-timers and the new *olim*.

[Page 318]

The first general assembly took place on October 9th 1950. It was a moving reunion after years of being apart. We related and shared memories–of various tragic experiences in the dark war era. Everyone felt as if we were one family. The yearly meetings are, for all the survivors in Israel, treated as a holy obligation even today. On the designated day, all the surviving Tishevitsers in Israel come together to the annual meeting and *haskore* in order to commune with the souls of our dear martyrs.

* * *

At the annual general meeting of 1964, a new committee was elected: Moshe Zamri (Singer), Pinchas Singer, Moshe Sachar, Pinchas Landau, Michal Bergman, Zvi Naor, Shmuel Knobl, Berl Spiz, and Berl Rov. The newly elected managers, at the first meeting, set as the only goal in their main work: immortalizing the memory of our obliterated community by producing a yizkor book as a monument for our martyrs. Naturally, work continued in all areas as before, but with more energy, searching for various ways to strengthen the contact among all Tishevitsers living in Israel. For that reason, we sometimes organized Purim celebrations, where we used to meet over food-covered tables and enjoy an intimate, pleasant atmosphere that brought happiness to all the participants. As mentioned above, the committee at the celebrations continued to pursue the same goal: what can we do so that, in our lifetime, a memorial to our shtetl shall remain? We convened a special conference with a larger number of chaverim. We co-opted chaverim: Ephraim Kuperstein, Meir Zwilich, Bat-Sheba Nir, David Goldman, Yoel Gam, and still years passed without any particular success in the task set.

In 1965, with the visit of our distinguished fellow townsman, Yakov Zipper from Canada and his wife, we again returned to the work of the pinkas. With the feeling that Yakov Zipper would edit our Tishevits "pinkas," we again took to the work. With a special zest and stubbornness the writer of these lines approached all the landsleit with the call to write what they were able to, and to collect all the materials they had, and send them in. Yakov Zipper also put out an announcement in the newspapers, and wrote to the landsleit about it. In particular, we worked especially hard on those who miraculously survived, and

[Page 319]

urged them to write about their terrible, tragic experiences in the bunkers and forests. We approached all the social institutions in the country and elsewhere in the world, libraries, archives, anywhere we could find material for the book. And after years of intense work, we were able to acquire important materials, and writing, and interesting photos.

And thanks to our distinguished fellow townsman–the author, and cultural activist, Yakov Zipper, who undertook the responsibility for this task, in spite of his daily intense work in the school system in Montreal (Canada), and did the most important job: editing the material for the book.

The committee of the Tishevitsers in Israel would like to thank and acknowledge all the chaverim in the country and abroad who shared their interesting articles for the book, and also those who expressed interest in, and helped in the publication of our Tishevits "yizkor book."

Photo: The first group of Tishevitsers in Eretz-Israel in 1933.

———

[Page 320]

Members of the Committee of Tishevits in Israel

Pinchas Singer

Moshe Zamri

Moshe Sachar

Shmuel Knobl

Pinchas Landau

Zvi Naor

Ephraim Kuperstein

Michal Bergman

Dov Spiz

[Page 321]

Afterword

The editors

Translated by Moses Milstein

Our thanks and acknowledgment to all who helped in putting together this pinkas both for their direct involvement, and for their help in acquiring materials. Particular mention goes to the researcher and wonderful *chaver* and noble person, Mordechai Bernstein, z"l, who gave us very important instructions for the historical sources regarding Tishevits. Thanks also to the chaver.

We very much regret, however, that with the best of intentions, we were not able to present a full and comprehensive look at all circles and levels of society. Certain institutions, old and new, especially those connected with traditional religious social life and a number of deserving individuals, are not properly pictured. We tried really hard to get the materials, and that is the main reason it took so long to put together. The fact is, however, that from certain sectors in general very few survived, and those we approached either promised and did not keep their word, or in general did not demonstrate an understanding of the whole enterprise. We strongly believe that what we did succeed in producing is an honest, respectful contribution to the immortalization of the holy congregation of Tishevits. *Chaval al de'avdin v'lo mishtakchin.*[1]

May their souls be bound in the bond of life.

Translator's footnote:

1.   Woe unto us, for he cannot be replaced

NAME INDEX

A

Adamczyk, 12
Adler, 102, 103, 104, 128, 129, 130, 132, 167, 172, 197, 198
Aharon of Tyszowce, 11
Alboim, 21
Alerhand, 198
Allerhand, 153
Ang, 112
Ansky, 13, 45, 174
Appelbaum, 163, 211
Asch, 23
Asher, 45
Ashpiz, 136, 153, 157
Atlas, 149

B

Baal Shem Tov, 12, 32, 104
Bahnhoffer, 191
Baker, 61
Balachowicz, 14, 16
Balegoleh, 47
Bandera, 166
Barg, 20, 198
Barg?, 218
Baschister, 199
Bashister, 45, 57, 131
Bashisters, 158
Becher, 198, 225
Becker, 65, 199
Bedyonny, 17
Ben Mair, 22
Ben Yosef, 176
Berdichever, 49
Bergleson, 64
Bergman, 55, 132, 200, 227, 228
Bergner, 100
Berl, 39, 65
Berman, 169
Bernstein, 10, 229
Bibel, 199
Biber, 83
Bicher, 14, 16, 90, 128, 198
Biderman, 200
Bimko, 23
Binberg, 200
Bishko, 12
Bitterman, 56
Blachman, 129
Blank, 199
Blecher, 47, 129
Blechervanik, 45

Blechman, 199, 200
Blender, 199
Blonder, 17
Blozer, 200
Bluzer-Kizel, 166
Boim, 219
Borg, 114, 157, 158, 218
Borik, 91
Borochov, 65
Borochow, 118
Botvin, 169, 170
Boxenboim, 129
Braun, 22, 132, 199
Brenner, 41, 157
Brick, 158
Brosh, 60
Brown, 160
Brush, 114
Bucharin, 23
Budyonny, 14
Bulak-Balachowicz, 17
Burg, 200

C

Chavkin, 66, 224, 225
Chazer, 45, 158, 174
Chmielnicki, 11, 185
Cordovera, 12
Crystal, 16
Czarniecki, 111
Czuma, 23
Czuta, 25

D

Danziger, 169, 202
Danziker-Neiman, 33
Deaf Shieh, 25
Derschitz, 202
Diamant, 55, 56, 58, 59
Diber, 157, 158, 159, 160, 161
Dicker, 202
Diker, 57
Dinezon, 23, 174
Domaszewski, 6
Dorenfeld, 41
Dornfeld, 14, 16, 132, 202
Douglas, 6
Droch, 202
Drori, 115
Dudzinski, 15
Dum, 161
Durce, 135
Dutche, 24, 167

www.ingramcontent.com/pod-product-compliance
Lightning Source LLC
Chambersburg PA
CBHW050411110426
42812CB00006BA/1859